D1491765

THE
JACOBITE GENERAL

KING JAMES VIII

From a miniature at Blair Castle.   Artist unknown

THE
JACOBITE GENERAL

by

KATHERINE TOMASSON

With a Foreword

by

THE RIGHT HON.
THE EARL OF PERTH

WILLIAM BLACKWOOD & SONS LTD.
EDINBURGH AND LONDON
1958

©

Katherine Tomasson 1958

PRINTED IN GREAT BRITAIN BY
WILLIAM BLACKWOOD & SONS LTD., EDINBURGH

DEDICATED

TO THE MEMORY OF

LORD JAMES STEWART-MURRAY
NINTH DUKE OF ATHOLL

whose kindly and ever-ready help, inspired
by his profound knowledge of the History
of his Country and his Family, made this
book possible

FOREWORD

By The Right Hon. The EARL OF PERTH

THE " Forty-Five " is one of the most romantic episodes in Scottish history. Countless stories have been told about it, scores of histories written, so that it might be judged that nothing new remained. Miss Tomasson's story of Lord George Murray, the Jacobite General, unfolded in this book, shows how wrong such a judgment would have been.

My qualifications for writing the foreword are few : the wish of the late Duke of Atholl, who gave so much encouragement in its writing but unhappily died before the book was finished, and the fact that many of the leaders were my forbears or their kinsmen. This includes Lord George Murray himself, whose great-grand-daughter Lady Amelia Sophie Murray married my great-great-grandfather, Lord Strathallan, whose grandfather was the Lord Strathallan slain at Culloden.

Against these fortuitous qualifications must be set a knowledge of the period which is woefully slight. It will therefore be for others to pass judgment on the story as told in Miss Tomasson's fascinating book. For my part I find much that rings true, even though it takes away some of the glamour and romance from Bonnie Prince Charlie. Much remains, including his great personal charm and spirit which alone made the impossible possible. Of those who were with him some were adventurers and sycophants, but the greater number, whether Chieftains or clansmen, showed a loyalty and devotion which has never been excelled. What opportunity for recrimination and intrigue there must have been in the retreat from Derby, when less than 130 miles from London and the Hanoverian throne ! Yet one of the most remarkable things was that in such bad times there was so little despair or disunity.

As one reads the book it becomes more and more clear that one of the main reasons lay in the generalship of Lord George Murray, who in adversity was instinctively looked up to by his fellow Chiefs as their leader in military affairs. How right was their instinct!

The advance of 5,000 Scots to Derby through a passive if not hostile country, and even more their ordered retreat, were great military feats. It has always astonished me that they should have been achieved. Perhaps a reason is that in those days the people of England as a whole did not feel that their way of life was at stake in the struggle between the Stuarts and the Hanoverians. They may rather have looked on it as a political struggle between two parties for the fruits of office, and not of concern to them. Their interests would be safeguarded whichever party were in power. Is it too far-fetched to look on the struggle as paralleled in Presidential elections in, for example, some South American countries? But even if this is a reason which enabled so small a force to penetrate so far into England, and even if the English generals were incompetent and blundering, any false move on the part of the Scots army would surely have led to their destruction. Lord George Murray, despite immense difficulties, never put a foot wrong in the advance or the retreat. He, and his fellow Chieftains, under their Prince, managed to guide and control their followers in their dealings with the local inhabitants in a way that would be the pride and praise of the best disciplined army to-day. Indeed, as one reads the story one is distressed at the double-dealing and meanness of those to whom they displayed such gallantry and good behaviour.

It will, I am sure, be of interest to the reader to know how this book came to be written. The late Duke of Atholl encouraged Miss Tomasson to browse through the family letters preserved at Blair Castle. The result was startling. She found nearly 1,000 letters of the Jacobite period which even the Duke did not know had ever been written. Many of these were from Lord George Murray to his wife. Presumably these had not been published in the five volumes of ' The Chronicles of the Atholl and Tullibardine Families ' because they were the private letters of husband and wife. But they showed Lord George Murray in so pleasant a light that it was clearly right that they should be edited. Miss Tomasson found then that she was embarking on a life of Lord George Murray which would have stopped at the " Forty-Five," for his campaigning letters had already been printed. Finally, this " life " was scrapped when she discovered that one manuscript was not, as was previously thought, a copy of ' Marches of the Highland Army,' but 79 pages of his notes for a history of the campaign written in the third person. These were probably written shortly after Culloden, when Lord George Murray was burning with indignation against the flatterers and fortune-hunters who had so misled the young Prince. In his ' Marches of the Highland Army,' written years later, he had become less bitter ; the earlier account was watered down and is therefore historically less valuable. Miss Tomasson then got down to writing a book which would cover his whole life. This, of course, in its turn meant reading everything about the campaign, memoirs of those who participated and so forth. She found that much material had often been overlooked or not received the attention it merited.

The story of Culloden itself is a story of confusion, but then undoubtedly the battle was a confused affair. Miss Tomasson, with the late Duke of Atholl, spent many hours in fighting the battle over again, using the great desk in the Charter Room at Blair Castle as the battlefield, and trying out with pasteboard pieces what movements as told by different accounts were or were not in fact possible. Apart from the new light that threw on the whole of the battle, curious facts appeared, such as that the first line of the Scottish army which charged Burrell's Regiment were at grips for only eight minutes, and that the stand of the two Jacobite cavalry regiments which saved the Highland army from total destruction, achieved their purpose in ten.

The first half of the proof of this book reached me just before I was going on a trip to the Far East. I read it on the aeroplane going out and was dismayed at having only the half to read, for I found it had much of the grip of a " thriller." The second half, which awaited my return, is of course the sad half, and shows the side of the hero's character which has often been quoted against him. I have particularly in mind his letter of recrimination to the Prince, but this at least shows that he had human weaknesses like anyone else. And his own reaction was not slow in coming : regret that he had not shown more patience in his dealings with the ardent and impetuous young Prince, and a strengthening of the deep loyalty to his King and the Stuart cause which surmounted and surpassed all else. If Miss Tomasson's book leads to controversy and yet further examination of the " Forty-Five," that will be good; for the history of the " Forty-Five " can always bear new light and new telling.

Peel

70 SOUTH AUDLEY STREET,
    LONDON, W.1.

CONTENTS

LIST OF ILLUSTRATIONS

ERRATA

Page 1, line 10: *For* Robert Douglas *read* William Douglas.

Page 39, line 1: *For* Loudon *read* Loudoun.

Page 49 (Footnote): *For* Woodhouseless *read* Woodhouselee.

THE JACOBITE GENERAL

PROLOGUE

" My son George was born at Huntingtower on Thursday, the 4th of October 1694."* So records Lady Murray, whose husband, the eldest son of the Marquis of Atholl, was nine years later created Duke of Atholl. In January 1697 she again wrote about her two-year-old son : " George is one of the finest boys that can be ; if ye heard him say the prayers it would make you laugh heartily. He takes a book and first he reads and then he sings the psalms in his own little fashion and then kneels down and prays for papa and mama and the cat and all the rest of his acquaintance."†

The Duchess, the eldest daughter of Robert Douglas, Earl of Selkirk, and Anne, Duchess of Hamilton (whose title he assumed), did not live to know that this child, of whom she was so proud, would make the name George Murray a well-remembered one in Scotland. She died when he was twelve ; and was thereby spared the knowledge that he and her other sturdy headstrong sons would stray far from the narrow fold in which she and her equally devout Calvanistic husband had striven to enclose them.‡

George was perhaps the most unruly of them all. He ran away from his school in Perth and sought sanctuary with his father's younger brother, William, Lord Nairne, who had married the heiress of a staunch Cavalier family. Lady Nairne was a woman possessed of a dominant personality. An eminent Jacobite historian credits her with having done more damage to Hanoverian interests than any other Jacobite in Perthshire ; and to her the Duke of Atholl attributed the ruin of three of his five sons. John, the eldest, had betaken himself to the wars and later fell at Malplaquet ; James, the third, was self-seeking and prudent enough to keep out of harm's way. But dreamy romantic William, and his wild young brothers Charles and George, were all quite ready to adopt their aunt's

---

* Entry in the Duchess's Bible at Blair Castle.
† Unpublished letter at Blair Castle.
‡ Like most members of the Atholl family they became Episcopalians.

A

views and became "convinced that the setting aside of the Royal line was an act of the highest injustice."*

Such convictions did not deter them from seeking commissions in the forces of Queen Anne—so anxious were they to escape from the oppressive atmosphere of a home ruled by a stern and difficult father and a disagreeable stepmother. Failing to settle at Glasgow University, George, at seventeen, was allowed to accompany Charles to Flanders as an ensign in the Royal Regiment. He landed there a few weeks before the long war of Anne's reign drew to an unexciting close. He spent the winter in sick-bay at Dunkirk, and the succeeding two years in peace-time soldiering. He was on leave in Scotland when the insurrection of 1715 broke out, and joyfully exchanged a cornetcy in the army of King George I. for a colonelcy in that of King James III. and VIII., as the exiled son of James II. was styled by his English and Scottish adherents. He commanded a battalion of Athollmen raised for Mar by his brother William, Marquis of Tullibardine, much against the wishes of their father who was a firm supporter of the Protestant Succession. During the five months' campaign Lord George earned the reputation of a strict disciplinarian and an able organiser; but having been chosen to raise cess in Fife, he missed the fight at Sheriffmuir. Charles, taken prisoner at Preston, died of an illness contracted during his harsh captivity. But after three years of exile in France and Italy his two brothers took part in the yet more ineffective Rising of 1719—William as Commander of the King's Forces in Scotland, George as a Major-General.

Although they had lost everything they possessed by adherence to the Stuart Cause, the two young men gained the friendship of the King for whom they had fought; and this firm friendship, so rare between a sovereign and a subject,† proved to be the motivating power in Lord George Murray's life. They were refused support by their Whig parent and the truce between England and France prevented them from obtaining employment, civil or military, in the

* Unpublished letter of Lord George Murray at Blair Castle.
† The exiled Stuarts always referred to the people of Great Britain as their subjects.
Throughout the book the same titles are used as those employed by the Jacobites, except in the case of the Jacobite and Whig Dukes of Atholl who are referred to as in the 'Atholl Chronicles' as Duke William and Duke James in order to avoid confusion.

French King's domains. Lord George, therefore, travelled to Turin and Venice in the vain hope of receiving a commission in the army of the King of Sardinia or the Republic of Venice. Had his money lasted he would have gone to Hungary or Prussia—where, in the service of Frederick the Great, he might have attained Field-Marshal's rank as did James Keith, a fellow fugitive from Glenshiel. As it was, he, who loved activity of every kind, was forced to lead an idle aimless life—a pensioner of his sorely straitened master.

Lord George strove, however, to fill in the many gaps in his education, which had been beaten into him " with rods "* in the days of his unruly boyhood. King James, generous and " kind beyond all imagining," not only sent him to the Paris Academy, but on several occasions paid his debts. Neither then, nor when involved in a rather foolish duel with Campbell of Glendarual, did the wild young man receive anything but the gentlest rebuke from the King, who in those early days was the only person to realise the sterling qualities of his turbulent and headstrong young follower. Staunch Protestant though he was, Lord George came to regard the gentle Catholic King, who bore his misfortunes with such fortitude and dignity, as the personification of a Christian hero. The recollection of such " infinite goodness and favour " never faded from his mind ; and his great desire in life was to repay the debt he owed his royal friend and master.

After eight and a half years of exile, Lord George risked his life by returning to Scotland to visit his dying father. King James had given him permission to do so, and to seek a pardon. This he obtained the following year, 1725, through the good offices of his brother James who, having remained loyal to the Government, was allowed to succeed to the Dukedom in place of the attainted Tulli-bardine. On disadvantageous terms Lord George obtained the lease of the old Murray lands round Tullibardine Castle, and thereafter his abounding energies were employed in making a living out of this long neglected estate.

Military fame, for which he had once ardently longed, had eluded Lord George, and his inherent military talents seemed in danger of being wasted. Poring over his cherished maps, he still traced the movements of British and foreign troops engaged in Continental warfare. But it was not upon the battlefields of France and Flanders,

* Unpublished letter of Lord George Murray at Blair Castle.

or as the mercenary of a foreign ruler, that his laurels were to be won. He was to battle once again in the Cause of his lawful and much-loved King, in his own land, and at the head of his own countrymen. Under his skilful leadership Highlanders were to perform deeds unsurpassed by any of their valiant ancestors, and on the blood-soaked field of Culloden, when all that they had striven for was lost, the fighting men from the hills and glens of Scotland won immortal glory that will never fade from memory.

CHAPTER I

THE EVE OF THE 'FORTY-FIVE

On 15th February 1744 George II. acquainted the Members of both Houses of Parliament with the startling news that the French threatened to invade Great Britain. The general alarm increased when it was reported that twenty-three French men-of-war had sailed from Brest and, joined by many more ships on their way to Boulogne, Calais and Dunkirk, had actually anchored off Dungeness. Admiral Sir John Norris, in command of a stronger fleet than France could hope to get together, was immediately sent out to protect the Channel. There were, however, only 6,000 troops in England at that time ; and uncomfortable news came from across the sea of the force of 15,000 men ready to embark under the leadership of the famous Marshal Saxe. It was rumoured that 3,000 were to invade Scotland under the Earl Marischal in an attempt to restore the " Pretender," James III., whose elder son, Charles, was known to have arrived in Paris with the intention of joining the invasion forces.

Lord George Murray had no foreknowledge of these unexpected events. He knew nothing of the hopes and fears of the Jacobite Party, for out of consideration for the brother who had procured his pardon, he had abstained from meeting Jacobite emissaries engaged in futile plotting. Pardon had been granted to him without his being forced formally to express contrition for his former deeds, or to swear never again to bear arms for his rightful King, whom he had promised to serve if the opportunity arose. But for fourteen years he doggedly refused to take the Oath of Allegiance to the hated " Hanover family." Then, in 1739, he had had to choose between his duty to the House of Stuart and his duty to the House of Atholl, which he had been brought up to consider of supreme importance. The fortunes of the Stuarts were at their lowest ebb. To him, as to any man conversant with world affairs, their Cause seemed dead. There was nothing whatsoever he could do for his Sovereign. But there was much he could do for his family, for there was considerable opposition to the re-election of Lord John Murray as Member for Perthshire. Lord George had a brotherly affection for his half-brothers John and Frederick, who served respectively in the army and navy, and whose frequent letters kept him in touch with the world from which he was so shut off. Their accounts of matters naval, military, and political had gradually imbued him with their own belief that the Guelphs were as firmly fixed upon the throne as the stars were fixed in the firmament. It was then that, conscious of his power of organisation, and despairing of King James's restoration, Lord George, after much heart-searching, decided to take the oaths which would enable him to bear a part in public affairs. The Whig Duke's kindly friend Duncan Forbes of Culloden helped him, as he had helped other Jacobites, to word his act of submission in the least painful manner possible. As Lord George wrote to his brother James :

> The principal, if not the only motive that induced me to qualify was because you had signified to me oftener than once how much it was detrimental to you the shape I was in. In the letter which you thought proper I should write, tho' the words were our friend's penning, yet the thought was my own—I mean as to the obligation that lay on me upon your account.*

Lord George considered " ingratitude the worst of all vices and that he who possessed it capable of any other vice."† He threw himself with " vigour and dilligence " into his brother's service. In his conduct of these election campaigns he displayed many of the qualities which later distinguished him as a General. He looked ahead and foresaw the possible moves of the enemy, and was thus prepared to circumvent his measures. He made it a rule not " to trust to incidents which might not turn out as he hoped," but he ensured success by preparing for any contingency that might arise. His defects were also apparent. Impatient of the slowness and blundering of his helpers, he wore himself out by undertaking duties which a less meticulous man would have allocated to underlings—with the result that he became irritable and difficult to work with. He did not suffer fools with gladness. He had no patience with religions or politics, or with men " who had only party interest at heart." But, though deeply interested in European politics, he

* Unpublished letter at Blair Castle.
† Ibid.

strove to escape embroilment in those at home about which his various relations held such widely divergent views. And he made a rule of listening to both sides of a question and withholding his own judgment until he heard the views of an impartial person. To him all forms of bribery and corruption were abhorrent,* and he noted with dismay how greatly they had increased in the seven years since the last General Election. " Most people in Britain now regard neither probity nor any other virtue," he told his wife. " All is venal. All seems to centre in self-interest."

" The decay of virtue and honour in our land since the [Hanoverian] succession is very remarkable, and the progress and barefacedness of vice is astonishing,"† wrote another Jacobite gentleman of the day, James Maxwell of Kirkconnel. To both these honourable and honest-hearted men, and to others of their way of thinking, the restoration of the Stuarts, the welfare of Great Britain, and improvement in moral standards were synonymous. To Lord George the effect of this opinion was strengthened by his intimate knowledge of the character of the Sovereign whom he had good reason to suppose would have made one of the best Kings to occupy the British throne. Firm and upright in character, and a good judge of men, King James was also broad-minded and tolerant. He had ever remained true to the protestation he made to Lord George's uncle the Earl of Panmure that he wished to reign over the hearts of his subjects and not over their consciences.

Lord George's detestation of the Whig administration was intensified after a visit to London in 1743. There he was confronted by the necessity of kissing George II.'s hand—for it was impossible to appear in London society without having attended Court. The very fact that Lord George in his voluminous letters to his wife gives no description of the most important event during his visit to England, gives a clue to what he must have felt as he kissed the podgy hand of the German princeling—so different from the slender hand of the King across the Water. Long years before, when he had decided to return home and to live in amity, if possible, with

* Lord George, unlike most people of his day, would never buy contraband goods.

† ' Maxwell's Narrative of the Prince's Expedition, 1745,' by James Maxwell of Kirkconnel.

Other references from letters at Blair Castle, few of which have been published.

his Whig kindred, he had been told by his exiled brother that only
" a person with a wrong turned imagination "* could hope to steer
an honourable course in keeping with his early life and principles.
For once William, the unpractical idealist, had foreseen these
difficulties with great clarity. And, as time wore on, Lord George
may well have regretted having taken the hated oaths. The very
year he did so Colonel Urquhart, the Jacobite Party Manager in
Scotland, died. He was succeeded by John Murray of Broughton
who, young and enthusiastic, was interesting other young men in
the seemingly moribund and leaderless Jacobite Cause. To one of
these, Lord John Drummond, the younger brother of the Duke of
Perth, who came to see him when home on leave from the French
service in 1741, Lord George opened his heart. Afterwards Lord
John wrote to King James :

> Lord George Murray desired me to assure Your Majesty how
> zealously attached he is to your interest, and how sensible he is
> and how grateful of all the favours you have bestowed upon him.
> That he is in the country suspected of less zeal for Your Majesty's
> service than formerly, which he thinks gives him the more
> opportunities of being useful to you. He keeps in with the
> Patriots and Republicans, and he assures Your Majesty that
> more of them are much more attached to your interest than is
> commonly imagined. He desired me to tell Your Majesty that
> not only is he ready to obey any of your commands in the country,
> but will be ready if he can be useful in any other manner of way
> to serve Your Majesty.

One genuine result of Lord George's apparent reconciliation
with the Government was the friendship that sprang up between
him and prominent members of the Whig administration ; for
unlike his Jacobite brother, who " shunned association with men of
noted Hanoverian principles," Lord George never allowed his
political opinions to mar his intercourse with those whose views in
other matters coincided with his own. He shared with Duncan
Forbes, the Lord President of the Council, many intellectual
interests, as well as a deep desire to see a betterment of conditions
for the people in the Highlands. He and Lord Milton, the Lord
Justice Clerk, took a general interest in agriculture, fisheries, and
other industries in Scotland. Robert Craigie of Glendoig, the
Lord Advocate, an old friend and neighbour of his early married

* Unpublished letter of Lord Tullibardine to Lord George, Blair Castle.

days, continued to rent one of Lord George's parks at Tullibardine. These friendships had not the political significance Lord George's detractors supposed. But they caused him to be looked upon with some mistrust by his former associates. A man ahead of his times and interested in the future, he gradually fell out of touch with those of his old Jacobite friends whose minds dwelt entirely in the past. Lord George's did not. He was intensely interested in all that was happening in the world around him.

In 1728 he had made a runaway match with Amelia, daughter and heiress of the late James Murray of Glencarse and Mugdrum and his wife Lady Strowan, who owned the estates of Strowan, near Crieff, and Arnhall, near Stirling. Lord George managed these properties as well as Tullibardine, near Muthill, in Strathearn. The old Castle, fast falling into decay, had been the seat of the Murray Lairds and Earls of Tullibardine, whose titles and lands on the death of the last Earl had been inherited by Lord George's grandfather the Marquis of Atholl. Duke James's two sons had died in infancy. His lands would, therefore, in the course of time pass to his elder daughter Jean, and the family honours to Lord George, whose eldest son, it was tacitly understood, would marry the young heiress, thus uniting the titles and estates. Johny had been sent to Eton at the Duke's expense—a matter of great satisfaction to Lord George, who believed in a public-school education; and feared that Johny would be spoilt if fawned upon and flattered at " an insignificant county school."* In return for all this liberality Lord George kept an eye upon the ducal seats at Blair Atholl and Dunkeld during their owner's absences when attending Parliament in London. He also strove to turn the coal-mine at Blairengone, near Alloa, sunk by his father thirty years before, into a paying concern. He studied books on mining, spent days underground, convened a conference of local coal-grieves (as colliery managers were then called) and sent to those unable to attend, questionnaires regarding pay, shifts, and fair working hours. He overcame difficulties with " ca' canny " colliers, addicted to filling their buckets with shale instead of coal; and he earnestly strove to improve both their working and housing conditions.

Lord George was always sympathetic with the poor. It distressed him greatly during a bad winter to see Low Country people begging

* Unpublished letter of Lord George at Blair Castle.

food from door to door, and he tried in vain to induce the Duke to buy stocks of meal to sell at a reasonable price to the still more necessitous people on his Highland estates. In 1742 he even suggested to Duncan Forbes that Highlanders could be enlisted to serve as soldiers in Scotland, thus providing employment for them, and freeing regular troops for service abroad. Another Jacobite Rising had then appeared to him to be a most improbable event ; but now, barely two years later, came this almost incredible news that King Louis was massing troops for the purpose of restoring the Stuarts to their long-lost throne. In three letters which he wrote to his brother in March 1744 Lord George tells of the effects of this news in Perthshire :

> All is very quiet at present, and I verily believe if the French have any intentions of making an invasion there are few, if any, in Scotland that now know their design. You know the country better than I can inform you. Whatever the private sentiments of some may be, yet I am persuaded they have neither head nor tail.
> Affairs in the Mediterranean and Italy I take to be the great point of view of the French in the first place. If we attack them there and consequently have a war with them, doubtless they will distress us in all shapes they can. But if they ground their hopes upon an insurrection in their favours in Britain, especially in the North part of it, I'm convinced they will be deceived.

> I cannot conceive how the French can think of making so desperate an attempt, especially Sir John Norris lying in the Downs, who doubtless will give a good account of their transports and men-of-war too, if he meet them.*
> What is talked by the country people is quite idle and foolish. Sometimes they say the Spaniards and French landed in Ireland, then in the North of Scotland, and that the Duke of Perth and his brother are gone to join them. Next day they have other reports as little grounded. Whatever I learn of any certainty, or worth while, you shall hear.
> Lord Strathallan was here again last night. It seems he heard it was given out that he had left home, and seemed to be very uneasy about it, lest upon such rumours he might be taken up. He has had a rupture upon him these several years. By what he said, I imagine if it were put to him he would very willingly give his parole that he would not stir from home. But he did not

---

* A sound prophecy. Sir John Norris sank or dispersed the ships of the French escorts and convoys which had escaped damage in the gales.

enter further upon that subject. I told him he had too good sense to join in any such design or attempt were he even in perfect health, for that the French wanted only to embroil Britain to gain their ends elsewhere. I believe he is of the same mind.*

If there were an invasion, to be sure, there would be single persons and disorderly people that would be glad to fish in muddy waters. But . . . who is it among them that, were they so inclined, could make any figure in a following or rising ? Thirty years has made great alteration in things, in men, and their minds. And were there any disturbances like to be in this country as long as the families of Argyll, Gordon, and your Grace's are united to the Government no commotions can be feared in the Highlands.†

Lord George prided himself upon being a " Citizen of the World " ;‡ but his letters to his wife and to his Whig brother reveal his wholly British outlook. Strongly as he disapproved of money being expended upon foreign wars, which benefited Hanover rather than Britain, he hated to hear of British reverses. Much reading had widened his outlook. His love for his King was unchanging. But his views upon many subjects had altered. As the years slipped by his former hatred of the Union lessened, and he perceived the economic benefits that had accrued to his country as the result of that measure. The spirit of patriotism, which in his youth had manifested itself in a longing to bring about the restoration of Scotland's Parliament and ancient privileges, gradually developed into an intense desire that the prestige of Great Britain should be upheld among the nations of the world. From the information he received from his brothers and friends in London, he believed as they did that Britain could well defend herself against invasion. As a gentleman farmer and a sportsman he mixed with men of every class. On his travels in the Highlands and Lowlands where he went to shoot and to buy cattle, and in the North of England where his son had been at school, he noted men's changed outlook. He probably saw clearly that the reactions of the people to foreign intervention would be very different from what they had been in the years of universal discontent immediately after the Union of

* Lord George was evidently unaware that Lord Strathallan had bound himself to appear in arms " in any event."

† ' The Chronicles of the Atholl and Tullibardine Families,' compiled by the seventh Duke of Atholl. (Hereafter referred to as the ' Atholl Chronicles.')

‡ Lord George to Lady George. Unpublished letter at Blair Castle.

the Parliaments and the accession of the Hanoverian dynasty. He
himself expected no solid help from France. The broken pledges
of 1715, and the animosity of the French Government against
exiled Jacobites, had imbued him with a deep mistrust of French
policy.

Lord George's views were shared by Robertson of Struan, who
emphatically declared that he " never expected any good from the
French, who were only making a tool and a fool " of Prince Charles
as they had of his father thirty years before. He believed the threat
of invasion to be a feint to cover some other move. This staunch
old Jacobite had been put into a " pett," deeming himself neglected
because no agent had been working in Rannoch or Atholl. So, at
least, Duke James's factor informed his master. He added that the
agents from France then reported to be touring the Highlands on
Charles's behalf were meeting with little encouragement except from
the Camerons and Macdonalds. Even they, he wrote, " have
declared that they'll never appear unless first they find England
invaded by such a considerable force as that there may be at least
a probability of prevailing ; and in that case they would endeavour
to make a diversion in Scotland."*

Lord George's letters of this period are curiously impersonal in
tone. But when he visited Dunkeld House about the middle of
March he heard news that stirred him deeply. There he found his
brother James's English wife, who had hitherto supposed the French
were merely playing at " peep-bo " with England, greatly agitated
by a report that the dispossessed Tullibardine had landed in Scotland and was lurking on the fringe of her husband's territory. The
Jacobite brothers had ceased to correspond since George's refusal
ten years before to send his eldest son to France to be " reared in
right principles " by William. As William had reduced himself to
such straits by giving away much of his pitifully small pension to
those worse off than himself, George believed that he was too
broken in health to come to Scotland. On being questioned, the
Duchess confessed that her only ground for belief in the tale was
that their cousin Lord Nairne and other disaffected persons had
paid several visits to Logie—the Marquis's supposed hiding-place.
" Country people and servants have a thousand stories at such
times which have no foundation but their imagination. It can do

* Unpublished letter at Blair Castle.

no service that such a rumour be believed," her brother-in-law told her sharply. Neither did he credit the story told him by Jamie Johnstone, who rowed him back across the Tay at Inver, to the effect that the Earl of Sutherland had gone North with five hundred men to search for Sir Hector Maclean and the Old Lochiel now also thought to have returned to Scotland. Lord George was so out of touch with Jacobite affairs that he supposed the last-named reputed conspirator to have been long dead. The ferryman, still steadfast in his attachment to his " dear Lord Duke " across the sea, must have wondered what effect the exile's rumoured return had upon his Lordship, whom many people believed had been won over to the Whig side.

On 20th March France declared war upon Great Britain; but a great storm two weeks earlier had so damaged the invasion fleet that the disappointed heir of the Stuarts, refusing to return to Rome, withdrew to Paris to devise a fresh scheme for the recovery of his father's kingdoms. Duke William had not been in Scotland; but a false report that he and Lord George had met at Dunkeld to conspire against their Whig brother caused Lord George to consider copying the example of the Duke of Gordon, who avoided being suspected of intrigues by going to York for the summer racing. Lady George vetoed the plan, and the family remained at Tullibardine, where Lord George entertained the Lord Advocate and later the Lord Justice Clerk. In consequence of these visits the host was suspected of Whig, and the guests of Jacobite leanings, so that thereafter none of them was wholly trusted by his own party.

Misunderstandings were apt to arise as a result of this masking of political opinion. Lord George's neighbour the Duke of Perth did not hide his own; but he avoided being suspected of the serious plotting in which he was engaged, by assuming the manners of a man who cared for little but pleasure and sport. Horace Walpole, who met him at York races, set him down as " a foolish horse-racing boy," and Lord George's judgment on this occasion was equally at fault. Thus, when the eager young man came to sound him in secret as to how he meant to act in the event of an insurrection, his host replied equivocally that he would lead out his brother's Atholl-men to serve the Government and then take them over to the other side. Perth assumed that this was said in jest. But a joking reply to a question asked in all seriousness did not commend Lord George to the Duke. Lack of confidence between these two men, each so devoted to and so important to the Cause, proved detrimental to it in the days to come. Yet Perth would almost certainly have stood Lord George's friend and answered for his absolute loyalty had he been as frank and open with him now as he was with Lord John.

Lord George spent the summer of 1744 in his usual congenial employments. He imported cattle and sheep from England, and had seeds sent up from London, so keen was he to improve his herds and flocks, and the crops. The walled garden which he made at Arnhall was the first of its kind to be seen in that part of the country ; and from the extensive nurseries he had planted round Tullibardine cart-loads of trees were sent every year to beautify the parks and to clothe the bare hillsides on the ducal lands at Blair Atholl and Dunkeld. An indefatigable traveller, he rode in all weathers about the countryside supervising affairs on all these far-flung properties.

During the winter he was assailed by difficulties that almost overwhelmed him. He had lent the money left him by his father to his brother James to save the Atholl estates from disintegration. The loan had been slowly and grudgingly repaid, and the Duke's languid efforts to evade immediate repayment by procuring George a minor Government appointment (fortunately, as it happened) came to nothing. Lord George and his family were often " pretty much pinched for money,"* for it was no easy task to live in a position befitting his birth on an income of little more than two hundred pounds a year, and he had at one time thought seriously of trying his fortunes in the Carolinas, or procuring an estate in Ireland where he believed farming could be made to pay by the application of modern methods of agriculture. Now his embarrassments became more acute than ever. The last winter had been especially severe. But never within living memory had the cold been so intense as during the early weeks of the fatal year of 1745, when a great frost in January was followed by a heavy fall of snow in February.

In two letters written to Duke James about this time Lord George says :

> It is really extraordinary the snow as high as the whins, so that there is no purchase for sheep and cattle but what they get out of hands. There is great loss amongst the sheep, and if this

* Lord George to Duke James. Unpublished letter at Blair Castle.

continue a little longer the country people will be mostly ruined. The corns and fodder you know were in a bad taking with the rainy harvest, and now the sheep and cattle are like to fare no better.

You seem to think a farmer can't want amusement and employment in the worst weather. Employment they may indeed find in seeing cattle fed and looking after them. But amusement there can be little in seeing so much distress, one day a cow casting her calf and another the ewes casting their lambs upon the snow!*

More snow fell at the end of March and early in April, when Lord George visited his Mackintosh kindred and friends at Moy. He wrote to his brother:

The losses by the hard winter are greater in the North than you can well imagine. The Members from the different counties will have better and certainer intelligence than I can pretend to give you. But since you desired me to write to you upon that subject, I'm sorry to tell you that thousands have lost their all. Good substantial tenants six months ago are now reduced to want. Many are throwing up their tacks and will either go to service or list for soldiers who were in good circumstances last year. The greatest part of the cows with calf are lost in most of the Highlands, and their other stock is in great distress, being in want of fodder. They had turned many of what remained to the hills and their nearest shielings. Had the weather now been favourable they might have made a shift; but these ten days past has been worse for the weakly cattle than what ever happened before. The cold is so nipping that weak and starved cattle are not able to stand it. A few days longer of such weather will destroy the whole cattle where there is no hay or straw.

Atholl in general escaped much better than most other parts of the Highlands, tho' they have had abundance of loss. But so good is the management of your farm that when the whole country suffers you are safe.†

An epidemic of " cattle distemper " at the end of April played further havoc with Highland and Lowland herds. Worry and anxiety, and perhaps some premonition of coming trouble, seemed to weigh upon Lord George's mind, so restless and unsettled he appeared to be throughout that summer. But to him, as to others, the news that Prince Charles had landed at Moidart on 25th July

* Lord George to Duke James. Unpublished letter at Blair Castle.
† Ibid.

with only seven followers—one of them the exiled Tullibardine—
must have come as a bombshell.

The Lord President posted to Inverness to rally Government
supporters and paused at Blair to interview Duke James. Unfitted
by long absences in England to cope with the security measures
suggested by his guest, the Duke decided to appoint Lord George,
so much better informed of local matters than himself, as Sheriff
Depute for the Shire. On 14th August he wrote to Sir John Cope :

> In consequence of what my Lord Advocate and the Solicitor
> wrote me, I have appointed Lord George Murray a Sheriff Deputy
> for this country to give the necessary directions for furnishing
> His Majesty's troops with everything required that the country
> can provide if they are to march northward by Crieff and
> Taybridge.*

Lord George, writing from Glenalmond that day about his hay,
was apparently ignorant of the honour conferred upon him. Anxious
to avoid an open breach with James, he hastened to Dunkeld at
his bidding. From there, on 20th August, he wrote to the Lord
Advocate, who learned nothing from his letter but what was already
known to the authorities :

> My Lord—I now (as I know it will be acceptable to your
> Lordship to hear anything of moment) send you this by express
> to let you know that this night about 9 a clock Glengarry came
> here to wait upon my brother—as he had given assurances he
> would upon this critical occasion. We all go to-morrow to Crieff
> to wait upon the General. Your Lordship will have much better
> intelligence as to what passes in the North than I can pretend to
> give you. What Glengarry tells us is this. That Lochiel and
> Keppoch attacked the two companies of the Royal† betwixt
> Fort Augustus and Fort William. There were four or five men
> of the regular troops killed, and the rest, being eighty-two, taken
> prisoners. Captain Scott was slightly wounded in the top of his
> shoulder. But they have not attempted anything against Fort
> William or Fort Augustus, and Glengarry is positive they neither
> will nor can. They have no cannon but small things of a pound
> bore. The ship that brought the invaders is gone, and there are
> not above twelve or sixteen that landed with the young Pretender,
> and nobody belonging to this country except my eldest brother.

---

* Letter produced at the trial of Sir John Cope.

† The Royal Scots, then usually known as " the Royals." Lord George
served as an ensign in this regiment in Flanders under his uncle the Earl
of Orkney, the first British Field-Marshal.

Lochiel's people, Keppoch's, Clanranald's, Appin's, and Glencoe's are the people that are joining and gathering to a head. Glengarry says he cannot answer for it but some of his people will be with them. But it is positive many of them will not, for he had assurances from them to the contrary, but thought it best to retire out of the country himself as he had reason to believe there would be attempts made upon him, as he had given Brother Atholl assurances of his coming to him if anything of this nature should happen. It is very late, so shall end with my best wishes that these troubles will soon be over.*

Lord George had assured King James long before that his attachment and fidelity would never alter; that he would " wholly give himself up to his duty, venture his life in his service, and ever remain his faithful servant."† But like the Perthshire Jacobites in 1719 he had not felt called upon to join the infinitesimally small number of Highlanders who had risen in arms on the western seaboard. At this early stage the enterprise seemed doomed to as swift suppression as had the landing at Glenshiel—that luckless undertaking which left an indelible impression upon all those who took part in it. Even in that attempt, timed to synchronise with a foreign landing, and supported from the first by Spanish soldiers, Tullibardine had experienced the greatest difficulty in inducing eight hundred unwilling Highlanders to join his banner, and he had only succeeded in marching them a few miles from the coast before they were dispersed by the enemy. Prince Charles had no foreign troops at his back and, as Lord George wrote later, " The fewness of the arms he had with him, being but about 2,000 stand, and the scarcity of the money, being but four or five thousand pounds, was another reason that made the attempt seem desperate from the beginning, and prevented many who were otherways well inclined joining in it."‡

But in his summing up of the situation Lord George failed to take into account the importance of the distress caused by two successive hard winters. The clansmen were now more ready and willing than in 1719 to make a wholesale descent upon the fertile regions of the south. Nor could Lord George conceive, when he went to Crieff with James (who was summoned to interview Sir

* Ormond's ' The Lord Advocates of Scotland.'
† Letter from Lord George to King James.
‡ Lord George's Unpublished Notes for a projected History of the Campaign.

B

John Cope) that the commander of the imposing Government army assembled there would be so foolish as to omit to provide any ammunition for the men who were about to march upon the rebels. Indeed many of his artillerymen did not know how to fire a cannon.* The previous year, while with the Lord President Forbes, Lord George had met and dined with Cope, and judged him to be a sensible man—an opinion which he changed when he learned that instead of remaining in Atholl to oppose the Highlanders' southward march, the General had turned aside to Inverness, leaving the whole country open to them.

Meanwhile the long exiled *de jure* Duke of Atholl sent summons to his vassals to rally round the Standard, and many a loyal man cast aside his sickle to take down the sword that he, or his father before him, had wielded in the same Cause. On reaching Dalnacardoch he ordered Blair Castle to be prepared for the Prince's reception. As he rode to Blair " men, women, and children came running out from their houses, kissing and caressing their master, whom they had not seen for thirty years before."†

On hearing the news Duke James fled precipitately from Dunkeld, sending word to Lord George to conduct his daughters to Edinburgh. Lord George accompanied the two girls as far as Stirling, where he found a responsible person to escort them farther on their way. From there he dashed off a hurried note to their father in which he gave not the slightest indication of his future intentions.

But he had already made up his mind where his duty lay. The Prince was now in Atholl with a thousand men at his back. The few Athollmen whom James had sent to join Cope had all deserted. Two thousand of their fellows might well be recruited for the Stuarts' service. And who but he himself could lead them? Poor loyal William had set out upon this expedition in a state of health in which no other man would have gone to war. He had been carried ashore, and had been held up by two stalwart Gaels when he was accorded the supreme honour of raising the Standard at Glenfinnan.

* A letter among the unpublished Newcastle MS. of Henry Pelham states that it was only discovered on the day after the army left Crieff that the soldiers were unprovided with bullets. This omission was repaired; but at Prestonpans many men had no swords. Some engineers put powder in the cannon without balls. Others put in balls and the powder after.

† ' Memorials of Murray of Broughton.'

Lord George could no longer stand aside. His kinsmen, Nairne, Mercer and Gask were hastening to Blair. His heart, like Lochiel's, got the better of his head. A torrent of pent-up emotion swept over him ; for nothing had ever altered his " way of thinking for the King and country's service," and the time had now come for him to fulfil his promise to serve the master whom he loved above all men on earth. But this time the cost would be infinitely greater than in the days of his hot impetuous youth, when no one but himself could suffer as the result of his action. The fact that ever afterwards his copy of ' The Office and Authority of a Justice of the Peace ' opened at the page dealing with the pains and penalties exacted for high treason reveals that he had pondered much upon the consequences of participation in rebellion. " Death," he maintained, " is not an evil, and not to be feared."* Now it was not only his own life, but that of his adored and delicate wife that he was placing in jeopardy, for she had been ill and was expecting a child in four or five months' time. He was putting the well-being of his entire family to the hazard, and possibly depriving Johny of the Dukedom of Atholl.

Lord George's heart was heavy with foreboding as he rode home along the familiar road to Tullibardine. It can have been no surprise to him to learn that during his absence a letter had been brought there by Gask's only son Lawrence Oliphant—a young man aglow with the same enthusiastic admiration for the gallant and adventurous Prince Charles that Lord George in his own youth had conceived for King James. The missive was from the Prince, compiled with the assistance of Lord Nairne, and it was an appeal to his father's old and valued friend to join the Standard.

Lord George's immediate task was to tell his wife of his decision. She was wont to call him her Don Quixote and to tease him about his tendency to run to extremes. But hitherto she had had implicit faith in the rectitude of all his actions. In this, the greatest crisis of their married life, she could not meekly acquiesce in his terrible decision. She could scarcely credit that he, who had worked himself into such a state of anxiety over her previous pregnancies, could desert her now. She strove with every argument to deflect him from his purpose. She argued, she pleaded ; but she did not chide him for his rashness. Gentle and loving, she remained true to her maxim that it ill became a wife to criticise her husband's

* Lord George to Lady George. Unpublished letter at Blair Castle.

conduct. Her constancy, as he ever affirmed, was " above all things in this life "* what he valued most ; and he paid tribute to her self-abnegation in a letter in which, when the painful interview was over, he announced his intentions to his brother James :

TULLIBARDINE 3rd Sepr. six in the evening.

DEAR BROTHER,

I wrote to you this morning from Stirling, and I hope Lady Jane and Lady Charlotte got safe to Edinburgh. I was not a little difficulted when you left this place, and gave me the charge of your daughters to bring them to Edinburgh, for to speak the truth, I was at that time resolved to take a step which I was certain you would disapprove of as much when you knew it, as it would surprise you to hear it.

I never did say to any person in my life that I would not engage in the Cause I always in my heart thought just and right, as well for the interest, good, and liberty of my country.

But this letter is not wrote with a view to argue or reason with you upon that subject. I own frankly now that I am to engage, that what I do may and will be reckoned desperate. All appearances seem to be against me. Interest, prudence, and the obligations to you which I lie under, would prevent most people in my situation from taking a resolution that may probably end in my utter ruin.

My life, my fortune, my expectations, the happiness of my wife and children are all at stake (and the chances are against me), and yet a principle of (what seems to me) honour, and my duty to King and Country, outweighs everything. If I err, it is only with respect to you. I owe obligations to nobody else—I mean the Court of London. If you find you cannot forgive me, yet sure you will pity me.

Think of what a weight there is upon my spirits. My wife is in a dangerous state—for it is no feigned illness. She has been bled since I began this letter, and God knows how she will be able to support herself in her present state of health, and the load that is on her spirits by my being determined to venture our all at this juncture. I must do her the justice to say that tho' she is much against my rashness (as she calls it), yet when she found me determined, she did not dispute with me upon it. For now that we have been together for above seventeen years, I can say, tho' sometimes she might differ in opinion with me, she has ever yielded to my resolutions. And the present proof she has given me of acquiescing to my will, makes so deep an impression upon me that nothing but so strong an attachment

* Unpublished letter at Blair Castle.

as I have to the Cause I am to embark in could make me do what in all appearance must disturb her future quiet and happiness.

. . . I will not venture to recommend her and my children to your protection. All I shall say on that head is, that a man of worth never repented of doing good-natured offices. After what I have said, you may believe that I have weighed what I am going to do with all the deliberation I am capable of, and suppose I were sure of dying in the attempt, it would neither deter nor prevent me. I shall conclude with declaring that should it ever be in my power to be of use to you, I would embrace the occasion with a grateful heart, and wish for nothing more than to be able to show you that I am, dear brother,

Your most affectionate brother and faithful humble servant

GEORGE MURRAY.

. . . I forgot to tell you that I never spoke or interfered with any of the Athollmen. But now they are up (as I hear) you will excuse my doing my best with them and others.*

It was Lord George's custom to leave all things in order at Tullibardine before setting out on a journey. But need for secrecy had prevented him from making adequate preparations for an absence which must be of long duration, and which might well result in his never returning permanently to his home. During the first few hours of the ensuing day he had little time to indulge in regrets or in uneasy reflections, for many matters required his attention before he took his departure. Although there was every likelihood of his seeing them again before the Prince marched south, he left his wife and children with a heavy heart.

As Lady George afterwards affirmed, she too had " much need of Divine assistance in bearing this so very hard and severe stroke "† which had fallen unexpectedly upon her. Thirteen-year-old Amie and eleven-year-old Jamie, home from their schools in Edinburgh and Alloa, must have felt utterly bewildered that their papa, who had some months ago acquiesced in their uncle James's proposal that their elder brother Johny should soon take up a commission in King George's army, was now riding away to fight for King James. But Georgy, who was only four and somewhat spoilt (for Lord George was no disciplinarian with his own " infantry," as he called

* ' Atholl Chronicles.'
† Letter of Lady George.

his children), was happy in the belief that his parent would soon
reappear, bringing home a fresh consignment of toys, as he did
whenever he had been away in Edinburgh.

Lord George rode down the long avenue of Tullibardine beneath
the branching trees, their leaves turned now to the dull green that
heralded the approach of autumn.   Former Lairds and Earls of
Tullibardine had ridden down it in olden times to do battle for
their King—men whose names have for the most part been lost in
the mist of time.   But Lord George's name was not to be forgotten.
He took with him only a few servants, but his strong character,
wide knowledge of affairs, and above all his gift of leadership,
made him a far more valuable recruit to the Royal Cause than
many a man who came with a large retinue of followers.   An early
historian of Perth, writing of the men of noble names who rallied
there round their Prince, very truly says : " The chief accession of
strength, however, was the single person of Lord George Murray,
the Duke of Atholl's younger brother, who made a remarkable
figure throughout the Chevalier's remarkable campaign."*

        * ' Perth : its Annals and Archives,' by David Peacock.

CHAPTER II

THE OLD ALLEGIANCE

AFTER three days' stay at Blair Castle the Prince and his followers were Duke William's guests at Dunkeld House. There they gathered round a table denuded of its silver-plate, all carefully hidden away by the Duke James's servants. Good food and musical entertainment, however, was provided for them, one of the performers being a stripling named Neil Gow. On their way to Perth a halt was called at Nairne House, where on this, the greatest day of her life, the Dowager Lady Nairne (whose husband had so narrowly escaped execution in 1715) enjoyed the honour of entertaining Scotland's heir to dinner.

Her nephew Lord George Murray was waiting on the highway to the north of Perth along which the Highland army must advance. It was late in the afternoon before the cavalcade came into sight, and the whole episode was reminiscent of another evening eight-and-twenty years earlier when he had waited on the Susa road in order to be the first Scotsman to salute King James on entering Italy. The handsome young Prince to whom he now advanced to pay homage seemed to greet him as kindly and courteously as his royal father had done—perhaps even more graciously ; for he was gifted with a charm that won men's hearts and drew them to him. But never, alas, was there to exist between the Prince and the man who sacrificed so much to serve him, the same trust and friendship that had marked Lord George's association with King James.

The Prince and his men rode into Perth just as the sun was casting its last declining rays upon the roofs and steeples of the Fair City. Although the townsfolk were mainly Whig in sympathy, Jacobites in the crowd acclaimed the Prince as loudly as their fathers had acclaimed Mar. The Athollmen among the forces came forward to give hearty greeting to the brother of their feudal lord whom none had expected to see among their ranks. John Murray of Broughton, the Prince's Secretary, wrote :

> The joy is scarcely to be imagined which the news of Lord George's joining occasioned amongst the vassals and followers of

the Atholl family, the cautious part which he had acted for many years never having given them any reason to believe that he had any inclination that way, and had made them give him up as a person lost to the Cause. But when they found that his behaviour had proceeded from policy, and not from principle, it was like all unexpected benefits, it created a double pleasure, and made them exert themselves with uncommon energy.*

Lord George met many old friends in Perth. But his great wish was to see his brother, so on the second day after the occupation of Perth he obtained permission to visit Blair Castle, to which the Jacobite Duke had returned to raise more men.

" Twenty years may make such an alteration in a man that he may indeed be quite a different person,"† Lord George believed. But as Commissary Bissett reported to Duke James, Duke William was still " the old man he was "‡ as far as fanatical loyalty to the House of Stuart was concerned. In appearance, however, he was sadly changed. Twenty instead of five and a half years might have divided the brothers in age; for George's fifty years sat lightly upon him. " The scabbard may wear, but the blade is still good,"§ was one of Lord George's sayings, and it could with truth be applied to his eldest brother; for his heroic spirit and devotion to duty had enabled him to endure fatigues which all had thought beyond his strength. It was his vehement insistence at the Council at Invergarry that the Athollmen must not be left to be corrupted by Duke James that had caused the Prince to lose no time in setting out upon his southward march.

The Whig historian Henderson makes much of a report that Lord George, observing that his brother William was distrustful of him, though accepting his services, " bound himself with a curse that he would be faithful and true." ‖ His further report that " a very sumptuous dinner was prepared, as Lord George was a great epicure, though very strong and courageous," may bear some relation to truth; for Duke James's cook Sandy Morrison, who had absconded from Blair on Lady Jean's mare, had been returned to the Castle by the Jacobites who had captured him in Glenalmond.

* ' Memorials of Murray of Broughton.'
† Lord George to Lady George. Unpublished letter at Blair Castle.
‡ ' Atholl Chronicles.'
§ Lord George to Lady George. Unpublished letter at Blair Castle.
‖ Henderson, ' History of the Rebellion of 1745.'

Anxious to propitiate his new master, he may well have exerted himself to turn out a feast of surpassing elegance for a guest whom everyone looked upon as a prodigal: it was an event to be duly celebrated.

George's philosophy had taught him to be patient under adversity, and " never to approve of resentment even for gross injuries.* But William's all-embracing Christianity had endowed him with the divine gift of not only forgiving but of loving his enemies. Not one of the many people who had persistently acted against his interests received so much as a harsh word from him. Had James, instead of his cook, been captured in his flight and returned to Blair, he would have received nothing but kindness from the brother whom he had left to starve almost to death in a debtors' prison in France.

Lady Nairne's second son, Robert Mercer of Aldie, had been drafted to Blair to act as the Duke's adviser, and soon afterwards his dauntless seventy-six-year-old mother braved the thirty miles drive to Blair and remained there with her favourite nephew William until he marched south; supervising his household, upsetting the pampered servants at the Castle, and doubtless advising him upon matters military, as she had formerly advised Lord Mar. The cousins had much to discuss. But Lord George said that he " had a great many things to do," and could not stay overnight with his brother.

For a few hours he rested at the inn at Moulinearn, then he left at three o'clock in the morning to resume his journey to Perth. Three hours later he indited a letter to William from Dunkeld, followed by another that evening, and one on each succeeding day. His long silence was indeed atoned for. Each letter was crammed with admonitions and instructions. William's messenger John Murray, who had failed to find him at Moulinearn, was " a fool and a blundering lad and not to be trusted with anything of moment." He himself could supply the name of a youth, good at figures, who would make an excellent secretary. " Clever runners " must be kept in readiness to carry messages between Blair and Perth. Thirty-five bolls of meal would be despatched to Atholl, and " cost what it will " the Duke was to buy linen, harn, or any suitable material to make pokes in which the men could carry it while marching.

* Lord George to Lady George. Unpublished letter at Blair Castle.

He must apprise this and that Chief of the intended march south, and yet keep the news a dead secret. He must muster his vassals speedily, and march by Tummel and Tay bridges so as to be at Tullibardine on 11th September to dine with His Royal Highness. Failing this, he could confer with him next day at Crieff, and he would find cold meat and liquors awaiting him at the house at Newton in Glenalmond, which Lord George used as a summer retreat.

"Did any of us make too much haste to join the Prince I am afraid we would be too much like a good milch cow that gives a great pail of milk and kicks it over,"* wrote the exasperated William. He refused to dismiss young John Murray, who became his most valued servant, and he chose for himself a better secretary than the "little picaro" who acted as his brother George's scribe.

On his return to Perth Lord George was appointed joint Lieutenant-General of the army with the Duke of Perth, who had risen from a sick-bed to join in the enterprise and arrived in Perth on 4th September, a day after Lord George. The Prince retained supreme command for himself. Of these appointments Lord George wrote in his notes for a projected history, written in the third person:

> The Prince having brought the Duke of Atholl with him from France was of infinite use to him. His name had great influence throughout the Highlands and made that country (particularly those who were well inclined) declare unanimously . . . Lord George . . . was extremely acceptable to the Highlanders having a great interest among them as he was reckoned heir to the Atholl estate and dignities. . . . His declaring did not only effectually determine the Atholl people, but had great influence throughout the rest of the Highlands and also in the Low Country. He had behaved with great caution in not having in anyways declared his sentiments for twenty years. . . . He had been a Brigadier by the King's Commission in the year 1719 so that there was nobody else in the army . . . who had a title to command equal to him.†
> The Duke of Perth got a Commission also as Lieutenant-General, his father having had one in the year 1715. He went back to Crieff where he had been (or in that neighbourhood) for some days before the Prince came to Perth, and having got the Stewarts of Appin, endeavoured to raise his own men and some others in those parts. But the success did not answer to his expectation, tho' he was at all pains and a good deal of expense.

* Jacobite Correspondence of the Atholl Family.
† Gordon of Glenbucket was a Major-General, but was then absent raising men on Deeside.

Lord George . . . ordered bread to be baked by all the bakers in the town for the Highlanders. . . . The Highlanders behaved very well whilst at Perth. They were none regularly paid [but] might have been kept in very good discipline had proper means been used. Horse to carry their baggage was the first thing they exceeded in. Some were wanted for those men who, either by disposition or other ways, have difficulty to march on foot. But all this was so inconsiderable had proper persons been appointed to have found horse for these uses, and any of the common men punished at first that transgressed that way there would have been no room for excesses committed of this kind which every day went to a greater height, the Prince thinking winking at such things was best in his situation; but it had quite a different effect. . . . The townspeople seemed very well pleased that so good a discipline had been kept in so far as none of them had the least reason to complain of any disorder.

Of his method of disciplining his men Lord George wrote further in his ' Marches of the Highland Army,' which he wrote from the Notes during his subsequent exile :

It was told me that all Highlanders were gentlemen, and never to beat them. But I was well acquainted with their tempers. Fear was as necessary as love to restrain the bad and keep them in order. It was what all their Chiefs did and were not sparing of blows to them that deserved it which they took without grumbling when they had committed an offence. It is true that they would only receive correction from their own officers ; for upon no account could the Chief of one clan correct the faults of the meanest of another. But I had as much authority over them all as each had amongst his own men. . . . At any time when there was a post of more danger than another [I] had more difficulty in restraining those who were too forward than in finding those who were willing.

The Lord President, who believed that his former friend had been drawn into the rebellion, " touched with pity for his eldest brother," wrote to Cope saying that he had heard Lord George was to " command all the Highlanders until the Earl Marischal, who is expected, arrives."* But neither the Earl nor any other commander was sent from overseas to supersede Lord George and the Duke of Perth, to whom King James had granted a Lieutenant-General's commission the previous year in full expectation that he would be serving under some distinguished French commander.

* Letters from Duncan Forbes to Sir John Cope and Lord Lovat.

Thus the thirty-two-year-old Duke, who had had no military training, was of senior rank to Lord George.

Although during his three years in the British army and eight months with the Jacobite forces Lord George had only been in action once—at the two hours' " scuffle " at Glenshiel—he proved to have an aptitude for strategy not unworthy of a descendant of William the Silent ; and he was destined to share with Montrose and Dundee the distinction of being a successful commander of Highland troops. From the first the Chiefs welcomed him as a leader who understood the characteristics of their followers, whom (to judge from their Memoirs) the Irish soldiers of fortune who accompanied him from France regarded as barbarians to be treated like the peasants of the various European countries in which they had served.

John William O'Sullivan, who had constituted himself as military adviser to the expedition, experienced great difficulty in inducing the Highlanders to carry out his orders regarding the transport of baggage. " The Prince was never easy but when this agreeable Irishman was with him. But the Scots looked on him only as a private gentleman of no more merit, and of less importance than themselves—yet engrossing all his favour and attention,"* wrote the Prince's Italian valet, who had evidently little liking for this well-fed forty-five-year-old soldier of fortune. The praises of a French Marshal (whom he had once or twice saved from the consequences of debauchery and neglect of duty) had given him exalted notions of his military attainments which, with the aid of the Marshal's patronage, had after more than twenty years of foreign service only raised him to a captain's rank. Since landing in Scotland his efforts in every direction had been unimpressive. At the head of a hundred men he was ignominiously repulsed by a sergeant and twelve privates when he attempted to storm Ruthven Barracks, which contained stacks of arms and ammunition sorely needed by the Jacobites. He also displayed bad judgment when, on learning that all arms had been hidden in Dundee before Keppoch arrived there to collect them, he sent to his assistance young Clanranald, who was not forewarned to take his best officers with him. " Nor were they acquainted with the thing until it was too late. But Mr O'Sullivan, who acted from the first as Quartermaster-General and Adjutant-General (two parts very incompatible), never asked

* ' The Young Juba,' by Michele Vezossi.

the advice of those who had knowledge of both the country and the people,"* comments Lord George. He committed " blunders on every occasion of moment, and . . . had certainly no knowledge of these affairs. Nor was he ever seen to do anything in time of danger . . . but left that danger and fatigue to others."†

On joining the Standard Lochiel had told Sir John Macdonald, a peppery old captain of Carabineers, that " having never carried arms, he did not pretend to know anything of matters military, but that he would take council with others that had that experience."‡ Sir John and Francis Strickland, who had both served in Spain, undertook to instruct him. They made such a bad impression upon the Highland Chiefs that neither they nor O'Sullivan, who considered themselves the only military experts with the army, were called in to the Council at Invergarry, where it was left to that ex-naval officer the long exiled Duke of Atholl to devise the successful plan for a swift descent upon the Lowlands.

" The Irishmen whom the Prince had adopted as his only counsellors on all occasions, men of the most limited capacities," were, from their " great confusion of ideas, very bad counsellors, and altogether ignorant of the nature and resources of the country, and the character of the Highlanders," wrote Lord George's newly appointed aide-de-camp James Johnstone, who had been introduced to the General by Lord Rollo's sisters from Duncrob. This observant young man thought the men whom Charles had brought with him from France were " a most extraordinary band of followers when one considers the daring enterprise on which they were entering which was nothing less than that of attempting to wrest the Crown of Britain from the House of Hanover which had so long been in possession of it."§

---

* Lord George's Unpublished Notes.

† Æneas Macdonald, in his account of the expedition in ' The Lyon in Mourning,' affirms that O'Sullivan remained in the safe shelter of a barn during the attack on Ruthven Barracks. He adds : " Mr O'Sullivan, an Irishman, is a remarkable man of whom the world has been greatly deceived, whether we look upon him as a soldier and a councillor, or for honesty and integrity."

O'Sullivan, trained for the priesthood, had acted as tutor to the son of Marshal Maillebois, who bought him a captaincy in the French army.

‡ ' Memoirs of Sir John Macdonald.' ' The Forty-Five and After,' edited by Alasdair and Henrietta Tayler.

§ ' Memoirs of the Rebellion of 1745,' by the Chevalier de Johnstone.

The fact that the Prince came to Scotland accompanied only by these Seven Men of Moidart has made his adventure appear the more daring and romantic. But it would have been far better had he ventured there alone, or attended only by the faithful, if infirm, Jacobite Duke of Atholl. Happy had it been for his Scottish followers if by some lucky chance at least three of his odd companions had been lost upon the voyage. Æneas Macdonald, the banker, persistently slandered by these Irishmen, fell from grace; George Kelly, the parson, returned to France; and Francis Strickland, the Prince's writing-master, died of dropsy during the campaign. But the three Irish followers, Sir Thomas Sheridan, Sir John Macdonald, and John William O'Sullivan, remained ever at his side continually poisoning his mind against the loyal Scots upon whose protection he had thrown himself.

" The Prince having lost all hopes of a landing in Scotland with an army of regular troops, ought to have been accompanied by officers distinguished for their talents in the art of war," opined the future Chevalier Johnstone. His views were shared by another shrewd commentator on events, James Maxwell of Kirkconnel, a Catholic gentleman in his late thirties who was one of the few south country lairds to join in the Rising.

One General officer of reputation in the world would have been of infinite service. Besides the advantage that might have been expected from his knowledge of military operations he would have certainly prevented all the contests for power and command. If anybody had been foolish enough to pretend to direct he must soon have dropped his pretensions, as he would not have been seconded by any man of science in the army. . . . It must be acknowledged then as one of the greatest oversights in the Prince's whole conduct his coming over without an officer of distinction. He was too young himself and had too little experience to perform all the functions of a General; and though there are examples of Princes that have been born great Generals they had the advice and assistance of old experienced officers—men that understood in detail all that belongs to an army. . . .

It was perhaps not agreeable to Lord George to serve under the Duke of Perth, who was certainly much inferior to him in years and experience. He thought himself the fittest man in the army to be at the head of it; and he was not the only person that thought so. Had it been left to the gentlemen of the army to choose a General, Lord George would have carried it by vast odds against the Duke of Perth who was much beloved and esteemed even by those who did not want to see him at the head of the army.

The two Lieutenant-Generals were described as the Prince's " right and left hand men."* But it was a little difficult to decide which was which. Although Lord George was punctilious in giving his fellow General precedence on all important occasions, Sir John Macdonald asserted that he " took upon himself more authority than was his due and set himself above the Duke of Perth, who made no protest.† The Duke, though gifted with many talents as well as with great wealth, was an unassuming man, and he did not consider that the perfunctory military studies he had pursued in Paris entitled him to give advice about planning a campaign, albeit he turned out to be one of the most hard-working officers and best scouts in the army. As a fellow officer said of him : " The Duke of Perth was a very brave man than whom there was not in Scotland anyone more zealous for the House of Stuart ; he had no will but to obey the orders of the Prince, and his creed was the commands of the sovereign are laws for all his subjects."‡ His polished manners, good-nature, the fact that he alone had not condemned the daring expedition to Scotland, and above all his hesitancy in proffering advice, greatly endeared him to his royal master, who from the first had told his followers : ' It is the obedience of my subjects I desire— not their advice.' "§

Noting that a certain dryness subsisted from the first between his joint commanders, the Prince avoided a possible clash by deciding to give them each the same number of men in battle, alternate command of the right and left wings, and supreme command of the forces on alternate days—an arrangement hardly conducive to the efficient conduct of an army.

While the Jacobites remained at Perth the Duke's energies were directed upon raising his tenants. This proved no easy task ; for he had spent so much money on bettering their circumstances and setting up industries that few of them were inclined to go a-soldiering. Owing to the better conditions that had prevailed in Perthshire during the two previous winters he and the Duke of Atholl experienced

* Unpublished Newcastle MS.
† Extracts from the ' Memoirs of Sir John Macdonald.'
‡ Lord Elcho's Journal.
§ Lord George's Unpublished Notes.

far greater difficulty than did the Highland Chiefs in inducing
men to take the field.   Athollmen were not coming forward in
sufficient numbers to form four battalions of the Atholl Brigade as
in 1715.   Besides, they had suffered more severely than any clan for
participation in that ill-starred rising, many of the private men, and
even some officers having been sold into slavery in the Plantations
after the surrender of Mackintosh's forces at Preston.

Nevertheless Lord George must have been as delighted as everyone
else by the youthful Prince Regent's energy and enthusiasm, and
the easy charm of manner which endeared him to the humblest of
his Highland followers.   Unhandicapped by shyness and ill-health,
he seemed in these first days to be far better equipped than his
father had been to become the successful leader of a difficult and
dangerous expedition.   He cheerfully shared the long marches of
his men, and pleased them by airing the little Gaelic he had learned ;
just as he had delighted his host at Blair by conversing in the old
Court Scots which the long exiled Duke still affected.   He had
displayed " great courteousness of manner " to merchants from
various parts of Britain who were attending the Fair the day he
entered Perth, and he treated the civic authorities there with all
the consideration that even Lord George could have desired.   It
is recorded that when he called upon one of them to discuss the
levy imposed upon the city, a Highland soldier attending him was
much disgusted to see the bailie wearing a large peruke while his
distinguished guest stood bareheaded.   He seized the monstrous
erection and reverently transferred it to the royal head, saying as
he did so : " It was a shame to see ta like o' her, clarty thing, wearing
sic a braw hap when ta very Prince hersel' had naething on ava."*

Cant, the earliest historian of the Jacobites' occupation of Perth,
describes Lord George as " the best statesman and general among
them."   He " took charge of everything, and attended to everything."†   Indeed there was no one else capable of doing so except
young Mr Murray of Broughton, who was occupied in raising levies
for the maintenance of the troops, as well as acting as a kind of
unofficial Secretary of State.   The handsome and soldierly Keppoch,
" that mirror of martial men,"‡ who had ten years French service

---

* ' The History of Perth,' by Thomas Hay Marshall.
† Chevalier Johnstone.
‡ ' Memoir of Macdonald of Keppoch,' by Dr Angus Macdonald.

LORD GEORGE MURRAY

Aged 43. From the portrait by Jeremiah Davison at Blair Castle

[Facing p. 32

Photo by] [IDEAL STUDIOS

LADY GEORGE

From the portrait by Jeremiah Davison at Blair Castle

[*Facing p.* 33

to his credit, Lord Ogilvy, who was but twenty, and the mercurial John Roy Stewart, who had served in both the British and French armies, were the only officers now in Perth to have taken part in any fighting except at Sheriffmuir, for the days of clan fights were over.

Keppoch had his hands full with his own regiment. Like his forebears he owed his fame to his own force of character rather than to the size of his clan, and as in the previous Rising, his regiment was brought up to strength by the inclusion of " loose men " from various parts of the Highlands, who were ever ready to serve under such a warlike leader. " They keep good discipline and pay for everything except Keppoch and Glengarry's men who commit disorders which cannot be prevented by their officers, who dare not discipline them for fear of desertion,"* reported James Kerr, a servant whom Abercromby of Tillybody had despatched to Perth to take note of the doings of the Highlanders. One amateur spy who sent reports to Whitehall described the Highland soldiers as " a most desperate crew resolved to do or die—determined and desperate men headed by an indefatigable young man of the same disposition."†

" Prince Charles is a very handsome man," commented a spy, who believed the Prince would march to Galloway in the hope of a foreign landing there. It was said that he waited only until his men were supplied with targes, which thirty-eight Perth joiners were engaged in making. On breaking into the Council House the Jacobites had found 150 bolls of gunpowder and 100 halberts and Lochaber axes ; and in the steeple yet more powder, which had been stored there since the year '15. Many of the Highlanders were equipped with arms brought from France, others with long brass-hilted broad-swords, antiquated muskets, and some few with Dragoon pistols stuck in their belts. Some were still unarmed, and the indefatigable Lord George set gunsmiths and blacksmiths to work making and repairing arms.

Poor James Johnstone, acting also as aide-de-camp to the Prince, who then had only one other aide—the aged and frequently intoxicated Sir John Macdonald—was kept so busy that he was only able to snatch about two hours sleep out of twenty-four. Lord George expected everyone under him to work as hard as he did

* Unpublished Newcastle MS.
† Ibid.

C

himself, and his recruits underwent a grilling course of drill on the North Inch. " From the first he showed an inherent military genius, for he invented a simple form of drill that was quickly picked up by the raw recruits. . . . He introduced discipline, he organized transport and commissariat, and he gained the confidence of the men."* The Prince took a lively interest in the training of his soldiers, though he had often difficulty in suppressing a smile at their initial awkwardness. A grand review was held on the Inch on 7th September, at which a spy reported that one of the leading officers wheeled his men about so adroitly as to give the Prince, as well as his adversaries, the impression that he had a greater number of men than was actually the case.

Lord George was Colonel of the first battalion of the Atholl Brigade, though pressure of other duties compelled him to delegate many of his duties to the Lieutenant-Colonel, Andrew Spalding of Glenkilry. Spalding, elderly and rheumatic, turned out to be such a complete valetudinarian that it was deemed best to leave him behind in Perthshire. Thereafter his duties were carried out by Robert Mercer and the exceedingly efficient Major, James Robertson of Blairfettie.

New verses were added to a song written in Lord George's honour in 1715 :

> Wha will ride wi' gallant Murray ?
> Wha will ride wi' Geordie's sel' ?
> He's the flower o' a' Glenisla,
> And the darling o' Dunkel'.
>
> See the white rose in his bonnet !
> See his banner o'er the Tay !
> His good sword he now has drawn it,
> And has flung the sheath away.
>
> Every faithful Murray follows ;
> First of heroes ! best of men !
> Every true and trusty Stewart
> Blythely leaves his native glen.
>
> Atholl lads are lads of honour,
> Westland rogues are rebels a',
> When we come within their border
> We may gar the Campbells' claw.

* Walter Blaikie's article on Lord George Murray in ' A Military History of Perthshire,' edited by the then Marchioness of Tullibardine.

> Menzies he's our friend and brother ;
>   Gask and Strowan are nae slack !
> Noble Perth has ta'en the field,
>   And a' the Drummonds at his back.
>
> Let us ride wi' gallant Murray,
>   Let us fight for Charlie's crown,
> From the right we'll never sinder,
>   Till we bring the tyrants down.

Believing that " nothing encouraged men more than seeing their officers dressed like themselves and ready to share their fate,"* Lord George wore the kilt while in Scotland, and advised William to do so too, and one was duly ordered for the Duke in Perth. This was an innovation. In the previous Risings most officers had worn tartan trews, as the Prince now did, for they were more convenient for riding. Few had marched all day at the head of their regiments as the Duke of Atholl's sons and the young Master of Nairne had done, and as Lord George continued to do during the present campaign whenever time permitted. The three hundred and fifty men in his battalion would hear no word breathed against him. One of them, Charles Gow of Glen Tilt, who lived to be nearly ninety, used to talk to Lord George's great-granddaughter Lady Amelia Sophia Murray of his much-loved commander, who was ever willing to share fatigue as well as danger with the private men. He described him as a very handsome, brave, and righteous man, or *Duine Firinneach*, the name by which he was known among the soldiers.

Once, in the company of the Prince, he met a sergeant and twelve men who had been pillaging. When asked what they had been doing, one of them answered : " The man who will not fight for his meat will not fight for his King." When Lord George understood that they were ill-supplied with rations he sent for Robertson of Blairfettie and complained of the negligence of their captain, Patrick Stewart of Inverslanie, who was at once relieved of his command.

As a civilian Lord George had always given thought for the well-being of those whom he and his family employed, and work-people on his own estate and employees at the Blairengone mine were never dismissed without being given time to find fresh employment and a new roof over their heads. Now, like his brother William, who had

* Lord George's ' Marches of the Highland Army.'

refused to leave the battlefield of Glenshiel until he had found a surgeon to tend the wounded and had provided money for their maintenance, Lord George directed his abounding energies to ensuring that his men suffered as little hardship as was possible while campaigning. He advised the Prince " to endeavour to get proper people for provisions and commissaries, for otherways there would be no keeping the men together."*

The Commissariat Committee which he proposed was not set up for some weeks. So, since the Prince's Secretary (who as Lord George conceded was " extremely active in whatsoever regarded the provisioning of the army "†) was overwhelmed with other duties, Lord George and Quartermaster-General O'Sullivan began to interest themselves in these matters. This brought about an early clash between them. With the Dukes of Atholl and Perth both apt to judge the hearts of other men by their own, O'Sullivan and the other adventurers who surrounded the Prince lived on terms of amity. They had taken every precaution that their master had with him no man of high military rank to stand in their way of achieving fame. But in Lord George they recognised a stumbling-block to their plans. They looked upon him with the jaundiced eyes of jealousy, and they determined to bring about his ruin. He was moreover an obstacle to the ambitions of the royal Secretary—or so at least thought Maxwell of Kirkconnel :

> Secretary Murray . . . from the beginning aimed at nothing less than the direction and management of everything . . . and . . . was almost the only personal acquaintance of the Prince in Scotland. It was he who had engaged the Prince to make the attempt upon so slight a foundation, and the wonderful success that had hitherto attended it was placed to his account. . . . Lord George was the man the Secretary dreaded most as a rival. . . . The Prince had the highest opinion of the Secretary's integrity and knew little of Lord George. Naturally affable, fond of knowing everything by himself, and willing to listen to everybody, he was eternally beset by those who had surprised his confidence. Gentlemen whose faces were not known to the Prince, and not agreeable to the faction, could hardly fight their way through a crowd of sycophants ; and if they did they were represented to the Prince as dangerous, at least insignificant people. . . .

* ' Atholl Chronicles.'
† Lord George's ' Marches.' Lord Elcho was President of this Committee.

> There were abundance of people in the army in no respect inferior to Mr Murray, but his early acquaintance gave him an opportunity of excluding most of them from his personal acquaintance. . . . Care had been taken by those about the Prince to exclude their betters from his person.

Sir John Macdonald was soon afforded a heaven-sent opportunity of representing the new Lieutenant-General to his master as an extraordinarily dangerous character. "A woman of the Macdonalds, who had lived long in the neighbourhood, bringing with her a man of Clan Cameron," called at his lodgings. The woman lost no time in telling him her business. She had come " on purpose to warn His Royal Highness that Lord George Murray was one of his greatest enemies. She had known him for many years for a scoundrel. He had a little before this time collected a number of his brother's vassals at Blair Castle to go to war. Those who came thought they were to join the approaching army ; but when they had agreed to do this Lord George had told them they were to join General Cope who would give them arms and money. Thereupon these people dispersed again. Twice Lord George had prevented her from being admitted to the Prince, knowing that she was aware of his doings. She was convinced that this man would betray and cause the ruin of the party and of his fellow Scots."*

Sir John listened with attention to the startling revelations of his excited visitor and immediately repeated them to his master. Throughout the campaign he informed all and sundry that this traitor who commanded the army planned to take the Atholl Brigade and the Glengarry Regiment over to the enemy when the opportunity arose. Both he and O'Sullivan spent their time in canvassing the men of these regiments as to their opinion of Lord George, and they set down in their respective Memoirs only such items of information as accorded with their own preconceived ideas.

With his usual supreme disregard of facts O'Sullivan wrote thus of Lord George :

> His character was not of the best, and his own friends and relations were afeared of it, and some of them spoke of it openly, especially a lady, who told the Prince he was not to be trusted, and that he would soon or late ruin the King's Cause. His presence was nevertheless thought necessary to determine the

* ' Memoirs of Sir John Macdonald.'

Athollmen to join—as I doubt it did, though few of them had any confidence in him at the beginning. But to do him justice as to his exterior he was a very active stirring man, knew the country perfectly well, and gave himself a great deal of pains. As he was a Brigadier in the year '19, the Prince made him a Major-General. A day or two later, finding that the Duke of Perth was Lieutenant-General . . . he would be made one too.*

The Prince, as his Scottish supporters were to discover, was "naturally of a suspicious turn of mind."† The treatment he had received at the hands of the French King and his Ministers, and the apostasy of the Skye Chiefs who had promised him their support, had not increased his confidence in mankind. He remembered that his grandfather had been betrayed by his trusted General, Marl-borough, and it is not surprising that he felt uneasy when told that the man whom he had now entrusted with the virtual command of his forces had solicited a commission in the Usurper's army, and had had his services refused.

Meanwhile there was amazement and consternation among the Whigs when it was learned that Lord George Murray had so unexpectedly thrown in his lot with the Jacobites. But feelings among men of both high and low estate, who had liked and respected him, was of sorrow rather than of condemnation.

The news was said to have roused his brother James's indignation even more than the temporary loss of his property, for George's tacit acceptance of the Deputy Sheriffship had now made the Duke appear a fool before the eyes of all men. There exists an unsigned letter, written in an unidentified hand, informing Lord George that his best friend had heard a rumour in Edinburgh that he had been seen among the rebels at Perth, and begging him to save himself from ruin " by instant withdrawal from their midst."‡ It is possible that Duke James was the dictator. He never forgave Lord George, who in after years believed him to be more his enemy than any man in the Government.

Fortunately the Whig Duke's resentment was not extended to Johny, who had a wretched enough time among the boys at Eton. He was obliged to remain there ; for as the son of a " rebel " he

---

* O'Sullivan's ' Narrative.' Printed in ' The Forty-Five and After,' edited by A. and H. Tayler.
  † Lord Elcho.
  ‡ Unpublished letter at Blair Castle.

was not permitted to take up the commission in Lord Loudon's Regiment which had been promised him a few months before. Though " quite shook " by the course Lord George had taken, the poor boy was less surprised than were the rest of the family ; for he wrote to his uncle that it was what he had always dreaded as his father " had been of that party always."*

On 9th September, Lord George found time to write a letter to his children which he hoped would eventually reach his eldest son :

As I only apprised you of my design in joining the King's Standard when I was on the point of doing it, whatever my fate may be I think it a justice I owe to you my children to give you my reasons, and that in as few words as I can.

Ever since I could form a judgment of things I have been fully convinced that the setting aside of the Royal line was an act of the highest injustice. The greatest virtue a man can be possessed of is justice, so I think any individual is obliged by the laws of God and man to do their best to contribute to what is just and right. I know others have different notions as to politics. But for my own part I declare that it is in justice to my King and Country that I gage myself. I am as much against Popery and arbitrary power as any person in the island, whatever danger there was at the Revolution times—and things are now so altered that I think it impossible for the Roman Catholic religion being established in Britain—and that for our liberties they are, in my opinion, at an end without another Revolution. Can anybody be persuaded that we are free when corruption and bribery are come to such a pitch that not only the Members of Parliament but even the electors are bribed ? Has not this evil increased every seven years these thirty years past ? It is come to such a pitch that the Ministers of the Reigning Family have openly declared that every man has his price. Has not the practice of these Ministers shown that by bribery alone they would rule ? God forbid that mankind should be so degenerate as these men would make them—tho' their success has indeed been greater than could have been conceived !

Has not infinite treasure been expended by Britain these thirty years in wars all entered into for and upon account of the Electors of Hanover ? The whole debts of the nation might have been extinguished by this time had it not been for these wars. None since the Peace of Utrecht have been for the interest of Britain— but merely for that of Hanover. Upon the whole I am satisfied there is much greater need of a Revolution now to secure our

* John Murray's letter to Duke James, ' Atholl Chronicles.'

liberties and save Britain from utter destruction than there was at the last—even if the King's right were not in question.*

On Sunday the 10th September Protestants and Catholics worshipped side by side in the great Kirk at Perth and next day the army set out for Dunblane. On the way there the Prince dined at Tullibardine. Lady George with her "sad afflicted heart" could not exult as she should have done at the honour accorded to her. Fortunately she had the support of her now very grown-up-looking daughter, whose one desire on leaving school was to help her mother. Neither could her sorely distracted husband enjoy the memorable occasion. He had left Perth well satisfied with the orderly way in which the newly raised regiments marched out of the city. But on the road to Tullibardine he had been insulted by Sir John Macdonald, who complained of his poor mount. Lord George had little sympathy with him. Although he gave all his own horses to the Cause, he did "not like to oppress the poor people by taking theirs. 'Whatever excuse we may have for our baggage, we have none for taking them to ride,' "† he averred, and he had even insisted upon returning some of them to their owners. He told Sir John that it was not his business to provide him with a charger. The newly appointed Instructor of the (as yet practically non-existent) Cavalry flew into a rage, and told the Lieutenant-General that he did not know his duties. He had acted without authority in having ordered four cart-loads of bread to come by Tullibardine, "for it was not in his power to alter the order of march in anything." Keppoch, overhearing the dispute, said that Macdonald must be "drunk or mad, if not both, and that it was best to take no notice of him."‡

Lord George found himself unable to follow this excellent advice when it came to dealing with Sir John's yet more trying fellow countryman, O'Sullivan. Accustomed to dealing in rough-and-ready fashion with Corsican brigands, the Quartermaster-General arrived at Tullibardine from Perth dragging along with him as hostages ex-Provost Cree and Bailie Sandeman, on the extraordinary pretext that the Postmaster's wife had not paid the £20 for which her absent husband had been taxed. Lord George, who during elections had been wont to treat civic dignitaries with every mark

* Unpublished letter at Blair Castle.
† 'Atholl Chronicles.'
‡ Lord George's 'Marches.'

of respect, had endeavoured to impress upon the Prince's followers
the need to do likewise. He had warned them " it would be of bad
consequence to show any severity at the beginning how much soever
they might deserve it ; and he had taken great pains to adjust
matters amicably regarding the levy."* Now all his good work
had been undone by the foolish blundering of a man who, incapable
of carrying out proficiently any of the duties allotted to him, was
for ever interfering with those of other people in his efforts to
impress his master with his overflowing zeal for the service. Lord
George realised clearly enough that this " imprudent step could
not but be looked upon by the town, who had paid the money
demanded of them, as a breach of what had been promised them—
that neither they nor their goods were to suffer by the Prince's
army."† He therefore put the case forcibly before his royal guest.
Old Sheridan, as was often the case, began to interfere, and " with
knit brows " said : " We must show these kind of people our power
or they will spit upon us."‡ Lord George, utterly disgusted by
this remark, persisted in his efforts, and " with abundance of
difficulty got the Provost liberate."

The dinner that had taken so much time to prepare was all too
quickly over. The Prince took his leave ; but many of his men
camped overnight in the park at Tullibardine. There they feasted
upon the remainder of the bread brought in the carts, and on the
ale, cheese, and milk provided by Lord George, who was to lead
them early the next day to join their comrades at Ardoch.

* Lord George's Unpublished Notes.
† Lord George's ' Marches.'
‡ Lord George's Unpublished Notes.

CHAPTER III

EDINBURGH AND PRESTONPANS

AFTER a night in the Park of Keir, near Arnhall, the Highland army " with Lord George Murray marching at their head " crossed the Forth at the Fords of Frew. They met with no opposition from the Stirling garrison, though as they had passed by the town " the Royal Standard was saluted by some cannon shot from the Castle."* The river was low after a long spell of fine weather, and on Touch Moor officers and men slept among the broom without other covering than their plaids. Lord George went the next day to bid the Provost of Stirling send bread, cheese, and ale for the Highlanders' midday meal on the field of Bannockburn—all of which provisions were duly paid for. To William he wrote : " I hope our good luck will continue. I believe there never were any troops that have made such vast marches, out so early, always dark before encamping, often skimped for provisions, and yet [in] high spirits. . . . The Low Country people seem to be much in our interest, and were it not for marauding I believe we would be welcome guests.† In his subsequent account of the campaign he recorded the events that took place after leaving Callander House :

> We were told there that two regiments of Dragoons which had retreated from Stirling were that night encamped betwixt Linlithgow and the bridge west of it. It was proposed to send a detachment to attack the Dragoons. A thousand men went about one in the morning which I commanded. There was not a hush to be heard the whole way. I was much satisfied to find the men could march in such order and upon any emergency were perfectly obedient, tho' when no enemy was near they were not so regular. When we came to the place by four in the morning we found the Dragoons had gone off the night before.‡ The rest of the army came upon us at Linlithgow about ten and we all marched three miles farther.§

* Lord George's ' Marches.'
† ' Atholl Chronicles.'
‡ All Gardiner's and half of Hamilton's Regiments were composed of Irish Protestants, who cared nothing for the King for whose service they enlisted. Colonel Gardiner dolefully told a friend that there were only ten men in his regiment on whom he could count. Actually sixteen out of 250 stuck to him at the Battle of Prestonpans.
§ Lord George's ' Marches.'

Mr O'Sullivan, who went with the Horse to reconnoitre and choose a fit place for the army to encamp and lie all night, did not incline to be out of sight and at any distance. Whether this proceeded from his not knowing the country or too great caution is not material; but the most of the officers observed it then and afterwards that he never exposed himself.*

At Gray's Mill, a few miles short of Edinburgh, an incident occurred which was the first open indication of the Prince's mistrust of Lord George, whom he had hitherto treated with marked favour. There he warned the newly joined Lord Elcho never to talk of his (Charles's) affairs in the presence of Lord George Murray, who " had only joined to betray him "†—an admonition that had little effect upon this new follower, who became a steadfast friend of Lord George.

The Prince and Lord Elcho, who had known each other in Rome, afterwards sat talking until the small hours of the morning. Meanwhile two burghers arrived at Headquarters to beg delay while consideration was given to the Prince's demand for immediate admittance to Edinburgh. They were received by Lord George, who advised his master to see them. This Charles refused to do, and merely renewed his summons to the Magistrates to surrender. Turning to Elcho he said : " Lord George has not the spirit to put this order into execution; you must do it for him." The Deputies overheard the conversation before the young officer emerged from the room and abruptly told them " to get them gone." Lord George followed them out and murmured to ex-Provost Coutts : " I know your pinch. You want to have the consent of your principal inhabitants. Make haste to town. You'll have an hour or two to obtain it."‡

Although this was said in Elcho's presence, the Prince in his wretched brooding exile afterwards persuaded himself that his Lieutenant-General had acted treacherously in parleying with the Deputies. He failed to realise the incorrectness of his own conduct

* Lord George's Unpublished Notes.
† Lord Elcho's Journal, part of which is printed in ' Jacobite Miscellany,' printed by the Roxburgh Club and edited by Henrietta Tayler.
   Unless otherwise stated all other quotations by Lord Elcho are from his ' Affairs of Scotland ' which, like Lord George, he compiled at a later date from this earlier account.
‡ Evidence at the Trial of Provost Stewart.

in speaking slightingly of the commander of his army before a junior officer.

Of the capture of Edinburgh by Keppoch and Lochiel's men (who slipped in through the gates opened for the Deputies' coach) there is no need to write. And of the victory at Prestonpans Lord George himself has little to say in his ' Marches of the Highland Army ' :

> Our whole line broke through the enemy. Some of them were rallying behind us, but when they saw our second line coming up they made the best of their way. We on the left pursued to the walls and lane near Colonel Gardiner's house. A Lieutenant-Colonel with five other officers and about fourteen common men of the enemy got over in the ditch and fired at us. I got before a hundred of our men who had their guns presented to fire upon them, and at my desire they held up their fire, so that those officers and soldiers surrendered themselves prisoners. Nothing gave me so much pleasure that day than having it so immediately in my power to save those men as well as several others.
>
> Never was quarter given with more humanity than was by the Highlanders—even in the heat of battle. . . . The wounded (who were many of the enemy) were taken as great care of as possible, and many of them were carried to Colonel Gardiner's house which was the next adjacent to the field of battle. Surgeons were sent for in all haste from Edinburgh, and nothing was omitted that could be done for their relief.

It was while the Prince's army were on the march to meet the enemy that trouble had threatened over the ever-recurring question of which regiment should occupy the coveted place on the right wing. The new scheme of drawing lots, agreed upon at Perth, had proved unworkable. Now that the honour fell to the Camerons, the Macdonalds refused to cede the privilege, which Bruce had granted them after the Battle of Bannockburn, of always fighting on the right. Lord George, called upon to give his opinion, said to the assembled officers : " In an army such as ours I do not see how any regiment or name can claim a right before another. If we are to be ruled by precedents, I could show that in the Civil Wars in King Charles's time the Athollmen had always the right in Montrose's army. But I think the agreement come to since the first setting up of the Standard is a very right one and should be the rule, not only in the march, but in the line of battle. Whoever's turn it is to have the front will have the right that day, if a battle should happen."*

The proposal was unanimously accepted by the officers present. But the rank and file of the Macdonald regiments held very different views, and they succeeded in ousting the Camerons from their place on the right just before the battle began. As the high-minded and selfless Lochiel had his men perfectly disciplined no trouble arose on this occasion. But Sir John Macdonald, who claimed distant kinship with Clanranald, swore that had he any command among the clan none should have the right but them ; and he freely gave it as his opinion that Lord George had devised the rule for the purpose of sowing dissension in the ranks. His words carried little weight just then, for Lord George had voluntarily waived the claims of the Athollmen and placed them in the reserve at this battle. But the mischief made among the Macdonalds by Sir John Macdonald, and another of Lord George's enemies in Keppoch's Regiment, was to bear bitter fruit in the future.

After the battle the Prince sent Lord George with the Camerons to Cockenzie House, where the enemy's baggage was guarded by 350 men, half of them Highlanders who had been recruited by the Lord President. Lord George's captive, Colonel Halket, was sent to summon them to surrender. This they did, thus saving much trouble, for the house had a court with a high wall in front of it which could easily have been defended. After a very thorough search Cope's military chest containing his papers and £3,000 was found hidden beneath some broken barrels and other lumber in a cupboard under the stairs. The officer in command at Cockenzie was Lord George's cousin Sir Patrick Murray of Ochtertyre, the son of Sir William Murray, his great friend and comrade in arms in the 'Fifteen.

Lord George ordered captured non-commissioned officers to make lists of the private men taken with them, and he found that there were half as many prisoners as there were soldiers in the Jacobite army. Country-people stood gaping at badly wounded redcoats, whom they refused to carry into their houses. Lord George ordered his men to take them there, which they did—though many officers experienced the greatest difficulty in inducing

* Lord George's Unpublished Notes.

their men to bury the enemy's dead, a labour which Highlanders deemed it beneath their dignity to perform. In consequence of this, many bodies left unburied that night were stripped naked by the women who followed Cope's army. Lord George, who, like the Prince and the Duke of Perth, was full of humanity for his wounded foes, lent his horses for disabled officers to ride to the house assigned to them at Musselburgh, and sent his own cold provisions and liquor to provide their evening meal. Having no guard, and fearing that drunken clansmen might break in upon them, they begged him to remain overnight with them. He did so, stretched upon the new-thrashed straw he had sent for as bedding, for the house was newly built and contained no furniture or grates. The worst casualties were sent to the more comfortable quarters at the Manse which had been prepared for the victorious General.

Next day the wounded in carts were carried in procession through Edinburgh, guarded by Highlanders and attended by all the bagpipes of the Jacobite army playing their favourite air of "The King shall enjoy his own again." The wounded soldiers were sent to the Infirmary of that city, where some of them obtained discharge by swearing not to bear arms against the House of Stuart for one year.[*] But others stole away on being cured.

Lord George "got what provisions could be possibly had to the common men prisoners who were that night in the gardens of Pinkie, and the night before got some of their own biscuit carried from Cockenzie House to Colonel Gardiner's court and gardens for their use."[†] He conducted the unwounded officers to Pinkie House, the residence of his cousin the Marquis of Tweeddale, the Secretary of State for Scotland, where they would be well lodged until Queensbery House in the Canongate was made ready for their reception. He rejoined them there that night, for he had not taken part in the triumphal entry into Edinburgh of the victorious army —headed by his cousin Viscount Strathallan who commanded the Cavalry. He himself had returned to the battlefield to give further directions about feeding the prisoners and removing the captured guns and baggage. There he had a further disagreement with O'Sullivan, who had been sent to take an inventory of these things. The Irishman had angered him exceedingly by offering unsolicited

[*] Boyce's 'History of the Rebellion of 1745.'
[†] Lord George's 'Marches.'

advice about placing troops before the battle, followed by an insulting reminder " to work for the service of the Prince and the general Cause."* The Quartermaster-General, incensed at his advice being contemptuously brushed aside, and seriously alarmed to observe his master to be " cup and can "† with Lord George, returned with all speed to Edinburgh. There he told a maliciously concocted story about the number of carts laden with booty which his Lordship had sent away as his own perquisites—a number that must have increased at every recital of the tale, for it had reached an unbelievable figure when eventually set down in his Narrative of the campaign.

Lord George had only time to send a messenger from the field to give his wife tidings of the victory and of his own safety. From the man's disjoined narrative she wrote out and sent William the most lucid account he received of the battle. It caused him to regard her as " a woman of much more valuable parts than could otherways have been imagined,"‡ and he thereafter entrusted to her the task of compiling reports of the enemy's movements in and around Stirling. On 29th September she received instructions from her husband about entertaining the captured officers who were being sent to Perth :

> Make ready beef and mutton, cold and hot. . . . It will be an obliging thing. . . . You need not dine in the big room with them, but send for the field officers (particularly Colonel Halket) and tell them that both you and I are most desirous to show them all the friendship in our power. . . . I have this pretty much at heart, so pray conduct it with your wonted discretion.§

Only sixteen of the sixty officers deigned to accept a rebel's hospitality, among them young Lieutenant Farquharson of Invercauld, who on this visit met Lord George's daughter, whom he eventually married. Many of the officers behaved shamefully on reaching Perth. They sent the Government information of their enemy's movements, and at the first opportunity broke their parole —a notable exception being Colonel (later Sir Peter) Halket. " The unworthy pack of prisoners—a troublesome and dangerous set of

* O'Sullivan.
† Ibid.
‡ Jacobite Correspondence of the Atholl Family.
§ ' Atholl Chronicles.'

people "*—sent to Atholl proved equally ungrateful for Duke William's kindness in feeding them like fighting-cocks and providing them with ale and pocket-money; and all but twenty-one of them broke out of jail. Some few officers wrote thanking Lord George for his courtesy, and this inevitably lent colour to the belief that he corresponded with the enemy.

During the ineffective blockade of Edinburgh Castle (29th September to 5th October) Lord George, like Lochiel, " lay in town for some nights, and was constantly visiting the guards and sentinels," although, as he adds, " I declared from the beginning as my opinion that it was impracticable to take it without cannon, engineers, and regular troops. Others thought it would be obliged to surrender for want of provisions; but General Guest was too knowing an officer to have neglected so material a thing, and I was sure we were not to stay long enough to bring them to any straits."†

This eighty-five-year-old officer and his yet more aged second-in-command General Preston (who was wheeled on his round of the sentries in a chair) were by no means lacking in spirit. They opened fire upon the city. Lord George, well aware that the half-moon battery of 9-pounders at the Castle gate could knock down the west end of the Weigh-house and kill the men in it, removed the guard of Athollmen to a nearby street. He congratulated himself on having done so when the men whom O'Sullivan, without consulting him, had left on guard at the West Kirk, were taken prisoners by a party of soldiers who sallied out from the Castle and looted several deserted houses. Even this simple action gave Lord George's enemies an opportunity to spread a malicious report that he corresponded with General Guest, and privately supplied the garrison with food and other necessaries. Broughton, who, whatever his faults, was acknowledged by political opponents to be in some respects a " very pleasant young man," had exposed himself to similar suspicions by yielding to the entreaties of the General's housekeeper that milk and butter be allowed into the fortress for her aged master, who could eat little else. His kindness was ill-repaid by the Whigs, who secreted messages in the pats of butter.

Outwardly, at least, the Prince's Secretary and Lord George

* Jacobite Correspondence of the Atholl Family.
† Lord George's Unpublished Notes.

PRINCE CHARLES

From the portrait by Giles Hussey at Blair Castle

[Facing p. 48

LORD GEORGE MURRAY

From the portrait of Lord George, in campaign dress, by a contemporary artist: at Blair Castle

[*Facing p.* 49

were still on excellent terms, and they sometimes supped together at a tavern to discuss administrative matters. As the two most able administrators with the forces they had one strong bond in common. Each looked upon the present hostilities in the light of a political disagreement rather than a civil war, and they felt no rancour against men whose opinions differed from their own. Neither scrupled to dine in public with the Earl of Breadalbane, Provost Stewart, Sheriff Campbell, or with Councillors, Magistrates, or bankers whom they knew. This made for harmony during the occupation of the city; but it must have appeared suspicious behaviour to such persons as were inclined to doubt the political principles of the man who led the Jacobite army.

A Proclamation signed by the Lieutenant-General forbade " despoiling any of the good people of Edinburgh or in the country by forcibly taking any of their goods without making fair bargain and payment . . . or any horse . . . except belonging to the army in time of action . . . without a signed warrant." These injunctions were so strictly enforced that Broughton further stated that there was " no instance in the history of any times in whatever country where the soldiery, either regular or irregular, behaved themselves with so much discretion."* As Edinburgh thieves, masquerading as Highlanders, broke into many country houses, trustworthy officers were stationed in each village to deal with them. Lord George, much incensed on hearing of robbery and murder being committed at Lord Somerville's house, expressed a hope that all such unauthorised intruders should be " summarily dispatched."† On their march to the capital the leaders of the army had exerted themselves to put a stop to all irregularities among their followers. Perth, a hunting and racing man who owned the best horses in the army, would career along a hillside whipping in with his hunting-crop men who had been running down sheep; Lord George had often dragged out men who had entered houses on pilfering intent, and had thrashed them soundly. Lochiel threatened to shoot any clansman who committed such abuses, and on the day they captured Edinburgh no Cameron would touch a drop of liquor on account of the promise given to his Chief.

Keppoch's and Lochiel's men, who were engaged upon the siege

* ' Memorials of Murray of Broughton.'
† The Woodhouseless MS.

D

of the Castle, and Lord Nairne's battalion of the Atholl Brigade, which usually had the honour of acting as the city guard, were quartered in the Lawnmarket, the Tron Church, and the lobby of the Parliament House. The rest of the army lay encamped at Duddingston, and only officers were billeted upon the citizens. " The polished and gentle " Lochiel, who knew Edinburgh better than did the other Chiefs, was chosen as its Governor. As " the politest man of the party, and for softer measures,"* he filled the post to admiration, and was so considerate that on learning that families of prominent Whigs who had fled the city lived in fear of molestation, he sent a couple of picked clansmen to each of their houses to protect them from insults. Yet his own wife, when journeying to the Lowlands, was set upon by Whigs, who slew one of her servants and mortally injured two others.

Lord George was greatly concerned for the safety and welfare of his nieces—left in Edinburgh by their casual parent when he fled to London. Apart from the bombardment from the Castle, there was danger in the streets from the " undesigned going off of some of the Highlanders' guns."† His cousin Mady Nairne, while standing at a window watching the Prince's entry into Edinburgh, had been struck in the head by a bullet from a boy's gun, which ricochetted off the wall. Lady Nairne's daughter, however, bore her serious injury with fortitude—expressing thankfulness that it had happened to her, whose principles were well known, rather than to a member of a Whig family. Actually the Duke of Atholl's sophisticated fourteen- and fifteen-year-old daughters were having a pleasant enough time receiving calls from captured officers on parole. But Jean, who was fond of sensation, declared that if Charlotte stayed much longer in the capital under gunfire from the Castle she " would lose her life out of fright,"‡ and that she herself expected every minute to be her last. Lord George rashly suggested that his wife should come to Edinburgh to keep them company, or to take them to her mother's house at Arnhall, where she was then staying. Her journey proved fruitless and dangerous. She reached

---

* ' Jacobite Gleanings,' by Macbeath Forbes.

† A contemporary letter. Another letter-writer recounts that after the Highland army withdrew from Edinburgh the soldiers from the Castle were " vastly rude to Lady Lochiel, going to murder her. She went to General Guest, but got no protection."

‡ ' Atholl Chronicles.'

Alloa ; but there her coach was attacked by a rabble of Hanoverian supporters, her wearing apparel was stolen, and her servants were made prisoners.

An opportunity was soon afforded for Lord George to assure himself that she was none the worse for her adventure, and also to allay her fears that he might have lost his " manly look,"* after so much stress and strain. He spent a few hours with her, when sent to Perth " to quicken the motions of those who were gathering thereabouts, and also to forward cannon and ammunition, &c. He ordered a post at Alloa, which saved at least twenty miles of very bad road, placing strong guards and batteries . . . and . . . put all in motion so that in a few days all would be at or near Edinburgh who were expected for some time."†

The Prince longed to pursue Cope to England ; and he always believed that had he done so immediately after the victory at Preston-pans he would have won through to London in the space of two months. Lord George, who had " a vast desire to be at hands with the Dutch,"‡ a thousand of whom had already landed on the Northumbrian coast, also thought this would have been the best time for such an expedition—had it been practicable. Unfortunately it was not. Many Highlanders had gone home with their booty and to help with the harvest which so few had been left to gather in ; and the ranks of the Atholl Brigade were depleted owing to Shian's 300 men having had to return to Atholl as an escort for the prisoners. Charles's refusal to accept a French proposal to ship them all to France weakened his own forces at this momentous time, and subsequently augmented those of his enemies, since almost all his prisoners escaped, or broke parole, and returned to fight on the Government side.

Everyone deemed it an act of insanity to attempt the invasion of England with only 1,500 men, for the smallness of their forces would discourage Englishmen from joining. Moreover, money had to be raised in the Lowlands to maintain the troops. The Jacobites had few cannon ; the Infantry were wearied by long forced marches ; and the Cavalry lacked horses, for many of the Highlanders from

* Unpublished letter at Blair Castle.
† Lord George's Unpublished Notes.
‡ Letter from Lord George to Duke William. Jacobite Correspondence of the Atholl family.

remote districts, imbued with the strange idea that the Dragoons' chargers were trained to " bite and tear " foot soldiers asunder, had slaughtered all that they could catch.

Money was raised by the levying of cess in Lowland towns ; but south of the Forth few men of standing joined the Prince, and in Edinburgh, as Elcho states, " not one of the mob who were so fond of seeing him ever asked to enlist in his service." Instead of the 10,000 adherents Charles had expected, not enough men came in to make up John Roy Stewart's so-called Edinburgh Regiment—to which Lord George had to transfer fifty Strathbran men from the Atholl Brigade.

The Presbyterian clergy, Whig to a man, had gained great ascendancy over the people in the Lowlands, where, moreover, feudalism was as dead as it was in England. Viscount Kenmure put the case quite clearly when he wrote to Broughton to say that he lived in a country " much debauched since 1715 so that it would have been dangerous to make preparations."* His Jacobite wife also wrote pointing out how different was the position of her husband, who could only bring out a few servants, from that of her brother the Earl of Seaforth—a Highland Chief surrounded by loyal clansmen. Seaforth had been out in 1719, when he and Lord George had been the only distinguished casualties at Glenshiel—but having been pardoned by the Government he felt in honour bound to keep his clan at home in 1745.

Lord and Lady Kenmure's letters were not shown to his master by Broughton, " who laboured nothing so hard as to keep the Prince in ignorance of what he most wanted [needed] to know."† As the English news-sheets were always read aloud to him by this assiduous Secretary, he knew nothing of the happenings south of the Border, except what Murray deemed it fit for him to hear. He placed entire faith in O'Sullivan's views about the British army, against which the Irish captain had never fought during his years of soldiering in Corsica, Italy, and on the Rhine ; and he readily believed all his favourites told him about the people of England—a country which none of them, except Broughton, had ever visited.

Blissfully unaware of the state of tutelage in which he was being kept, and of the fool's paradise in which he lived, the Prince remained

---

* Letter of Lord Kenmure to Murray of Broughton.
† Kirkconnel.

content to see everything and everybody through the eyes of the wrong people. Vain and self-centred like his half-Polish, half-French mother, he was often at a loss to understand the temperament, as well as the views, of his father's British subjects. Throughout his stay in Britain he rarely saw a situation as it really was; and since he was no judge of men, he seldom formed a sound estimate of the characters and capabilities of those with whom he came in contact.

CHAPTER IV

THE MARCH TO THE BORDER

To give impetus to recruiting Broughton gave out that Macleod, Macdonald of Sleat, Lovat, and many of their clansmen were marching to join the Standard, and that the Prince's brother Henry, Duke of York, and Lord John Drummond had landed with foreign troops in Moidart. To Glengarry's son, Angus Og, who had gone home to raise the remainder of his father's clan, he wrote: " The Ferrol Squadron have landed the Duke of York with 5,000 Spaniards with two Lieutenant-Generals, three Major-Generals, 300,000 Spanish pistols and arms for 4,000 more men at Whitehaven, and the Earl Marischal is at Dunbar with six Irish regiments and Lord John Drummond's Royal Scots Regiment from Dunkirk. In all, 4,700 men commanded by the Duke of Berwick."*

Such stories, heartening to Angus Og in remote Glengarry, had not the same exhilarating effect upon the officers in Edinburgh, for they soon learned of their falsity. " It was with fictions such as this that the Secretary deceived everybody into embarking in this enterprise," wrote young Lord Elcho, who had been drawn into it by the assurance of his former friend Broughton that the Prince had 6,000 men with him at Perth—instead of only 2,000—and that he had come from France accompanied by the French General O'Sullivan and the Spanish General Macdonald. Most of the leading officers began to feel a growing distrust of this " bankrupt Tweeddale laird," who had obtained such an ascendancy over their young leader.

It is small wonder that Elcho wrote somewhat bitterly of the Prince's Council, which met daily at ten o'clock in the drawing-room of Holyrood House during the six weeks that the Jacobite army remained in Edinburgh.

> The Prince in this Council used always first to declare what he was for and then he asked everybody's opinion in their turn. There was one-third of the Council whose principles were that Kings and Princes can never either act or think wrong, so in consequence they always confirmed whatever the Prince said. The other two-thirds who thought that Kings and Princes thought sometimes like other men, were not altogether infallible, and that the Prince was no more so than others, begged leave to differ from him when they could give sufficient reason for their

* ' Memorials of the 'Forty-Five,' by Rev. A. Macdonald.

difference of opinion, which very often was no hard matter to do. The Prince and his old Governor Sir Thomas Sheridan were altogether ignorant of the ways and customs of Great Britain, and both much for the doctrine of Absolute Monarchy. They would very often, had they not been prevented, have fallen into blunders which might have hurt the Cause. . . .

Governors and flatterers amongst his father's courtiers had always talked of the Hanoverian Family as cruel tyrants, hated by everybody, and only kept possession of the Crown because they had enslaved the people. . . . He himself knew nothing of the country or the strength against him. As he could not bear to hear that the Government had any friends, his favourites . . . used to represent the King as a hated Usurper who would be deserted by everybody upon the Prince's appearing. As for his armies, they made the Prince believe they were small, disaffected, and ill-provided with everything. . . . All the successes he had had as yet he attributed more to the men's consciences not allowing them to fight against him than to the power of the broadsword ; and he always believed he should enter St James's with as little difficulty as he had done Holyrood. . . . But he had difficulty in persuading other people of these notions who were anyways acquainted with the English soldiers. . . .

Schemes were very ill-formed, and as the Scots had their lives and fortunes depending they sometimes took the liberty of representing against them, which the Prince took heinously amiss. There was people about him that profited of his displeasure to represent the Scots to him as a mutinous people and that it was not so much for him they were fighting as for themselves, and represented to him all their bad behaviour to King Charles I. and II. and put it in the worst lights. . . . Prejudices in favour of Passive Obedience, Absolute Monarchy, the Roman Catholic Religion, and consequently the Irish who professed it, had been strongly inculcated into the Prince's head by Sir Thomas Sheridan who was infinitely fitter to bring up Jesuits than Princes . . . and in company used to argue that the nation had usurped every privilege they possessed from their Kings. All the subjects of Great Britain are the King's property, and in consequence a parcel of slaves. As most of the gentlemen who had joined the Prince had very different principles it is easy to imagine what uneasiness it gave them to be governed by people whose heads were filled with those ideas. But as the French says " Le vin etoit verseil falloir de boire." And as the Prince in his conversation used always to swear he would never lay down his arms as long as men would stick by him, nobody ever thought of asking terms from the Government, but on the contrary to stand by the Cause whether good or bad as long as it would last.*

* Lord Elcho, ' Affairs of Scotland.'

The Council, at first comprised of eighteen members, became unwieldy after the inclusion of the colonels of all regiments. As Lord George wrote :

> A few of those in the Council of War desired to be in His Royal Highness's room almost every night about seven when things of a private nature were talked of, as it was thought the Council of War was too numerous. His Royal Highness was advised only to call a Council of War upon an emergency for it was found inconvenient to have such a number of the officers attending because many of them should be necessarily employed with their regiments ; or upon other duties.*

So Elcho's Major, Maxwell of Kirkconnel, was much concerned about the " dissensions and animosities " that had already arisen between the Prince and his Councillors :

> The Council was insensibly divided into factions and came to be of little use when measures were approved of or condemned not for themselves but for the sake of their author. Some schemes were given out to get more money and arms very early, but the Secretary and his assistants had already too much business with the management of the army, small as it was. They had no leisure to pursue methods of increasing it, and they dreaded nothing so much as the interference of other people.

Kirkconnel admired Charles's ability to maintain "tolerable decorum " among his adherents ; but much was due to the Duke of Perth's refusal to allow himself to be set up in opposition to his fellow Lieutenant-General in Council. The Duke, however, felt it his duty to support his master's measures—as did three or four others of the sixteen Scottish Councillors. Among their number was that " staunchest Jacobite in Scotland," Lord Nairne, one of whose relations afterwards informed Bishop Forbes that the " disputes and cangling . . . were owing to the haughty, restless, unaccountable temper of Lord George "†—a rather surprising statement ; for in the voluminous family correspondence there is only one reference to any display of irritability on his part, and that was during an election when, as now, he was both overwrought and overworked.

Regard for the Prince prevented these ultra-loyalists from quarrelling with fellow officers who opposed them. Lord George's assertion at the time of Culloden that " from the beginning of the

---

* Lord George's Unpublished Notes.
† ' The Lyon in Mourning.'

whole affair until that time there had never been the least dispute or misunderstanding between the officers* " is not so fantastic as it sounds. The unanimity among the Scots was remarkable. The " gentle Lochiel " had steadfastly adhered to the advice sent him by his uncle Allan Cameron " to keep on good terms with . . . neighbours, and let byegones be byegones, as long as they continue firm in the King's interest," and other Chiefs had followed his example. Unlike their turbulent ancestors, to whom a civil war was a heaven-sent opportunity to wreak vengeance upon some hereditary foe, most of them had taken the field actuated by a sense of duty and loyalty to their King. Since some of the more powerful Chiefs had sunk into a state of indolence or decrepitude, Keppoch and Lochiel had taken the leading part in Highland affairs ; and the previous year had, with Old Glengarry, entered into an agreement to check crime and aid the cause of law and order in their domains. They had also directed their energies to bettering the condition of their clansmen, whose lives they were not prepared to hazard in the same reckless fashion as their forebears had done.

Young Clanranald, Angus Og of Glengarry and Lord Ogilvy, who had brought out their father's men, were mere boys, and Ardshiel who led the Stewarts of Appin, " suffered from a lethargy." Keppoch and Lochiel had travelled in Europe, but the only Councillors who knew much about England were Lord George, Lord Kilmarnock (who would never contradict the Prince's views), and the youthful Lord Elcho, who had been educated at Winchester. Erudite Lord Pitsligo knew more about the country under the Plantagenets than under the Guelphs, and he had a tiresome habit of holding up business by seeking an historical precedent for any measure that was proposed.

Because of his wide knowledge of contemporary affairs at home and abroad, Lord George was looked upon by the Chiefs as their spokesman. Few save Keppoch and Cluny Macpherson had known him prior to the Rising ; but all felt that his interests were their own. As his words " had greater weight in the Council than the Duke of Perth's or O'Sullivan's," he usually " brought the majority over to his opinion."†

* Lord George's letter about the Battle of Culloden, ' Lyon in Mourning.' Referred to in Browne's ' History of the Highland Clans ' as the Particular Account.

† Kirkconnel.

Lord George therefore became the chief instrument in thwarting many of the most cherished schemes of the Prince, who began to regard him not only with suspicion, but with intense personal dislike. To those who offered him the incense of flattery (to which he had become accustomed at his father's Court, where he was looked upon as the rising hope of the Cause), Charles was indeed a gracious and a charming prince, whom all supposed to be endued with every noble and manly quality their fancy painted. But those who offered him advice that did not please, or who in any way offended him, he treated with rudeness—a habit that had caused much concern to his Governor, Lord Dunbar. The idol of his father, brother, and the doting Sheridan,* he had never learned the need of adjusting himself to those around him, or of concealing his likes and dislikes. Like a spoilt child he appeared to imagine that smiles and graciousness would obliterate all remembrance of past rudeness or misunderstandings. Too self-centred to reflect on the effects his actions had upon others, he did not realise how damaging it was to his own interests to withhold his confidence from the commander of his army and his leading officers. He sprung upon them schemes which he had evolved in secret with his unofficial advisers. If the Scots did not like them he sulked; and threw himself upon the protection of his little band of Irishmen. Their soothing speeches were a pleasant contrast to the forthright utterances of Lord George Murray, who never in times of leisure had been an

---

* According to to a tradition in the Sheridan family Sir Thomas was the son of a Protestant Irish officer killed at the Battle of the Boyne and " Princess Hélène," a daughter alleged to have been born to James II. and Anne Hyde before their marriage, and was thus a nephew of James III.

Prince Charles's ill-balanced, pious mother had shut herself away from the affairs of the world long before she left it. His father was immersed in business, as was his Protestant Governor the Earl of Dunbar, who acted also as Secretary of State. The boy had thus fallen unduly under the influence of his over-indulgent Sub-Governor, whom he came as near to loving as it was in his nature to love anybody. Sir Thomas had thought more of usurping his master's place in the heart of his royal pupil than of instilling much wisdom into his head. He was indeed " scarcely an adviser, rather an adorer, of the traditional sanguine Irish temperament." Balhaldy, a secret agent in Paris, warned King James that his son was completely in the hands of Sheridan, whom he described as both " pernicious and dangerous." His former pupil's letters to his father, though couched in the Prince's " own style and manner," were devised by the old scholar who abetted him in concealing from the King his warlike designs, which some believed were of Sheridan's devising.

adept in the composition of pretty speeches—an art in which he acknowledged himself deficient.

Lord George's intercourse with King James had ill-prepared him for dealing with his son; for the King, who considered "dissimulation unworthy of a Prince," had never represented a military situation as other than it was to the loyal friends who risked their lives in his service. In his youth Lord George had sought counsel upon all personal matters from his old master; now he found himself in the extraordinary position of being unable to confer with his young master upon matters affecting the Prince's most vital interests. After years spent in studying contemporary Continental campaigns he was now, paradoxically, allowed to take little part in planning what he himself was supposed to undertake.

Charles himself had very little knowledge of military affairs. He had not attended a Military Academy; and no foreign Prince had dared to incur the ire of the British Government by permitting him to serve in their armies. At the age of thirteen he had spent ten days at the Siege of Gaeta, and had been thrilled by the experience. But, hating books, he had never troubled to learn anything further. He "was very badly educated; he knew nothing of geography or of history, and he believed that the whole country was his property and that the word subject meant slave," recorded Lord Elcho. And Sheridan . . . "who did not like the Scots, in teaching him the little history that he knew had given him to understand that the Scots had taken part against his great-grandfather, Charles I." When they had met in Rome Elcho had been surprised that the Prince had not taken the opportunity of learning more from him about conditions in Great Britain; nor had he attempted to study such matters during his months of inactivity in France.

Undoubtedly Charles had lacked the power of concentration to devote himself to preparing ground for the invasion of England— to which country he had not even sent a secret agent at the time when he sent Broughton to Scotland. And even now in Edinburgh he failed to realise that a matter of such magnitude should not be left in the hands of civilians such as his Secretary and his old tutor. Such terms as strategy and tactics were meaningless to him. He knew exactly what he wished to do and where he wished to go; he refused to see (or was incapable of seeing) the obstacles that blocked his path.

Admittedly Lord George interfered in matters outside the province of a General. He was obliged to do so, and to exercise his functions as a leading member of the Prince's Council. His inexperienced young leader had no Secretary of State or Attorney-General to advise him on civil or legal matters. He was incredibly immature for his four-and-twenty years, and had no conception of the duties of a Regent. The throneless King had had no opportunity to "unboy" him, as Charles I. had done his sons by early initiation into affairs of state ; nor had the Prince acquired a knowledge of the world, or of men, such as King Charles's sons gained during their hard years of exile.

The library catalogue at Tullibardine tends to show that Lord George was well versed in the history, laws, and constitution of England and Scotland ; and he now put his knowledge to practical use by opposing Sheridan, whom he hotly accused of ignorance of the law. He had become reconciled to the Act of Union, and wished only for his country's fairer representation in the House of Lords. He stood for the laws of the land and the Parliamentary rights of a free people. He was perhaps the only Councillor who realised that Charles, by his autocratic action in abolishing this Act by a stroke of the pen to please the Scots, had acted as arbitrarily and uncon- stitutionally as his grandfather James II., whose use of the Dis- pensing Power had cost his family three Crowns. King James had considered septuagenarian Sir Thomas long past useful employment, for he had had three strokes and often dozed during important discussions. To so a modern-minded man as Lord George Murray the Proclamations he concocted must have seemed a hundred years out of date. Even Kirkconnel thought them " not well calculated for the present age." That issued in Edinburgh against the summon- ing of Parliament in London, and threatening with pains and penalties those who attended it, was laughable. But another, in which Catholic Sir Thomas expressed his dislike of the Ministers of the Presbyterian Church, would have had bad results if published. When his Councillors suggested the rewording of his Manifestos the Prince replied with hauteur that " it was beneath his dignity to enter into such reasoning with subjects."*

In Edinburgh Jacobite officers laboured with unremitting zeal to turn their undisciplined followers into an efficient fighting force.

* Elcho.

In an amazingly short space of time the gentlemen volunteers were transmuted into well-drilled cavalrymen. Broughton's seventy Hussars remained somewhat unruly and earned the censure of Lord George ; but the Aberdeenshire Cavalrymen did gallant work throughout the campaign under the command of old Lord Pitsligo, who, though now frail and shrunken and dressed more like a waggoner than a colonel, was as indefatigable in carrying out his duties as when " out " in the year 'Fifteen. The crack troops were the Life-Guards commanded by Lord Elcho, who had won his colonelcy for gallant conduct on the field of Prestonpans, his military experience up to that time having been confined to a few days as a guest of honour at the Headquarters of a foreign army. Their young commander was justly proud of his men, and wrote :

> They were all gentlemen of family and fortune, and they did not amount to above a hundred. Yet I may say there never was a troop of better men in any service, the uniform blue and red, and all extremely well mounted."*

> Nothing in the campaign was more adroit and effective than the work done by the mounted portion of the force. For the most part without experience in warfare, acting for the first time in concert, traversing an unknown country, the Cavalry never failed to bring timely information of the whereabouts of the enemy, nor, when occasion required, to act as an efficient screen to the manœuvres of the Highland army.†

The Prince, who delighted in such spectacles, wished to hold a grand review of his troops at Duddingston, and Lord George must

* Elcho.

† ' Memoir of David, Lord Elcho.' When the march began Lord Elcho's troop, which led the van of the army and was usually sent on ahead to enter every town, was comprised of only seventy men. The other thirty had been relegated to the second company, only fifty strong, commanded by a veteran of Queen Anne's day, Colonel Arthur Elphinstone, who a few months later succeeded to the title of Lord Balmerino—a name which he was to make for ever glorious.

Jacobite historians condemn Elcho for seeking to make terms with the Government after the secession of arms, and for bitter censure of the Prince, who at the time of the writing of the Narrative had sunk into a state of perpetual debauchery. In his ' Impartial History of the Rebellion of 1745,' the Whig historian, Boyce, is fairer to Lord Elcho and says : " He had a greater share of both learning and virtue than is common to those of his rank. His person was graceful, and his deportment engaging, and all his conduct was heightened with such benevolence of mind and sweetness of manner as gained him general esteem. As he engaged in the Rebellion from principles, so he acted his part in it with all the candour and spirit natural to him."

have had to employ considerable ingenuity to prevent him from
doing so and giving the enemy a heaven-sent chance of counting
their number—a task which the General rendered more difficult by
dispersing the men to winter quarters. No reliable accounts were
ever sent to Whitehall, and it was believed that the Prince had
far more followers than was actually the case.

Lord George, in addition to his other duties, was supervising
affairs in Perthshire, and wrote to his brother William :

> DEAR BROTHER,—I write once more by His Royal Highness's
> special commands, who desires you to come in person, and all
> the men possible, with the utmost expedition and join him. Any
> that are coming from the north you must leave orders about
> following you, and wait for none but such as have joined you
> before this comes to your hands.
>
> It is certain that all depends upon expedition, and the moment
> you join us His Royal Highness will march for England, if he do
> not march sooner. Everything is in great confusion in England,
> particularly in London, where credit is at a stand. The greatest
> Banquiers have stopped payment. All would go to our wish if
> we could march immediately. Settle everything with Lord
> Strathallan about the police of the country, civil and military.
> Adieu. I hope to see you before I write again.

This hope was not fulfilled. Three days later he wrote again :

> The Prince Regent is in the utmost concern for the precious
> time which is lost by your not coming up. I have wrote to you
> so often by his orders upon that subject that I can add nothing
> to what I have already said, only it seems the opinion of everybody
> if you delay any longer it will be the utter ruin of the Cause.*

As a modern writer has stated, few men have ever worked as poor
Duke William worked in his capacity as " Governor of Atholl and
Commander of the King's Forces benorth the Forth." But it was
beyond the power of even so devoted a Jacobite as he to gather in
his men more quickly. And while he struggled valiantly to do so
the Highland army dallied in Edinburgh for six fatal weeks awaiting
the expected arrival of his thousand men and the return of the
deserters, nearly all of whom eventually rejoined their colours.

Some weeks earlier Marshal Wade, sent north at the head of
Government troops, had declared : " England is for the first comer,
and if you can tell me whether 6,000 Dutch and the ten battalions

* Jacobite Correspondence of the Atholl Family.

of English, or 5,000 French or Spanish will be here first, you know our fate."

Five thousand more Dutchmen and regiment after regiment of seasoned British soldiers withdrawn from Flanders had landed in Northumberland, and others from Ireland had disembarked at southern ports. But there was not a sign of any foreign troops being sent to the assistance of the Prince.

Leading Jacobite officers had been told of letters from Marshal Saxe, the Duc de Bouillon, and the Prince of Campo Florido giving assurances of French and Spanish help ; but they were never shown these unconvincing missives. Neither were they allowed to suspect the fact that no such promises had been given by either country, or that Charles had sailed to Scotland without either King James's or King Louis's knowledge or consent, and that since his arrival there he had taken no steps to ensure that French soldiers would be sent to the help of the Scots now actually in arms. Sir John Macdonald was, in truth, perfectly justified in saying that " as no one in Scotland knew what was happening in France, the French were probably equally ignorant of what was taking place in Scotland."

The insignificant Protestant parson George Kelly, who had gained the royal favour by his ability to tell a good story, had been sent to France with news of the recent victory. Priding himself upon being the originator of the plan to invade Scotland, Mr Kelly dilated so much upon its wonderful success that the French Ministers felt there was little need to help a prince, whom they were informed commanded anything from ten to thirty thousand men. He would, they argued, be better received in England without the backing of foreign troops. The Prince allowed a month to slip by after his entry into Edinburgh before he sent another emissary to France—namely, Lord Elcho's brother-in-law Sir James Stewart of Goodtrees—a much more " proper person, being of a clear head and an honest heart," thought Lord George. But unfortunately Goodtrees loitered on his journey, carrying with him to France Lord George's cousin Susan Cochrane, the flirtatious widowed Countess of Strathmore. By the time he eventually set out the North Sea was infested with British men-of-war convoying troops to Britain, and such small supplies of arms as the French felt disposed to spare for the Scots had to be landed at Montrose and Stonehaven.

" Many wished well to the royal Cause," wrote Lord George later regarding the people of Great Britain. " Great numbers would have looked on and would have turned to that side that had success. And those who for their own interest were zealous for the Hanoverian Government would easily have been mastered." But this success, he felt sure, could only have been achieved if the French had supported " the Prince at the beginning of his attempt in a proper manner " before the British troops had been recalled from Flanders. But he was sufficiently clear-sighted to realise that the chance of a successful attack upon weak and disorganised forces had slipped by. He was, therefore, unable to share the Duke of Perth's belief that the British army " would go up in smoke," or to foster their master's fond illusion that " regular troops would never fight against him because he was their lawful Prince."* Desertion was not a tradition in the British army. It had happened only in the reign of James II. when the country was in the grip of a religious panic.

None of the officers, Englishmen or Scots, captured at Prestonpans, and comparatively few of the soldiers (not even Loudon's Highlanders) transferred their allegiance to the Prince. As they marched through Perthshire to Atholl the Duke of Perth's enthusiastic mother had persuaded some prisoners to enlist in his service ; but over sixty of these reluctant recruits took advantage of their liberty to bolt for shelter among their friends in Stirling Castle. Lord George, primed for years by his half-brother Lord John Murray with all manner of regimental gossip, was well aware that no gentlemen of Jacobite leanings served under the Georges as those of an earlier generation had served under Queen Anne. He probably correctly surmised that army men serving at home and abroad must consider that the Scots had stabbed them in the back by rising in rebellion while Britain was engaged in a Continental war.

By the middle of October, after this long stay in Edinburgh, a feeling of frustration began to spread among the higher ranking officers who attended Council meetings and realised how badly their master's affairs were being conducted ; for their own efforts were useless if they should not meet with adequate support from foreign troops and English supporters when they crossed the Border. And now, so careful had Charles been to conceal his carelessly conceived

* Elcho.

plans for establishing contact with English supporters from anyone likely to question their efficiency, that it was probably not until the middle of October that his military counsellors woke to the horrifying realisation that he had established none at all.

About the 16th of October the army, which had been encamped at Duddingston since the Battle of Prestonpans, struck their tents and went into quarters in the neighbouring villages. Reinforcements from the North came in daily. The design of marching into England had been formed before this time. But it was concealed from the most part of the army, and especially from the common people of the North whom no threatening nor force would have drawn into their measures if the scheme had been previously communicated to them. But now it was necessary they all should know it, and that proper dispositions should be made for their marching.

Upon this their Councils fluctuated, their harmony was broken and great heats arose amongst them. A Grand Council of War was called, but with little success. Some complained that they were betrayed and should immediately return homeward and concern themselves no more in a Cause that could not be supported without treachery, fraud, and falsehood. They reasoned to the purpose following : We were many months past flattered with the promise of a powerful force, money, arms, and ammunition from France and Spain. We expected upon the Prince's landing that these would soon follow, and we cheerfully joined his Standard. After our success at Preston we were told with confidence that the French were actually embarked and waited only for a fair wind. That the Dutch troops durst not sail. That the British forces should be detained in Flanders. That an almost general revolt would soon appear in England. The time was fixed and the names of the principal men were given us. And we were assured that the rest of the Highland clans particularly the Macdonalds [from Skye], Macleods, Frasers and Mackenzies should join us. But how great are our disappointments! Not one article of those promises performed! No hopes of a French army. The Dutch are arrived! The British forces daily land! No appearance of an insurrection in England! and no hopes that the clans will join us! Shall we march into England to be cut to pieces by superior force, and have no place of retreat ? Shall we any longer be bubbled by faithless French promises ? Shall we remain here to be chased into the mountains in the winter season ? No. Let us return and lay down our arms. 'Tis not as yet too late to hope for clemency ?

This is not a speech put into their mouths. My information from gentlemen of their number is unquestionable. These were

E

> the sentiments of many of the most judicious in the army. The
> truths and facts could not be denied ; the reasoning could not
> be answered.

So wrote an anonymous but well-informed Whig historian, who
believed that the Jacobites did not recross the Forth because
" persons of the greatest distinction among them . . . had gone
too far to look back, and some were mere agents to play the game
of the Court of Versailles, and unconcerned about the consequences
to Scotsmen."*

Half the Councillors had certainly advocated withdrawing to the
Highlands—a motion only defeated by the votes of Perth and Elcho.
All were much influenced by the words of the Marquis D'Eguilles
who had come over on one of the French ships bearing a letter from
King Louis.† The Prince was instructed not to reveal the contents
to his followers, who were only told that a large body of troops
would be sent over. D'Equilles, however, told Charles " not to
push things too far, or run the risk of a battle without being obliged
to it, for that if he kept his army entire the French would assist
him, whereas if he was defeated they would certainly not send
troops to the country."‡ In conversation with some of the principal
officers this self-styled Ambassador led them to understand that
" it was all one to France whether George or James was King of
England, but that if the Scots wished to have a King for themselves,
then the King of France would help them to the utmost of his
power "—a statement well in keeping with the policy of the French,
who ever desired a weak and divided Britain.

* 'History of the Rebellion in the Years 1745 and 1746,' edited by
Henrietta Tayler.

† Although he had been sent from France for the express purpose of
ascertaining the exact position of affairs in Scotland, Sir John Macdonald
alleges D'Eguilles was " unable to obtain from Murray and Sheridan any
details for his dispatches to France." Nor was O'Sullivan more helpful.
His one thought seems to have been to insert among the Ambassador's dispatches a reminder to Marshal Maillebois to solicit for him the coveted Cross
of Saint Louis, and a letter to King James's Paris agent to say that he hoped
he would not be accused of conceit by saying " all the different affairs were
given him to manage " and to remind His Majesty of his constant zeal and
fidelity. " H.R.H. is pleased with me, and the people of the country, Lords,
and others, are friendly to me and appear, if I may say so, to have confidence
in me," added the self-satisfied Irishman.

‡ Though aware of this the Prince's excuse for leaving his followers after
Culloden was that he was going to France to solicit French troops.

" The mind of the Prince, however, was occupied with England, and he seemed little flattered with the idea of possessing a kingdom to which, however, the family of Stuart owed its origin and its royalty." About a week after the above-mentioned meeting he proposed to march to Newcastle to fight Marshal Wade. He was sure Mr Wade " would run away . . . and . . . a great body of English would join him, and that everybody in London was for him." His Councillors said they hoped it might be so. But " it was time enough to march into England when his friends in that country sent for him." They also reminded him of the King of France's advice " not to search a battle immediately, especially in England, where if the army was beat the affair ended." So wrote Lord Elcho, whose own opinion was that " the enterprise was bold, nay rash, and unexampled. What man in his senses could think of attempting the conquest of England with 4,500 High-landers. It is true they were brave, resolute and determined to fight to the very last, selling their lives as dearly as possible— having no alternative but victory or death."*

If Wade came to Scotland the Prince's officers were ready enough to fight him : but at a Council convened the following morning the Prince could only induce them to march as far as the Border. There all " could learn their business better than in Edinburgh where the inaction of the army began to cause desertion."† In the evening he gathered his leading officers into his room and again pressed for an attack upon Wade. But Lord George and the rest were still against it.

> The Chiefs represented to the Prince that nothing could be more ridiculous than to attempt the invasion of England with a handful of men when it was defended by 50,000 regular troops and a numerous Militia. Some of the Chiefs even told him that they had taken arms and risked their fortunes merely to seat him on the throne of Scotland ; but they wished to have nothing to do with England. However the Prince pretending that he had received letters from several English Lords assuring him that he should find them in arms on the Borders ready to join him with a considerable force, the Chiefs of the clans suffered themselves at length to yield.‡

* Lord Elcho's Journal and Narrative.
† Elcho.
‡ Chevalier Johnstone.

Nothing short of three crowns would content the Prince. " I
see you are determined to stay in Scotland and defend your country,"
he had exclaimed. " But I am not the less determined to try my
fate in England though I should go alone." Such statements from
their ardent young leader had invariably shamed his followers into
yielding to his wishes. They did so now. But it was only by *one*
vote that the decision to invade England was carried.

> It being determined to march for England, horses, carriages,
> and provisions of all sorts, were called in from the country. They
> promised to return the horses how soon they should find others,
> and to pay each servant sixpence a day. . . . They had provided
> above 100 waggons and carts, besides a great number of trunks,
> chests, and baskets, with horses for all their carriages, and for
> mounting some hundreds of men, and a company of what they
> called Hussars. Their train of artillery consisted of eleven or
> twelve pieces of small cannon. And the better to disguise their
> motions, billets for quartering were sent to all the towns and
> villages on the east road to Berwick. . . .
> They set out for England on a mere chance, without any
> rational scheme, or any solid ground of hope. Spies and mes-
> sengers were dispatched before them to learn the motions of the
> King's army, and to inform their friends of their having marched.
> They had, however, but bad encouragement, for some refused to read
> the Pretender's letter, and some of the emissaries were seized.*

So records the Whig historian. But there was no other course
open to the Prince than to try his fortune in England. He had no
further " means of raising money enough to entertain his army in
Scotland," a fact recorded by both O'Sullivan and Kirkconnel.
The latter was well aware of the precarious situation :

> The Prince's orders were obeyed in places far distant from his
> army, and by people that were in their hearts very ill-affected
> towards him. But all this was rather glaring than solid. Unless
> he could make himself master of England, all that he had done in
> Scotland would avail nothing.
> The public money that could be come at was not sufficient to
> pay the army, and private contributions were now at an end.
> They had been pretty considerable, and a great resource. But
> people had given in the beginning what they could afford, or
> were inclined to give, and the supplies from France had been
> very inconsiderable. Besides there was such a desertion among
> the common soldiers, that the army was not really as much

* 'History of the Rebellion in the Year 1745 and 1746,' edited by Henrietta Tayler.

augmented as people generally imagined, and it was thought nothing but action would put an end to this desertion, which was imputed to the idleness and leisure they had had.

Alexander Gordon, a Jesuit priest whom the Prince had interviewed two days before the march began, was sent to France with the false report that 12,000 Foot and 1,000 Horse were already in Edinburgh, though in actual fact the Prince had not as yet succeeded in recruiting 6,000 men, a poor figure compared with the 14,000 whom Mar had gathered round him thirty years before. The English Ministry's summing up of the danger threatened by this present uprising was tolerably accurate. In 1715 they had placed the price of £100,000 upon the head of King James : in 1745 they placed only £30,000 upon that of his son.

Equally untrue was the statement sent to France that several thousand more Highlanders were on the march to Edinburgh, and that a hundred invitations had come from nobles in various English counties, as well as enough money to maintain the troops. Not a single guinea, letter, or invitation ever came from anyone in England or Wales—a fact which some of the Councillors suspected from the first, since none was ever shown to them.

Under such circumstances Lord George looked forward to the proposed invasion with no more relish than did other level-headed officers. By marching south they were abandoning the chance of any supplies reaching them from France ; for owing to the vigilance of the British Navy, the few arms and supplies sent over in November had had to be landed at Montrose and Stonehaven. It appeared more than doubtful if a landing could be made on the coast of England. But Lord George had twice witnessed the disastrous results of waiting in the Highlands while the Jacobite forces melted away and those of the Whigs increased. Such a course must not be adopted for a third time.

At the next Council meeting the Prince induced his unwilling Councillors to support a plan which he brought forward after they had consented, though hesitatingly, to advance to meet Wade who was still at Newcastle :

His Royal Highness seemed determined to march straight to Berwick. This was represented by Lord George Murray as of very dangerous consequence, for it was a walled town and a General officer with at least 300 regular troops besides Militia

in it. Highlanders were not fit for making a siege, and the cannon
they had could do no hurt to the walls, six of them being four
pounders and the rest three and two pounders. General Wade
was about Newcastle with an army stronger than that of His
Royal Highness. He proposed going into England by Carlisle,
which although walled and a castle, yet they would be unprepared.
It was believed no regular troops were there. He would march
one part of the army by Kelso as if the design were to march into
England by Woolerhaughhead and go to Newcastle, which would
hinder them sending any troops to Carlisle. After halting a day
at Kelso that part of the army would take the right-hand road to
Jedburgh and in two days more they would get near to Carlisle.
At the same time the other part of the army with the cannon and
heavy baggage would march straight for Carlisle by Moffat, the
road from Kelso to Carlisle not being fit for carriages. All would
meet the day appointed near to Carlisle. His Royal Highness
did not approve of this, but said he would march straight for
Berwick with the whole army. But next morning he told Lord
George as he found the officers were of the same opinion as to
the march he would follow his plan. The necessary orders were
accordingly given and in such a way as it was generally believed
the whole army was to march towards Newcastle.*

Lord George's was the only possible plan. Even had they
bypassed Berwick by taking the road from Kelso to Newcastle,
Wade would in all likelihood have retired behind the walls from
which he could not have been dislodged. He would thus have been
left free to follow on their heels and crush them in a pincer grip
between his own force and the army marching up from the south.
And each of these armies was twice the size of the Prince's command
—unless a miracle happened and ten times as many Northumbrians
mounted the White Cockade as in the last Rising. This indeed
was a most unlikely event in view of the thousands of Government
soldiers now assembled in Northumberland ready to nip rebellion
in the bud. If, however, the Prince's forces entered England by
Carlisle " Wade would have to make a long march through difficult
country in the depth of winter, and the [Jacobite] army could
maintain itself on the western hills while awaiting a French landing,
a rising of the English Jacobites, or the reinforcements expected
from Scotland. If, on the other hand, Wade was met on his own
ground a single defeat would be fatal."†

* Lord George's Unpublished Notes.
† Ibid.

Lord George set out upon the march with a heavy heart. He wrote to his wife before leaving :

EDINR., 1st Nov. 1745.

MY LIFE,—I entreat and conjure you to take care of your health, and next to that I recommend to you our dear children.

Happen what will, it is a comfort to me that I leave them a parent so affect. and so capable of advising them. Virtue is preferable to all the riches in the world attended with vice and folly. You cannot hear from me in haste (perhaps never), for, except things go beyond expectation, I do not think of any sure way to convey our letters.

Remember what I said at parting at your own house, I am of the very same opinion still, but God may order it otherways. To Him I recommend you and my dear babies.

Bid Amie read history, use exercise, and endeavour a contented mind, but I advise her not to be a bigot to any sect or party. Farewell.

Once more as the greatest proof of your friendship (of which I have had such inumerable instances), take care of yourself, and prefer peace of mind with a morsel to riches and everything else on earth. Adieu.

I ever have been and shall be yours whilst

GEORGE MURRAY.

We march today.*

That same morning Lord George with pipes skirling marched through the streets of Edinburgh with the last troops to be withdrawn from the capital. He led them to the rendezvous at Dalkeith. There the Jacobite force was brought up to 5,000 Foot and 500 Horse by the arrival of Duke William at the head of 1,000 Athollmen and Macphersons. The Atholl Brigade was now 1,000 strong.

The Dukes of Atholl and Perth commanded the second column that took the road to Moffat, but Lord George accompanied the Prince and the main body of the army on the march to the Border. Near Jedburgh he crossed the Tweed with a small party to make a feint of advancing upon Berwick. The recent rain appeared to have rendered the river impassable. "Lord George accompanied by Murray of Solzarie and Robertson of Easter Bleaton instantly jumped into the river and forded, while the soldiers looked on with

* 'Atholl Chronicles.'

amazement from the bank. When Lord George and his two companions got out of the deep strong current they leaped and danced in the river to show the soldiers that there was no great danger, and to encourage them to follow, which they instantly did. . . . After fording the river each man got a glass of gin and a half-penny roll."* Another day when Lord George and his staff were dining at a Border farm some straggling Highlanders walked in, but perceiving who was there, backed out without a word. When Lord George asked the farmer's wife what they had to pay, " Oh, nothing," she said. " Well," was his Lordship's reply, " I believe we have saved you more than we have got."†

According to the nameless Whig historian the soldiers had been induced to undertake the march on the assurance " that the French only waited till the British forces should be drawn northward and then they should make a descent in the South of England ; that their friends in England were ready to join as soon as the army entered English ground ; that the towns would throw open their gates, and that they could not but find plenty of money and provisions in that opulent kingdom."

The main army, which Lord George had rejoined at Jedburgh, boldly entered England on 8th November, and the following day was joined by the other column led by the Dukes of Atholl and Perth. The encirclement of Carlisle had to be postponed owing to a false report that old " Grandmother Wade " was marching westward, which caused the Jacobites to turn aside to Brampton. Lord George, however, proved correct in his forecast that the Government forces would neither intercept them on their western march nor venture to slip into Scotland in the rear, where they would be in danger of their being trapped between the Prince's army and that which Viscount Strathallan was gathering at Perth.

One thousand Highlanders, imbued with a superstitious reluctance to cross the Border, had deserted on their way thither, leaving the Prince with an army of the size with which it had been deemed unsafe to attempt the invasion of England. But his adversary had even more recalcitrant troops with which to deal. Before the Scottish army had left Edinburgh Marshal Wade's Dutch officers

* ' Atholl Chronicles.'
† ' Prince Charlie in the Border Country.'

flatly refused to march their six thousand men northward until matters concerning their pay and their horses had been settled to their satisfaction. Nor were they or Wade himself more inclined to march westward to the aid of gout-ridden Colonel Durand who, with eighty Invalids and the terror-stricken local Militiamen, was responsible for holding the crumbling citadel of Carlisle. Just as obligingly as Cope had stepped aside to allow the Jacobites to overrun the Lowlands, so now his aged colleague, anxious to avoid disaster, remained stock-still at Newcastle leaving them free to invest Carlisle—the Gateway into England.

CHAPTER V

CARLISLE

LORD GEORGE was offered the supreme command at the Siege of
Carlisle, but because of his lack of experience in siege warfare he
preferred to undertake the posting of the beleaguering forces and
to leave the care of the batteries to Perth, who had studied fortification
in Paris.

Lord George Murray said he was persuaded Carlisle might be
easily taken, there being no regular troops in it, and offered with
half the army to make the attempt. The Duke of Perth was of
the same opinion and said he would undertake to raise a battery
at a convenient distance, so that he hoped in a few days to oblige
the town to surrender. This was agreed to. His Grace was to
take charge of the battery, and the other the blockade.

Lord George Murray next day before he left the Prince (who
was to stay at Brampton till he knew what motion General Wade
would make) desired to know upon what terms Carlisle, should
it offer to capitulate, would be received. He thought it would
save time, which was precious, to know as near as could be what
His Royal Highness would desire of the town. Then he could
send word to the Prince if the terms were accepted of; in which
case the Prince would have nothing more to do but to receive the
keys if the town agreed to what should be proposed. But he was
told orders would be given time enough about that, and that it
was a civil affair to capitulate with the town and that no General
officer had any concern about it, &c.

On Wednesday the 13th [November] the town was blockaded
on all sides with six battalions, which considering the great
circumfrance on both sides of the river Eden, was too few, the
posts being at such a distance that the militia within the town
might easily have beat up one of the quarters before assistance
could come from another. Yet the service being of such consequence most of these six battalions were willing to be on guard
night and day, being in small villages under cover. The greatest
difficulty was where the battery and cannon was to be raised so
as not to be annoyed from the cannon and small arms of the
town. The Duke of Perth was indefatigable and took all the
pains possible, employing most of his own regiment in the works
whilst the rest kept guard the first night. Next morning he had

abundance of difficulty to keep his men from abandoning the works and guard of the trench, which many of them did. Had he not stayed with them almost the whole time himself they would have abandoned them for none of the men had ever seen such work before and it was a storm of frost and snow all night.

Lord George Murray to relieve him offered to go as a volunteer with two or three hundred other volunteers out of the Atholl Brigade to guard the trenches. For tho' they were very willing to go on with him as volunteers to guard the trenches for twenty-four hours, yet they absolutely declined it as a duty except all the army would take it in their turns. Indeed the danger was nothing in comparison of the fatigue in staying twenty-four hours in frost and snow in the middle of November—and that to men who had had execrable hard duty in the blockade besides, for the six battalions at Brampton were to have no share in it as was determined by themselves in the Prince's presence in a Council of War. But the method Lord George Murray fell upon of doing the thing by volunteers had the desired effect because the men strove who should go with him.

Very luckily on Thursday the 14th about an hour before the guard was to be relieved the town hung out the white flag. There was but one man killed, an Irish officer standing out of the trench jeering they could not fire cannon like gunners from the town. At the very time a cannon ball went through his throat.

It is impossible to conceive how ill the quartermasters did their duty. Three of the regiments who were next to the town upon the blockade got scarce any provisions (the country people having in these villages left all their houses) and did not get orders to come to town till the second night after all those who had been at Brampton came in. Then they were lodged in the Castle in vaults and a ruinous house without coal, candle, meat, and drink.*

The Quartermaster-General's orders were so muddled that Lord George " managed to have several deputies appointed to take away O'Sullivan's powers."† Unfortunately they proved to be equally useless ; and the arrangements of the Commissariat Committee had also broken down.

By declining to take full command at Carlisle, because, as he frankly admitted, he " understood nothing of sieges," Lord George unwittingly offended the Prince. Charles retaliated by sending all orders to the Duke of Perth who, observers noted, had for some time been given " all the preferences," so that Lord George " felt his

* Lord George's Unpublished Notes.
† O'Sullivan.

authority to be counterbalanced by that of the Duke."* And now to increase his annoyance, after so much stress had been laid upon the fact that no General had any concern in such matters, Perth was appointed to act jointly with Broughton in negotiating the city's terms of surrender.

Lord George's contribution to the final triumph had, in fact, been as great, and his task as difficult as that of his colleague. He was the only commander who could induce the men to assist in the siege, for Highlanders detested such work and were impatient even when employed as sentries. Even the inimical Secretary admitted that he had placed the beleaguering forces with " so much judgment that the few French officers then in the army allowed they had never seen anything of the kind better executed."† This was written some years later by a chastened Broughton. At the time it is doubtful if his growing jealousy of Lord George would have allowed him to pay him compliments. There was now a decided coolness between the two men ; for Lord George already suspected the duplicity and mendacity of the Secretary ; and he strongly resented his determination to take " everything upon him, both as to civil and military.‡ Broughton, who had been allowed to arrange about the capitulation of Edinburgh, may well have suspected Lord George of a design to clip his powers as well as those of O'Sullivan. Fearful of interference, when sent to Carlisle to meet the Deputies he stopped at his quarters to procure a guide " without sending any message or otherwise taking any notice of him." On his return to Brampton he learned that Lord George had written to the Prince asking to be relieved of his commission as his " advice as a General officer had so little weight,"§ though owing to his " attachment to the Royal Family, in particular to the King," he desired to serve in the ranks as a volunteer. The Prince replied :

> I think your advice ever since you joined me at Perth has had another guess weight with me than what any General could claim as such. I am therefore extremely surprised you should throw up your commission for a reason which I believe was never heard of before.
>
> I am glad of your particular attachment to the King, but I am

* Kirkconnel.
† ' Memorials of Murray of Broughton.'
‡ ' Jacobite Memoirs,' by Robert Chambers.
§ Ibid.

very sure he will never take any proof of it but your deference to me. I accept of your demission as Lieutenant-General, and your future services as a volunteer.

CHARLES *P.R.**

" Lord George's unfortunate reference to his especial affection for King James had offended the Prince, who could never comprehend that to the older Jacobites his father was King and master, and he merely the Prince of Wales. He also believed that although Lord George would have made ' a very good Dragoon,' he knew very little of the General."† That persistent mischief-maker Sir John Macdonald also averred that his military knowledge was out of date, and that although some of his plans were good he had not the ability to execute them. It was only because the English were even more ignorant of the art of war that they had been drubbed at Prestonpans. He described the letter of resignation as a most " impertinent letter," and he and his crony Colonel Strickland declared that this was a " very good occasion to get rid of a dangerous man, suspected by all the army except Sheridan and three or four others whom he had persuaded of his ability and honesty."‡ The very fact that Lord George would never take any advice from O'Sullivan caused the Prince to be as doubtful of his military qualifications as of his fidelity.

A man of the name of Ranald Macdonald, described as " a kind of officer in Keppoch's Regiment "§ (and in all likelihood the husband or a near relative of the Macdonald woman who had called upon Sir John in Perth), was at this time circulating all manner of falsehoods about Lord George. His name was only revealed in 1805 by Captain Alexander MacNab of Inishewen, Glendochart, who in extreme old age wrote ' A Vindication of the Conduct of Lord George Murray,' under whom he had fought during the campaign. Inishewen wrote :

> A subaltern officer [Ranald Macdonald] told me he had lodged
> with a widow who informed him that there was a principal

* ' Atholl Chronicles.'
† Inishewen's ' Vindication.' This was said during the Prince's wanderings to John Roy Stewart, who then upheld Lord George. Later this somewhat mercurial poet wrote his well-known ' Seven Curses Upon Lord George Murray.'
‡ ' Memoirs of Sir John Macdonald.'
§ Inishewen's ' Vindication.'

personage in our army who corresponded closely with the Government. She believed his name was Lord George Murray. This she said she had heard from a gentleman who lodged with her. I asked him why he did not impart this intelligence. His answer was that he thought it unnecessary as the gentleman was from home who knew the whole affair. I then desired him whenever he got to his billet that night to wait upon his colonel and communicate this piece of intelligence to him. But this he did not perform, as I afterwards understood from the colonel himself. A few days after the same subaltern told me of some bad usage he had received from Lord George Murray before the year 1745 when he had charge of a part of the Duke of Atholl's property in Strathbran with other lands in the neighbourhood to guard against depredations and carrying off cattle by the Highlanders of his country. The annual salary of such an office was called in those days blackmail. From all which relations I strongly suspect he was actuated by motives of revenge and was the sole propagator of this groundless calumny raised against Lord George. From my own observations Lord George's conduct was not only blameless but likewise true and loyal to his Prince from his first entering into the service till the whole was over.

Ranald was probably the originator of a story that since crossing the Border a clansman in a scuffle with a wayfarer had broken his stick, and inside the severed shaft had found a message from Duke James bidding George win pardon by deserting with the Atholl Brigade in the heat of battle.*

Kirkconnel records Lord George's reactions to this campaign of slander that had been launched against him :

Lord George soon came to know the suspicions the Prince had of him and was affected as one may easily imagine. To be sure nothing could have been more shocking to a man of honour and one that was now for the third time venturing his life and fortune in the Royal Cause. The Prince was partly undeceived by Lord George's gallant behaviour at the battle, and had Lord George improved that opportunity, he might perhaps have got the better of the Secretary. But his haughty and overbearing manner prevented a thorough reconciliation, and seconded the malicious insinuations of his rival. Lord George did not altogether neglect making his court; upon occasions he was very obsequious and respectful, but he had not the temper to go through with it. He now and then broke into such violent sallies as the Prince could not digest, though the situation of his affairs forced him to bear with them.

* This was a method employed by Duke James's henchman, Commissary Bissett, when sending messages to his master.

Many people have wondered why Lord George took no steps to refute the charges levelled against him. He had no time to do so. From Edinburgh he had written to William of having " more business on my hands than any one person can manage—more than ever came to the share of one man."* Once the march began he was even busier. Neither could he wholly vindicate his own conduct at the time of his resignation, or later, without exposing the weakness of the Prince's character. This he would not do. To the end he faithfully carried out his brother William's injunctions to be as careful of their young master's honour as of his own. His decision was right; and in keeping with his character. But history is the poorer for his reticence. Because of it writers have for years been left to say the Prince was right, his Lieutenant-General wrong— or the other way about—according to their own predilections or preconceived notions. But none was able to bring forward much convincing evidence to back such assertions.

Kirkconnel in his account of the campaign records Lord George's dislike of contradiction, impatience of advice, and his determination to have his own way in all things. Such criticism is understandable from one who, as a simple Major in the Life Guards, had no seat in the Council Chamber, and thus had no real opportunity of gauging the situation with which the Lieutenant-General was confronted. But the true state of affairs is revealed with startling clarity in an unsigned letter of the period recently discovered at Blair Castle :

> Some of the Irish . . . found fault with him, as he never courted their favour and did not apply to them—but always directly to the Prince himself. As many things regarding the operations of the War, which were both his own and all the principal Scots officers' opinions, were directly opposite to [what] Sir Thomas Sheridan, O'Sullivan, &c., were determined upon, they made the Prince believe that Lord George Murray was haughty and opinionate, as he was often obliged to declare his mind very freely.
> They therefore made the Prince believe those who were for delays had bad views. This was not done in any Council of War. If Mr Sullivan carried anything contrary to the opinion of the Scots officers it was in private ; for when at first there was frequent Councils of War held Mr O'Sullivan never differed from the rest, or if he did it was in private.

* Letters from Lord George to Duke William. The Jacobite Correspondence of the Atholl Family.

Lord Elcho, an astute young man, listened with disgust to the Prince's diatribes about his General, and with amused scorn to O'Sullivan's oft-repeated assurances that had he a thousand lives he would give them all to his master. He was amazed that Charles could be taken in by the stories of such men as the Quartermaster-General and the Secretary, both of whom were known to be liars. But as he wrote in his ' Journal ' :

> The Prince was extremely credulous and readily believed whatever was told him by those he had confidence in. . . . That which the Secretary Murray insinuated in the hearing of the Prince against my Lord George Murray exercised such an influence on the Prince's mind that in spite of the convincing proofs of attachment to his Cause that my Lord George Murray gave every day, he detested Lord George so heartily that he spoke of him as one who would betray him, although no one bore himself better than Murray on every occasion.
>
> Lord George knew of all these rumours, and so had confined himself to doing his duty as a soldier without offering any advice. [He] was a man of spirit, very brave, and one that would not let himself be ruled by anybody—and with good reason. [As] head of the Scots, the Prince and the Irish did not like him. The Scots on the other hand liked him much, and had great confidence in his capacity.

Maxwell of Kirkconnel shared his commanding officer's belief that Broughton was for ever reminding the Prince of his General's previous acceptance of Hanoverian rule, and of his friendship for his Whig brother. Others suspected Broughton's own fidelity to the Cause, and a rumour was current among the enemy that he had been condemned to be hanged for treachery, but had been pardoned at the last minute by the lenient Prince. As the worried Secretary wrote, his " ears were daily stunned with so many falsehoods not only charged upon himself, but on Lord George Murray and others, that he laid it down as an unerring maxim not to be swerved from to give credit to nothing till such time as he had the most convincing proof."* He and Lord George wrote with much irritation about each other's conduct at Carlisle ; but at other times they gave each other praise where praise was due. The Secretary never sought to curry favour with the Whigs by abuse of his former master and

---

* All quotations from ' Memorials of Murray of Broughton,' or his alleged ' Genuine Memoir.'

comrades, in whose estimation he was for ever damned after he had turned King's Evidence to save his life. In his own account of the campaign Lord George fulminates only against O'Sullivan and Sir John Macdonald. He evidently realised that the Secretary, who had nothing to gain by furthering French interests, and everything to lose in the event of defeat, essayed by devious means to deflect the Prince from courses upon which he was obstinately bent, but which were obviously against his best interests. In the present crisis Broughton seems to have acted with sound good sense. Realising that the sympathy of the Chiefs was with Lord George, whose " seeming disgust " they attributed to his (Broughton's) advice being so much followed by the Prince, he at once informed his master of what he had heard. He further declared that as his " interest was the thing in his life which he had most at heart . . . he would absent himself from Council."*

With some pique Lord George wrote to his brother that he had supposed he would have stood his friend upon the occasion. But evidently so stout a Royalist as Duke William had not been able to condone the slightest opposition to the young master whom he loved as dearly as he loved the King. The need to save Charles from the effects of his own rashness was entirely lost upon this devoted Jacobite, " who in spite of all he had suffered since the 'Fifteen, was no less sanguine in what he called the Royal Cause than he had shown himself before."† William could see no fault in those he loved. Nor could he understand George's dislike of Charles's associates. To him any man who loved, or appeared to love the Prince was a friend and brother. He got on well with Sheridan and Strickland and even with crusty old Sir John, for their views on Absolute Monarchy and similar subjects were entirely in keeping with his own. He was, moreover, truly fond of Broughton, who had sought him out in Paris and treated him with much respect and kindness in the days of his rule.

The Duke, however, arranged an abortive interview between his brother and the Prince at Headquarters, where Lord George had a quite friendly talk with Sir Thomas about the misunderstanding his reference to his especial devotion to the King seemed to have caused.

* ' Memorials of Murray of Broughton.'
† ' Genuine Memoirs of John Murray, Esqr.'

F

At the time of his resignation Lord George had written to William : " In the manner things are conducted I can be of more use charging in the first rank of your Athollmen than as a General, where I was constantly at a loss to know what was doing. I had no authority in the station I was in. Others acted as general who had not any call, but used His Royal Highness's name. In the drudgery I was employed ; but anything of moment was done without my participation."*

These statements have caused many people to suppose that Lord George threw up his commission in a fit of pique. Nothing could be further from the truth. Even Broughton admits that his chief cause of complaint was that Perth, who was a Catholic, had been allowed to negotiate the terms of surrender. Kirkconnel records the consternation the news of Lord George's resignation caused among his fellow officers, who had " a much greater opinion of his capacity than of the Duke's, though nobody had the Cause more at heart than his Grace " :

> The command of the Duke of Perth had like to have had bad consequences. It was not as much relished by some of the Prince's friends as by his enemies. They said that in England Roman Catholics were excluded from all employments civil and military by laws anterior to the Revolution. These laws, whether reasonable or not, ought to subsist until they were repealed ; that a contrary conduct, without a visible necessity for it, would confirm all that had been spread of old from the pulpit and from the press of the Prince's design to overturn the constitution of Church and State.

Lord George had anticipated the reaction of the English to Perth's command. But as his obvious successor it would not have come well from him to point this out to the Prince. Before leaving Scotland he had, however, induced Lord Elcho and others to mention the bad effects of " having a Catholic at Council, or in any public employ." The Prince replied that " if when in England his friends found fault with it, he'd follow their advice ; but in his present situation he did not see how he could propose to the Duke of Perth not to come to Council nor act as Lieutenant-General. Sir Thomas Sheridan was a Counsel [Councillor] that was given

* Extracts from letters in ' Jacobite Memoirs.'

him by the King.* Chiefs or Colonels that were Catholics had as
much right as others to know at least what regarded the army, or
what was to be undertook for the Cause, since they contributed as
much to it as any, and that Sullivan was the only military man in
the army." Yet now, in spite of such a warning, the Prince had
committed the major blunder of setting aside the Protestant and
appointing the Catholic General to make terms with the civic
authorities of the first English city that fell into his hands. Elcho
deplored such a decision :

> The Prince had always shown a great shyness for Lord George,
> and had affected to give all sort of commands to the Duke of
> Perth ; now again at the Siege of Carlisle, where people thought
> it would have been more proper for Lord George as he was a
> Protestant to have signed the capitulation in which there was
> question of securing the people in the enjoyment of their religion,
> than the Duke of Perth who was a Roman Catholic.

What Lord George had foreseen soon came to pass. An article
in a Whig newspaper pointed out that the " Pretender's " Councils
were directed by his Popish followers. Sir Thomas Sheridan, whose
pontifical mein caused an English crowd to mistake him for the
Archbishop of Canterbury, was likened by the writer to Father
Petre, whose bad advice had brought about the downfall of James II.
He also voiced the loud complaints of the citizens of Carlisle that a
Papist (however courteous and considerate) had been chosen to
treat with them. The officers' alarm increased. They talked " with
great warmth " about their new commander's religion. Lord Elcho
set down in his ' Journal ' :

> The principle people in the army met, and when the Prince
> came to Carlisle delivered a petition to the Prince begging
> that he would discharge all Roman Catholics from his Council
> . . . and . . . that when there was any question of capitu-
> lations wherein there was mention of securing the liberties
> of the Church of England, that Protestants might be employed
> to do it preferable to Roman Catholics. They concluded by
> desiring that Lord George Murray should be desired to take back
> his commission.

---

* At his son's request King James had reluctantly sent Sir Thomas to
keep him company in Paris, with the admonition to be kind to and to take
care of the old man whom he himself thought was quite unfit to undertake
the journey.

The Chevalier Johnstone had also much to say upon the same subject.

Lord George . . . possessed a natural genius for military operations, and was indeed a man of surprising talents, which had they been cultivated by the study of military tactics, would unquestionably have rendered him one of the greatest generals of the age. He was tall and robust, and brave in the highest degree, conducting the Highlanders in the most heroic manner. . . . He slept little, was continually occupied with all manner of details, and was altogether most indefatigable, combining and directing all our operations. In a word he was the only man capable of conducting our army. Vigilant, active, and diligent, his plans were always judiciously formed, and he carried them promptly and vigorously into execution. However, with an infinity of good qualities he was not without his defects. Proud, haughty, blunt, imperious, he wished to have the exclusive ordering of everything, and feeling his superiority, he would listen to no advice. There were few persons it is true in our army sufficiently versed in military matters to be capable of advising him as to the conduct of operations. . . .

Lord George possessing so many qualities requisite to form a General, gained the hearts of the Highlanders ; and a General who has the confidence of his soldiers may perform wonders. Hence, possessing the art of employing men to advantage, without having time to discipline them, but merely taking them as they came from the plough, he made them perform prodigies of valour against various English armies—always greatly superior in numbers to that of the Prince—though the English troops are allowed to be the best in Europe. Nature had formed him for a great warrior ; he did not require the accidental advantage of his birth.

A serious split in the Jacobite army was averted by the prompt action of one of Perth's friends, who represented the case to him. Declaring that he " never had anything in view except the Prince's interest and would cheerfully sacrifice everything to it," the young Duke " most readily resigned, showing himself willing to promote the Cause in any state, and giving a notable example of a brave warrior, willing to command and willing to obey, and willing to sacrifice for the common good his rank, his money, and his life.* To add to his magnanimity the Duke, who was still the Colonel of his own regiment, offered to take charge of the baggage when the army marched, as Lord Ogilvy had threatened to throw up his

---

* Captain Daniel's Progress. Blaikie's ' Origins of the 'Forty-Five.'

commission and serve as a volunteer rather than his men should be " employed in such dirty work."*

" The Prince was thus compelled (though much against his will) to request Lord George to withdraw his resignation. This he consented to do. The Secretary was banished from the Council table, " which seemed to quieten Lord George a good deal,"† although he remained suspicious that his enemy secretly undermined his authority. Broughton still had too much of the ear of his infatuated master, who regarded him as " one of the honestest, finest men in the world,"‡ and therefore the " misunderstanding in the Council did not end with the Duke of Perth's command. The rancour between Lord George and the Secretary still continued, though it did not break out on every occasion and sometimes gave way to the common good, particularly when the whole seemed to be at stake."§

> One reason that weighed amongst many with me not to give up command was the persuasion I found everybody had (tho' I believe it was being too partial to me) that I was of absolute use to the service and could not be spared. Add to that that I could not leave so many brave men who were engaged.‖

So Lord George wrote later to his wife. But it was with misgiving rather than elation that he resumed command ; for, as he told William, he had realised for some time that " things must go to utter confusion."¶ He was, moreover, oppressed by a heavy sense of responsibility for the safety of his Sovereign's son and all who had ventured on this risky expedition into a seemingly hostile country, where almost everyone evinced a " great dislike to the Cause."** And it was not only from his enemies that Charles needed shielding ; but also from his so-called friends. Both Sheridan and O'Sullivan were a menace on account of their inability to see how matters really stood. Lord George, though always intensely irritated by methodless and muddle-headed people, had always striven to deal patiently with those whose faults seemed to proceed

---

* Letter of Lord Ogilvy to Lady Ogilvy.
† 'Memorials of Murray of Broughton.'
‡ 'Genuine Memoirs of John Murray, Esqr.'
§ Kirkconnel.
‖ 'Atholl Chronicles.'
¶ 'Jacobite Memoirs.'
** Elcho.

from the head, and not the heart. But a state of emergency was no
time for a display of Christian patience. Compromise, or a policy
of give and take, was out of the question at a time of crisis, when
one false move might bring about irreparable disaster.

Lord George resolved to remain and to fight the evil councillors
who surrounded the Prince. He did so with such thoroughness
that their hatred of him grew—as did the lies they told about him.
Few people in his own day or since have realised the cruel disabilities under which he laboured—disabilities which prevented
him from rising to the same great heights as those former champions
of the Stuart Cause, Montrose and Dundee. The two great Greames
had supreme command of their armies, and none above them to
interfere with their plans. But Charles did interfere. And " whenever he interfered he made mischief."* When Lord George produced some well-thought-out and carefully laid plan, it was often
sabotaged by his enemies at Headquarters. He was, in fact, as
uncomfortably circumstanced as the unfortunate Generals of the
Covenanting armies who had been under the guidance of a flock of
black-gowned Ministers knowing nothing of the art of war.

During election contests it had been Lord George's custom to
look ahead, and also to survey the situation as far as was practicable
from the point of view of the opposition, in order to be able to
forestall possible moves. By continuing this practice during military
operations he was usually able to circumvent the manœuvres of
the Government commanders however scantily he was supplied
with information about affairs in England. " If I did not always do
what I would, at least I am sure I did what I could,"† were the
words with which he later wound up his account of the adventurous
marches upon which he led the small but gallant Highland army.

On the whole march from Edinburgh only one Border laird had
attempted to join the Jacobite forces, and owing to the Prince's
failure to forewarn supporters in the districts through which the
army was to march, this far from enthusiastic recruit arrived on
the road after it had marched by, and forthwith returned to his
home. Although the Jacobites met with no opposition on their
way to Carlisle, they met with many " sour faces "‡ along their

---

* Note to the Memoirs of the Chevalier Johnstone.
† Lord George's ' Marches.'
‡ Letter of Lord Ogilvy to Lady Ogilvy.

route, and in the city and the surrounding villages the inhabitants showed the greatest fear and dislike of the invaders. Three recruits came in from Northumberland; four from Cumberland, one of whom was too infirm for soldiering. Another at once slipped out of the ranks, and a third remained for the purpose of acting as a Government spy. The Prince's officers, particularly Lochiel and Lord Ogilvy, noted these things, and were filled with foreboding.

CHAPTER VI

THE ADVANCE

ALTHOUGH the Prince " found himself miserably disappointed in his expectations since entering England," he resolved to advance farther into that country. Such a move was not expected by Wade's officers, who never supposed that he would risk being trapped between their army and that which was marching northward under the command of King George's second son William, Duke of Cumberland, who had superseded Sir Jean Ligonier. Assuredly his hoped-for English supporters would never risk declaring for him and being trapped as Derwentwater's men had been between Wills's and Carpenter's armies at Preston thirty years before. Veteran regular officers, who had taken part in that campaign, noted the change that had taken place in the minds of North Country folk. The lessons of that earlier ill-starred Rising had been well and truly learned by both Whigs and Tories. The English Ministry did not repeat the mistake of driving Jacobite suspects into premature rebellion by threatening their arrest; and the once disaffected Northumbrian squires evinced no inclination to lose their lives or lands by embarking on a venture doomed to instantaneous suppression in a county teeming with Government troops.

But Charles chose to disregard his royal father's warning that it would be the ruin of the Cause if he invaded England without being invited there by the principal peers or the assurance of French help which, in view of King Louis's neglectful treatment of the Prince, seemed unlikely to be forthcoming. His head was still in the clouds. He supposed that Tory peers (of whom only Lord Barrymore ever corresponded with the exiled Court) would flock unsummoned to his Standard. Unlike King James, he lent ear to the far-fetched statements of unreliable Jacobite agents, or of favourites whose only object was to please. He even believed the fabulous report of King Louis's emissary Butler, who, after visiting several English country houses and listening to tales told over wine cups, had expressed astonishment that a Hanoverian still sat upon the throne, since all the country was said to be for King James, and the Archbishop of Canterbury, the Lord Mayor of London, and at least five Dukes were certain to come over to his side. In olden times Lancastrian, Yorkist, and Tudor claimants had possessed themselves of the Crown by winning over to their side great noblemen whom the occupant of the throne had counted upon as his own supporters. Since the establishment of a standing army the only invader who had met with success was the wily and experienced William of Orange, who before embarking upon the attempt had offered rewards to statesmen and generals if they would desert their royal master King James.

Charles had no experience in diplomacy; and no aptitude for moulding men and events to his purpose, save by the exercise of his personal charm upon the Chiefs with whom he came into personal contact. He had not even troubled to establish contact with English supporters by letter. Yet at the Council meeting convened at Carlisle he " again pretended he had received fresh letters from his friends in England assuring him that he should find them in arms on his arrival at Preston. The Chiefs represented in strong terms the danger of penetrating further into England," for the English " who had promised to join him on the Borders had vanished into smoke."*

The Prince's now thoroughly depressed followers were more inclined to remain where they were, or else return to their own country from which they received disquieting intelligence. The Scottish nation as a whole evinced little desire to see " the auld Stuarts back again," and in spite of the initial fear of allowing Scottish peers to raise volunteers to repel the Jacobites, before long there were more Scotsmen in arms against the Prince than for him. He seemed indeed to have more active enemies among the Lowland Scots than among the apathetic English. Edinburgh had resumed allegiance to the House of Hanover; and there had been local outbreaks against the Jacobites in various towns. The most serious occurred at Perth where Oliphant of Gask, the Deputy-Governor, had been confined for a night in the Council House until his redoubtable mother-in-law Lady Nairne hurriedly got together an armed force which she despatched to his rescue. If the French ultimately landed it was now perfectly obvious that they must do so on the north coast, since the English Channel was guarded by the British

* Anonymous Whig History.

fleet. The Prince, however, persisted that they would land in the south, and that if he marched there " everybody would receive him with joyful hearts and he would meet with no opposition."* Broughton, who was Treasurer as well as Secretary, produced a sounder reason for advancing—namely, that there was not enough money to maintain the army unless they levied cess on other towns. Lord George, though proffering advice with " more caution in consequence of the recent circumstances at Carlisle which led to his resignation,"† warned his master that the project " was attended with such danger to his person and all with him that he believed nobody would advise him to march south with so small an army. But if he did desire it, he was persuaded the army would follow him."‡ This the other leaders agreed to do—lest " it was said afterwards that had the army marched to Lancashire the English would have joined."§

While they debated upon these matters their best chance of inflicting a sound defeat upon the enemy slipped by. On 16th November Wade set out for Carlisle at the head of an army which, had the Jacobites but known it, was in a poor fighting condition. The seventy-two-year-old Marshal had grown miserly with advancing years. His " ill-timed economy " had disastrous effects upon the health and morale of his men. Many of them had come from Flanders suffering from dysentery and in a downcast state after the unsuccessful campaign there ; and their spirits had not improved since meeting with Cope's defeated Dragoons. Both British and foreign soldiers, used to spending the inclement months of the year in winter quarters, had suffered greatly in the camp at Newcastle, which was partially under water. On their march to Hexham they were forced to lie all night in the snow upon an open moor, where tents could not be pitched owing to the hardness of the ground. Wade, moreover, grudged every penny he had to spend in providing them with bread, firing, or even straw to lie upon. Sick, shivering, floundering in the snow, and heartily disgusted with their commander, who had furnished them with " scarcely a morsel of provisions," they would have proved no match for the hardy Highlanders

* Elcho.
† Lord George's Unpublished Notes.
‡ Lord George's ' Marches.'
§ Elcho.

to whom snowdrifts were no impediment on a march.* The Dutch, Swiss, German and Irish, composing more than half the army, cared nothing who sat upon the British throne. The Dutch were disposed to be troublesome and insolent, and the " damned runaway Dragoons," as their commanding officer called them,† would almost certainly have bolted as they had done at Stirling, Coltbrig, and Prestonpans and were to do yet again at Falkirk. Panic-stricken, and convinced of the invincibility of Highland warriors,‡ they would have been the best heralds that could have been sent southward to announce the Prince's coming.

A second victory (more especially one on English soil) would have shaken Whig morale. It might also have cleared Northumberland of Government troops and have caused North Country Jacobites to pluck up sufficient courage to show their colours. But because he had sent no spies there, Charles knew nothing of the sickliness of the British soldiers and of the insubordination of the Dutch. As Sir John Macdonald relates, even O'Sullivan tried to induce Broughton or the aged Sheridan (who now acted as both Foreign and Military Secretary) to establish a system of espionage.

> O'Sullivan and I begged John Murray and Sir Thomas Sheridan to send out spies, and repeated to them ceaselessly that it was impossible to succeed unless by a miracle, without knowing the resources and the movements of the enemy. . . . These two men were unable to comprehend the usefulness of the exchange of letters ; thay had the great defect of being ashamed of appearing to learn anything from anybody, a false pride prevented their seeing that there is no shame in not knowing what one has no opportunity to.§

* Lord Elcho wrote : " I have seen the Highlanders whom the night had overtaken in their journey shaking off the snow in which they had slept all night, and then continuing their journey as if they had slept in a fine bed."

† Information regarding the state of Wade's troops is derived from officers' letters in the unpublished Newcastle MS.

‡ So great was the fear of the fighting powers of the Highlanders that from Edinburgh word had been sent that all volunteers were to come, if they could, in Highland dress, and an alternative Highland uniform was devised for Elcho's Life Guardsmen. As Kirkconnel wrote : " The English army, officers as well as soldiers, had such a terrible impression of Highlanders that they thought they had no chance with them unless they were greatly superior in numbers, and they were mistaken as to the real number of the Prince's army—fear generally magnifies a terrible object."

§ ' Memoirs of Sir John Macdonald.'

To the Prince the word espionage was as meaningless as the words strategy and tactics. Although there were excellent Jacobite spies in England (one of whom worked at the London Post Office) he had never thought of getting in touch with them—with the result that their reports were still sent to his father's agents in Paris. From France he had sent no one to prepare the ground for an insurrection in England as Broughton had done in Scotland; and during his long stay in Edinburgh he had sent only one emissary across the Border entrusted with the stupendous task of summoning the gentlemen of all the northern counties to arms. This plausible John Hickson, a vintner from Perth, had been recommended by Sir John Macdonald.* Puffed up with the importance of his mission, he comported himself indiscreetly, and was captured with all his letters at Newcastle, and forthwith turned King's Evidence. A second messenger, despatched to report upon Wade's movements after the Jacobite march began, also failed to return.

Thus it was not until he reached Penrith on 22nd November that the Prince heard that Wade's army was in motion. He waited there for a day in the vain expectation that " Grandmother Wade " would come up and give him battle. But his Cavalry scouts brought back word that the veteran maker of roads had been seen struggling back to Newcastle the previous evening. He arrived there with a thousand sick soldiers in his train.

Before the Prince came to Penrith Lord George, who had preceded him there, had left the town where, as an irate Whig resident fretfully complained, Highlanders swarmed all day like bees. The army was divided in half so that the second column could occupy the billets vacated by the first—an arrangement that had the double advantage of keeping the Prince and his General apart. So Lord George had none to say him nay, and was free from undue interference. He had with him some Horse, including the Life Guards and Horse Guards, three battalions of the Atholl Brigade, and Lord Ogilvy's and Glenbucket's Regiments—all misleadingly referred to as the Lowland Regiments. At Penrith Lord George detached 120 men to take possession of Lowther Hall where Lord Lonsdale used to entertain him when he visited his eldest son at his school at Lowther. His former host had, however, absented himself from home just when his services as Lord Lieutenant of the County were so much needed.

* 'Memoirs of Sir John Macdonald.'

The men of Westmorland seemed more friendly than those in Cumberland; but none came forward as recruits. In Lancashire the invaders received a chilling reception, except from an elderly doctor who rode over from York to give the Prince his blessing. He was the only adherent from Yorkshire—where the Duke of Perth had spent a summer horse-racing and endeavouring to stir up enthusiasm for the Stuart Cause.

Lord George found a more useful friend in Lancaster who procured two spies, " whom he despatched, one to Yorkshire, the other into Staffordshire to get intelligence of Marshal Wade and the Duke of Cumberland's armies."* " Hereafter," says young Johnstone, " he was always informed of whatever took place in the armies of his enemies, and often by means of his emissaries even knew all the movements they intended to make, [and] had a great advantage over them for they were totally ignorant of everything that related to our army."

Poor Duke William was less fortunate in his contacts, for he was accosted by a local " medical man of high reputation " named Henry Bracken, whom he and Lord Balmerino had met in Paris, and who now begged an introduction to the Prince. The medico sent the Government a report of all he saw and heard. He and the Vicar, who had intercepted Jacobite messages, were obliged to flee from the town when the Highlanders came back to it and pillaged their houses. The Vicar's elderly wife effected a spectacular escape through the cellar window.

On entering Preston the Jacobites were " met by a great concourse of people and welcomed with the loudest acclamations of joy."† Two Welsh gentlemen from Glamorgan joined there, and thirty-nine recruits were whipped up in adjacent villages by a Mr Daniel as the result of his chance meeting with the Duke of Perth at a wayside inn. But the Prince's method of recruitment caused consternation among the townspeople; and his own followers protested strongly when they saw two Irish officers (Sir Francis Geoghagan and Captain Brown, of Lally's Regiment, to whom he had given commissions to raise English regiments), arrayed in their French uniforms with the Catholic Order of St Louis on their breasts, parading the streets to the sound of drums.

Most of these officers in the French service, sent to Scotland in

* Elcho.
† ' Memorials of Murray of Broughton.'

October with guns and other supplies from France, possessed, according to young Johnstone, " no other knowledge than that which usually forms the whole stock of subalterns, namely the knowing how to mount and quit guard." Not one of them held higher rank than that of captain. But to ensure that they should have better pay on their return to France the Prince promoted them at once—some even to the rank of colonel. A notable example was that of Richard Augustus Warren, a bankrupt merchant from Marseilles, who after a short period of service as a volunteer in the French army and six months in Scotland (where he was never in action) found himself at the end of the campaign both a colonel and a baronet. Lord George and Lord Elcho were ready to admit that there were men of worth and honour among the new arrivals ; but it was the worthless ones who became the favourites of the easily flattered Prince. He could not resist their wheedling tongues ; he even granted a commission to a captured Irish Dragoon whose secret reason for never wishing to rejoin his regiment was the uncomfortable knowledge that he would have to face the charge of having murdered his sergeant.

Such rank favouritism infuriated the Scots, for men of birth were serving at their own expense as volunteers in the over-officered army. Their indignation increased when they learned that the command of any English regiments that might be raised would be given to Sir Francis Geoghegan and Captain Brown. Commenting on the conduct of the Secretary, who to please his master handed over to Irish Colonel Bagot the command of the troop of Hussars raised by him for his sixteen-year-old nephew Sir David Murray, Elcho wrote :

Nothing displayed the Prince's want of insight better than to see him throwing himself into the arms of some Irishmen who had come from France to make their fortune. He took more pleasure in their company than that of the Scots.

There were many misunderstandings in the army of the Prince. He never consulted the Scots Lords, but was entirely under the influence of his Secretary Mr Murray, and Mr Hay. People had a low opinion of the capacities of Mr Hay, who though honourable, was a man of very limited intelligence. Everything was regulated by their counsel.

Mr Murray, who knew very well that the Prince was always to be in the hands of somebody, and who had governed him a

long time himself, introduced Mr Hay about the Prince in order
to keep out other people he was more afraid of, so that the Prince
had one or other constantly with him.

Lord George Murray, Lord John Drummond, Lord Ogilvy
and I did not like Mr Murray and looked upon him as a dishon-
ourable man. Time has shown that we were right, but what
annoyed us most was the preference that the Prince gave on every
occasion to the Irish—he gave no thanks to the rest of us. They
were of his own religion and paid always more court to him in
their discourse. As they had nothing at stake, and were only
there to gain his favour and protection, whatever he proposed
they were for.

As they knew that we disliked them, they inspired the Prince
with a hatred towards Lord George Murray, Lord John Drummond and Mr Macdonald his old banker, who was ever true to
him ; and in fact he had no braver or more honourable men in
the army than these. We saw this with distress, and in general
the Prince was not loved by the principal Lords in his army.

He did not seem to have the least sense of what they had done
for him, but on the contrary would often say that they had done
nothing but their duty as his father's subjects were bound to do.
He had a notion of commanding this army as a General does a
body of mercenaries, and so let them know only what he pleased,
and they obey without enquiring about the matter.

Private gentlemen who had no command in the affair were
very much to be pitied, and some such there were of very good
estates who never either spoke to the Prince or ate with him.
And as he knew nothing of the country he used to look upon them
in the light of common Dragoons.*

Intercepted letters of Jacobite officers reveal their discontent at
failing to obtain an introduction to the Prince ; and Kirkconnel
endorses everything that his commanding officer wrote concerning
the neglectful treatment of loyal Scottish volunteers :

All those gentlemen that joined the Prince after Murray were
made known to the Prince under the character he thought fit to
give them, and all employments about the Prince's person and
many in the army were of his nomination. These he filled with
such as he had reason to think would never thwart his measures,
but be content to be his tools and creatures without aspiring
higher. Thus some places of the greatest importance were given
to little insignificant fellows. . . . The Prince had in his army
abundance of good subjects had he known them, but it was

* Compiled and condensed from Lord Elcho's Journal, and his ' Affairs
of Scotland.'

impossible unless he could have read in people's countenance at first sight what they were capable of—besides an eternal hurry of business that allowed him no opportunity of making a general acquaintance.

Although he expected from his Scottish volunteers " more zeal, more resolution, and more good manners than in those who fought merely for pay,"* Charles showed far less regard for them than for regular officers from France. If, instead of marching with the clansmen, he had at times ridden with his gentlemen volunteers, or with his Scottish officers, he might have heard something of their discontent and of their uneasiness about the aspect of affairs in England. On the march he saw less of his principal officers than he had done even in Edinburgh. Not only was the army divided, but each leader was occupied with the command of a regiment, and they could no longer assemble for their early evening discussions in his room. The devoted Perth was the leader of whom he saw the most. But the Duke had now little opportunity of talking over affairs with other high ranking officers. He was therefore unable to bring about a better understanding between them and his master, or even to warn the latter of their possible refusal to march much farther through England. His frail health had never permitted him to be a roisterer, and he had always taken sparingly of the food and wine laid in such profusion before his guests at Drummond Castle. But now on returning from arduous scouting expeditions (when he sometimes rode down three horses in a day) he was so utterly exhausted that he retired to his room to an unappetising supper of bread and milk, which was all that he could eat, where he sat up in a chair all night, for he was unable to get his breath if he attempted to lie down upon his bed.

Preston was a town of unhappy memories for Duke William and Lord George. Their great-grandfather the first Duke of Hamilton and his army of 30,000 men had been routed there by Cromwell in 1648, and as a result the Duke had died upon the scaffold. Their own uncle, Lord Nairne, and their brother Charles had narrowly escaped execution after the Jacobites' surrender there in 1715. During his two days' stay in the town Lord George must have thought much of this brother, nearest in age to him and his constant companion in school and University days, who had fought so

* The Prince's letter to the Chiefs at Falkirk.

bravely at the barricade erected beside the Church, and accounted
for many of the enemy with his own hand.

As the Athollmen " knew well what their kin had suffered there "
Lord George decided to " break the spell and lay the old bogey,"*
by leading them across and billeting them on the south side of the
Ribble Bridge, which local superstition affirmed would never be
crossed by an invading army. Well knowing the " superstitions
of the Highlanders," he believed, he said, in " falling in with their
humours in such small matters, though these things may seem of no
consequence."† Lord George, though born in the reputedly
haunted Castle of Huntingtower, where his earliest days were spent,
was himself entirely devoid of superstition. He had been immensely
amused on the march to Prestonpans when " a sow attempting to
cross the ranks had been stabbed by twenty dirks and had expired
(making such squeaks as can be imagined)."‡ It was accounted as
unlucky for an animal to cross in front of men going into battle as
for men to turn their backs on their first sight of the foe.

As both columns of the army were reunited at Preston a Council
was convened there. The officers began to murmur that they had
come far enough ; but the Prince assured them of being joined by
many fresh adherents at Manchester. The so-called French
Ambassador the Marquis D'Equilles, who in compliment to the
Scots arrayed himself in Highland garb, offered to lay bets that his
fellow countrymen were either landed or would land within a week.
" Every puff Monsieur D'Equilles made was to encourage people
to join and keep up the spirits of those that had," recorded Lord
Elcho, who still thought that instead of pinning his faith on specious
French promises of a large-scale invasion, the Prince should have
seized upon the offer to send over the Irish Brigade in fishing-
boats before British regiments had returned from Flanders. The
Skye Chiefs, Elcho believed, would then have joined ; the Prince's
army would have been augmented by several thousand men and
Wade's weakened by the loss of his 6,000 Dutchmen. These
had been released after the fall of Dendermond on the undertaking
that they would not serve against the armies of King Louis for a
specified period.

* ' Memorials of Murray of Broughton.'
† Lord George's Unpublished Notes.
‡ Lord George's ' Marches.'

G

Lord George proposed marching with the van of the Jacobite army to Liverpool to secure some much-needed money. He had heard of the panic among the merchants there, and says :

> They were putting much of their valuable effects aboard the shipping. Yet they would have given a good deal of money to have prevented any part of the army coming into their town. He knew that he could have marched up the Mersey and crossed it near Warrington tho' they had broke the bridge as well as all the others on the river. He would have been at Macclesfield as soon as the other part of the army who were to have gone by Wigan and Manchester.*

Subsequent information showed that Liverpool was so badly prepared for defence that the raid must have succeeded. But instead, Lord George was ordered to proceed to Wigan. The road was lined with people standing at their doors to wish the Prince success, wrote Lord Elcho, " but if arms were offered them and they were desired to go along with the army they all declined and said they did not understand fighting."

The English peasantry had long ago thrown off the shackles of feudal service and were wholly unacquainted with the use of arms. So also were the gentry. Few Englishmen now served in foreign armies, and none of Jacobite leanings in that of Britain. All were quite unfitted to be of use in the present insurrection, and they later alleged that their reason for not coming out " was the want of officers to lead their undisciplined men, which the Prince could not spare."†　He had all too few who had seen regular service to lead his Highlanders. But he could well have sent some gentlemen volunteers across the Border to encourage North Country sympathisers to prepare in secret to assist him. Such Intelligence Officers might even have established contact between English and Welsh adherents, co-ordinated some plan of action, and above all have prevailed upon friends of the Cause to send information to Scotland regarding the strength and movements of the enemy. The issue of a contest so vital to the Scots was viewed with indifference by the English, who cared nothing for the White Rose of the Stuarts or the White Horse of Hanover. As one landed proprietor declared, he minded not if the devil were King so long as he was left in peaceful possession of

---

* Lord George's Unpublished Notes.
† Laurence Woulfe's Report.

his estates. Tories were not prepared to risk their fortunes for King James, whose health they had so often drunk. Nor were the Whigs more ready to hazard their lives for King George. The Government experienced the utmost difficulty in raising three or four English volunteer regiments, which in the end contained only a fraction of the number of men who enlisted in their service in the Highlands and Lowlands of Scotland.

The exiled Stuarts were imbued with the idea that their English and Scottish subjects suffered untold miseries under foreign domination—an impression gained from letters which came to Rome from adherents whose families had been ruined by participation in former Risings. But in point of fact the early Georgian era was a period of great commercial prosperity, and the thoughts of Englishmen were centred on more material matters than religious controversy or dynastic problems. Jacobitism now meant mere sentimentalism, or vague discontent. Tories grumbled, as English folk will always grumble. So, too, did many Whigs who fancied that their country was looked upon by their new rulers as a province of Hanover.

But as that shrewd observer of events, Horace Walpole, observed, dissatisfaction with the reigning house did not " proceed from love for the other." For almost a century and a half the English had become accustomed to being ruled by sovereigns who were not of their own race. They had not therefore the same devotion to the Stuarts as the Scots had to their ancient line of Kings. The Scots now out with Charles were the sons of men who had fought for his father, for whom many of the older men had themselves drawn the blade. The English were the great-grandsons of Cavaliers who had rallied round the Prince's great-grandfather Charles I. to battle against Parliament-men who sought to overthrow the old English way of life as well as the prerogatives of the Crown. When they had fancied that their religion and liberties were threatened few Englishmen had stood by James II. or had essayed to restore his son.

The average eighteenth-century Englishman had no particular reason to dislike the German race, or the German dynasty now reigning over Britain. The early Georges, uninterested in the country and its inhabitants, seldom showed themselves to their new subjects. But these Hanoverians had at least the merit of being of the same religion as the majority of their subjects, and were probably regarded as only a degree less foreign than the Italian-born Prince

of Scottish, Polish, and French stock who now came at the head
of a Scottish army to seek the British Crown. Unless they held
strongly Jacobite views, Englishmen had no wish to have a King
forced upon them by their ancient enemies across the Border, and
several decades were to elapse before their valiant deeds in British
battles overseas made kilted Highlanders popular figures in England.
Had their other hereditary foes from across the Channel descended
upon the shores of Britain, the apathy of the people might well
have given place to fervent patriotism and impelled them to fight
the invaders to the death—a contingency which seems never to have
been visualised by the Scottish Jacobites, whose own country had
formerly maintained close alliance with France.

The Prince's Irish friends were very much perturbed by the
lukewarm attitude of their co-religionists in the so-called " Stuart
Province " of Lancashire, where Protestants had been showing much
zeal in assisting the Government, and a pitiful list had been sent to
Whitehall of disaffected Papists—all of whom seemed to be aged,
infirm, or wandering in their wits. The Irishmen were too ignorant
of English affairs to be aware that the terms " Catholic " and
" Jacobite " were no longer synonymous, or that the Catholic clergy
had advised their flocks not to entangle themselves in the rebellion
for fear of worsening their own position, which had improved
immeasurably now that local authorities were disposed to wink at
the once strictly enforced penal laws. Sir John Macdonald, however,
laid the whole blame upon Sir Thomas Sheridan for failing to
contact Catholic priests in Lancashire before the invasion began—
an omission more likely to be attributable to the old gentleman's
dislike of writing letters than to his alleged reluctance to upset the
sensibilities of English Protestants.

Lord George had friends in the County Palatine whom he visited
when he came to see his son at school. His father had been born
and bred at Knowlesley, which the famous Charlotte de Trémouille
had held so gallantly for Charles I. Her husband, the Earl of Derby,
had been defeated fighting for the King at Wigan—another of
Lord George's great-grandparents to seal his loyalty to the Stuarts
upon the scaffold. But on such matters Lord George had no time
to dwell. In his ' Marches of the Highland Army ' he left a full
account of the life he was leading at this time :

I was always early in the morning employed in some necessary work. Anything that was readiest served for breakfast, and I commonly dined betwixt four and five, and no supper. Anybody who had business with me or anything to say had access at all hours, whether I were at meals or in bed. On some occasions I have been waked six times a night and had either orders to write or letters to answer every time. As I mostly commanded a seperate body of the army I had many details that in a more regular army would belong to different people. I not only wrote the orders myself when I commanded a seperate corps of the army, or directed them. But to any officers that was to go upon a party or upon an outpost I endeavoured to explain everything that might happen, and answered any objections that could be stated, besides giving the orders in writing, by which means there was no mistake or confusion, and the officers did their duty with cheerfulness and made their reports with exactness. . . .

In the whole time we were together I did not go into a house or stop at a door to take so much as a glass of water till I came to my quarters; but I often went into houses to turn out others. I thought I could not reasonably find fault with others in that if I did not show them a good example. I never took the least thing without paying the full value. My horses were either all my own breed, or bought before the Standard was set up. Fodder and corn I got often out of the magazines, as others did. I had a servant who dressed my meat, and though when I had supper at command (which was oftenest the case) I had always some of the officers that dined with me. Yet I seldom had anything but broth, a piece of boiled meat and a roast, and one bottle of rum or brandy in punch, served as a liquor when we had not good ale. Our expense was very inconsiderable, and I never heard of an army, generally speaking, so temperate. In many parts of England I was quartered in private houses, and they had their dinner prepared (knowing who was billeted upon them) when I came in towards evening. Many would not take payment. But I always left at least a guinea in the house, which was more than would have paid the expense.

At Manchester the Prince was received with far greater enthusiasm than in any other English town. "We expected that at least 1,500 men would have joined us here, for the whole country is well disposed," wrote O'Sullivan. "But very few joined, the reason being . . . that there was no foreign forces." The men who did come forward to enlist seemed unlikely to be of much use. Lord Elcho records: "Everybody was astonished to find that all that was to join was about 200 common fellows who it seems had no subsistance, for they used to say by way of showing their military inclination, that they had for some time been resolved to enlist in whichever of the two armies came first to the town." The Duke of Perth expressed the opinion that they would have enlisted with the Devil if he had offered them a shilling. These English recruits showed enough spirit to insist upon choosing their officers from among the sons of local merchants and tradesmen, instead of serving under Sir Francis Geoghagan and Captain Brown. The latter was " a very rough sort of man, and so well fitted to command the banditti of which that corps was composed," thought Elcho. The other Scottish officers thought otherwise. The Prince was thus compelled to rescind the promise given to his Irish friends and hand over the command to the only Englishman of standing who joined the Jacobites—Francis Townley, a Catholic gentleman who had served in Spain and had providentially been granted a colonel's commission by King James. The new Manchester Regiment was reviewed on St Andrew's Day in the churchyard of the Collegiate Church—a depressing place for such a ceremony.

Since no Council meeting was convened during the day's halt at Manchester, several leading officers met together and gloomily summed up the situation since entering England. They had received no encouragement " from any person of distinction. The French had not landed, and [they were] only joined by 200 vaga-bonds. They had done their part ; and as they did not pretend to put a King upon the throne of England without [the people's] consent it was time to represent to the Prince to go back to Scotland." Lord George, Kirkconnel states, had this " all along in view if there was no insurrection in England and no landing." On this occasion he counselled patience, and said : " We should make a further trial and go the length of Derby. If there is no greater encouragement to go on, I will propose a retreat to the Prince."

But as they proceeded on their way it almost seemed as if " every Jacobite in England had been annihilated."* On the banks of the Mersey the Prince was greeted by a few non-combatant supporters from Cheshire. But there was no message from Lord Barrymore (who in spite of his seventy-eight years had been expected by the

* Contemporary Letter.

Prince to fly to arms), or from Sir Robert Grosvenor, Sir Watkin Wynn, and the Welsh Jacobites whom he had hoped would come to join him on the march. Charles was unaware that the two baronets had actually subscribed towards raising troops to oppose him. He had, it is true, sent a letter to Lord Barrymore which Sheridan entrusted to a Carlisle grocer to deliver—the Englishman at first selected to carry it having run away within a few hours of joining the forces. Lord Barrymore was unfortunately away from home, and the bewildered grocer, uninstructed how to act in such a contingency, handed the missive to his Lordship's Whig son Lord Buttivant. Meanwhile Lord Barrymore's Jacobite son had gone to Wynstay to concert plans with the still loyal, if timid, Sir Watkin Wynn, and arrived at Derby just two days after the Prince had left, bringing word that three hundred Welsh Jacobites were ready to meet him when and where he commanded.

From the first the Prince had employed the strangest emissaries to conduct negotiations (if such they can be termed) with prospective English followers. His friends in France had indeed been justified in their prophecy that his affairs would never prosper as long as he continued to place his chief trust in persons who were " unknown, low-born, of no weight, and so useless."* His bald, peremptory orders to his known supporters to appear in arms forthwith gave no assurance of French backing, no instructions what the recipient was to do, and no reliable information of his own intentions. Delivered by unknown and untrustworthy-looking messengers such letters were indeed unlikely to induce North Country gentlemen of Jacobite persuasions to fall in with his commands. If messengers were sent to supposed Jacobites in London or the provinces the recipients were far too cautious to reply, for as Kirkconnel bitterly records : " Whatever the dispositions of the army and the city, it is certain the Prince had no intelligence of either."

Apart from the Lancashire recruits only ten Englishmen and two Welshmen joined in the attempt to restore the Stuart to the throne, and few of them were useful recruits. On crossing the Mersey a touching incident occurred when an octogenarian lady, who as an infant had witnessed the homecoming and restoration of Charles II.,

* Lady Clifford to King James. ' King over the Water,' by Andrew Lang and Annie Shiel.

presented her purse with all the money she had to his great-nephew. This loyal lady, who all her life had sent one-half of her income as an annual gift to the King over the Water, was the only person in England who is recorded as having given so much as a guinea to help to effect his restoration to the throne.

No friends came forth to join the Prince; but his enemies were now closing in. Lord George's two spies returned to him. One of them reported that Marshal Wade was marching ponderously down the Great North Road, and rumour had it that he would move across country into Lancashire. Lord George's invaluable aide-de-camp Colonel Ker of Graden (who acted in the same capacity to both the Prince and his Lieutenant-General) had been sent to Newcastle-under-Lyme to gain intelligence. Ker, who had served in the Spanish army, proved one of the best officers with the Jacobite army—and the most reliable and efficient scout. He returned with word that Cumberland's army was quartered at Coventry, Stafford, and Lichfield.

On 2nd December an informal meeting was held at the Prince's Headquarters at Macclesfield.

Here, according to the anonymous Whig Historian, " the people seemed mightily against the Prince, and vast numbers had run away from the houses. It would seem that they had expected an engagement, for they spent the evening scaling, firing, and putting in order their pieces. It was first thought they would march into Wales. But perceiving that this would coop them up, and reduce them to great necessities in a mountainous country [with] which they were not acquaint, they abandoned the project as imprudent." After much argument, " what Lord George Murray offered was agreed to. Viz., to go straight to Derby. And as the Duke of Cumberland with his army was at Lichfield, Coventry, and Newcastle-under-Lyme, he thought it would not be amiss to make a feint with some part of the army as if it was intended to attack him, which would make him wait there upon the road; and in the meantime give him the slip and go to Derby."

So with a strong mobile column composed of the Atholl Brigade and Elcho and Kilmarnock's Guards, Lord George set out for Congleton. " The Duke of Kingston with his regiment of Horse left that place pretty much in a hurry," recorded Lord George, who, after pursuing this newly raised regiment for several miles along the Newcastle road, returned to Congleton to enjoy the good dinner prepared there for the Whig officers. " Geordie's Wullie," as the Scots called Cumberland, was misled to believe that Wales was the insurgents' objective, and he obligingly withdrew to Stone by way of Stafford. His chief spy, an Irish Protestant known variously as John Weir, or Vere, fell into Lord George's hands and gave him a written list of the Duke's forces comprising 8,250 Foot and 2,200 Horse. Against his Councillors' advice the Prince released the man, who hovered about in the vicinity of Derby. He later gave such damaging evidence at the trials of sundry Jacobites that it suited the Prince's friends to shift the blame for his release upon Lord George.

The following morning Lord George's column turned off to the left and marched by Leek to Ashbourne. After sending Lord Elcho ahead with a small detachment of Guards to warn the townspeople of Derby of the Highlanders' approach, he waited on the road until the main body of the Jacobite army came in sight. He then continued towards the town. Two of the only three Derby men to join in the Rising rode out to meet him—a butcher on a horse, and a stocking-frame worker on a mule. The butcher, a loquacious fellow, furnished the Prince's General with much useful information about the movements of the enemy and the political leanings of local notables. The Duke of Devonshire's newly raised " Derbyshire Blues " had beaten a hasty retreat towards Nottingham on hearing of the Jacobites' approach.

Unlike the exuberant O'Sullivan, who thought it a " fine sight to see the illuminations of the town,"[*] Lord George was not impressed by the ringing of bells and the acclamations that greeted the Prince on his entry into Derby. Although the Highlanders had behaved in the most exemplary fashion throughout the march, and " the little disorder which had happened was made by the women and vagabonds that had followed the army from Edinburgh,"[†] the people of the towns and villages through which they had recently passed feared them and " seemed much more enemies than friends of the Cause."[‡] Lord George's hopes that a victory for the Jacobites

---

[*] O'Sullivan.
[†] ' Memoirs of Sir John Macdonald.'
[‡] Elcho.

would bring the English to the winning side were dashed. For how could 4,500 men hope to obtain a lasting victory when, counting the Militia and new Volunteer regiments, 60,000 men were in arms against them—and all much better armed than they ? Even if Lord Strathallan had gathered together the hoped-for number of recruits in Scotland, the Prince's men would still be outnumbered by more than six to one. But his Highlanders had routed an army of their own size in Scotland ; the Prince saw no reason why they should not rout three of twice their size, even though they were based on their own country and two of them at least were composed of better trained and steadier men than any Cope had commanded.

In his Notes about the campaign Lord George records bitterly :

> The King had been regularly proclaimed at every town upon the road, the people not seeming much affected one way or other. Ringing of bells and illuminations everywhere as His Royal Highness passed ; but most of the magistrates left the towns not to involve themselves whatever might happen. Few of the people would have inclined to fight for either side. They left that to those who were paid for fighting. At the Proclamation and the Prince's entering of the town there was loud " huzzaing." But they were ready to do the same to either side ; and did.

While the Prince at supper talked gaily of his expected triumphs, his Lieutenant-General sat up late with his host Lawyer Heathcote. Together they went through the lists of those who had subscribed to raise troops for the Government in order that a like levy might be imposed upon them for the maintenance of the insurgent army. Lord George was, however, up betimes next day and walked along Full Street to the Earl of Exeter's town house where his master had established his Headquarters. The Prince had drawn on his bonnet and was about to step out to take the air when he was accosted by his visitor, who lost no time in coming to the point. "It is high time to think about what we are to do," he announced. Charles, now wholly out of touch with his officers, was completely taken aback. He himself was in a buoyant mood ; for the previous night he had received a letter from his optimistic friend Parson Kelly, and another from Lord John Drummond who had sailed to Montrose with 1,000 of the 10,000 French troops, which he said were all on the point of sailing, and included the whole Irish Brigade and several other French regiments. " What do you mean ? " I thought it was resolved to march on," cried the Prince ; for he had not apparently

realised that the news he had received would make his officers the
more eager to return to Scotland to join forces with these newly
landed allies. " Most of the principal officers are of a very different
opinion and think they should march back to Ashbourne and join
the army in Scotland,"* Lord George replied sombrely.

In a subsequent letter to a friend, Lord George explained the
unusual nature of the momentous gathering held at Exeter House
on that fateful morning of Thursday, 5th December 1745. "Councils
of War were seldom held and were out of request from the time the
army marched into England," he wrote. " What happened at Derby
was accidental by most of the officers being at the Prince's quarters."†
Thus commanders of battalions and squadrons, as well as such
Councillors as happened to be at hand, were summoned to a hastily
arranged conference in the long oak-panelled drawing-room of
Exeter House. Lord George set down a circumstantial account of
all the matters discussed at that historic meeting :

> Most of the principal officers of the army being met at His
> Royal Highness's quarters in the morning of the 5th he spoke of
> the next day's march and of going on to London. As the marches
> had been very quick few of the officers had met together—at
> least since they left Macclesfield. Being fatigued they were very
> glad to get to their quarters ; and taking care of their men with
> other necessaries had taken up all their time. So now they
> found it highly proper to come to some resolution as to their next
> motion. Many believed His Royal Highness was not come to
> such a length without having encouragement from the great men
> at London or the Army. Those who had at least hoped of a
> landing in France found things were now brought to a crisis.
> If they marched forward two or three days would determine their
> fate. An army not five thousand men, brave men indeed, but not
> disciplined, surrounded with a number of the best disciplined
> troops in Europe and four times their number. One army within
> twenty miles on their right hand (Duke of Cumberland's) of at
> least 9,000 men ; another on their left (General Wade's) as
> numerous tho' not quite so near; a third in their front as numerous
> as either [consisting of Guards and Horse, with troops which
> they would bring from the coast where they were quartered.
> So that there would be three armies made up of regular troops.
> . . . Upon a misfortune it could not be supposed one man could
> escape, for the militia, who had not appeared much against us

* Statement by John Hay. Appendix. ' Home's History of the Rebellion.'
† Lord George's Letter to Hamilton of Bangour, 1749. Home's Appendix.

hitherto, would upon our defeat possess all the roads and the enemy's Horse would surround us on all hands. The whole world would blame us as being rash and foolish to venture a thing that could not succeed, and the Prince's person, should he escape being killed in battle, must fall into the enemy's hands.]

After a long silence His Royal Highness spoke of the order of march and who was to have the front. At last Lord George Murray said that he believed the first thing to be spoke of was how far it was prudent to advance any further. His Royal Highness turned to some other of the officers who also said that they did not see how they could extricate themselves out of so imminent a danger, for that their hopes of a French landing or a powerful junction in England had failed. The Prince seemed thunderstruck—as if they were against his obtaining a victory and a certain Restoration. He expressed himself as convinced of both.

At last Lord George Murray, seeing the uneasiness of everybody, desired leave to represent his thoughts upon so critical a juncture. Tho' he had not talked with any of the officers upon it, yet he now thought himself obliged to declare his opinion expressly as by what he observed most of the officers seemed to expect it. He said he was as desirous to see a happy Restoration as any man in Britain. He was ready to sacrifice his life and his all whenever there was an occasion. Tho' they were at present in a very dangerous situation, yet he hoped it was not desperate. If they went on another day it was not possible to save His Royal Highness. Both his life and all those brave men with him must be inevitably sacrificed. Suppose he should even beat the Duke of Cumberland, it would cost him the lives of a great many of his best men. He would not advance his affairs by it for the remains of the Duke of Cumberland's army would join the other which was still betwixt him and London—especially the Horse. The other army, if they thought they had not him secure enough, would by lining the hedges, by cannon, or other impediments retard his march and kill many of his people. By that time General Wade would come up and join the others and so surround his army and either kill or take everyone prisoner. Even suppose he could shun fighting with the last two armies he would be so disabled by the loss from fighting the first that he would make but a poor figure with the remains of his army should he get to London. Could it be expected that anyone would join him as long as the two other armies with the remains of the first were at his heels? For his part he could see but one way to be extricate out of such a difficulty, and that by a sudden and quick retreat. A safe and honourable retreat was often preferred to a victory, for the one is the effect of skill, and the other often of mere chance. For his own part he did not pretend to much skill, but if His Royal Highness would trust him with the management he could venture to assure him to bring the army safe back to Carlisle the very same road they came. He knew the country, and he had studied the ways. Even suppose the Duke of Cumberland should march quicker than he believed he could and got to Warrington as soon as they (or even some hours before them) by taking the right hand they could keep midway between him and Mr Wade's army. But he knew that no regular troops could march with the Highlanders suppose they were equal at setting out. If His Royal Highness marched next morning he would have two days' march of them. As for General Wade's they were further back. They had the country to cross, and his army would be much fatigued and were very sickly, so that should he come in their way they need not fear to fight him.

As we knew our quarters we would not be kept under arms at night till billeted. Every man would take the quarters that had been allotted to them in coming up, so that the night being long, men would be well refreshed and need not halt a day till Preston.

All he desired was not to have any embarrass with the cannon and carriages, but that His Royal Highness would give orders for it to go in front and so early that it might not stop the marches. For his own part he should always be in the rear in the retreat, and that every regiment should take it in his turn. [He] concluded with saying that he hoped by the time they came to Carlisle they would have good accounts of their friends who he knew were waiting to join them. Time might produce much. The French and all Europe must have a good opinion of them if after making so bold and long a march and so near to London they could make a safe and honourable retreat. He would think his life well bestowed should he lose it the day he returned to Carlisle—provided he were a means to bring His Royal Highness and so many of his brave countrymen safe back, which he hoped in God, if His Royal Highness would trust him, he would accomplish. But if there were any other advice offered to His Royal Highness which should seem better he would willingly go in with whatever should be thought for the best.

All the other officers were exceedingly pleased and applauded much what was proposed. Only the Duke of Perth, seeing how very much His Royal Highness was bent upon going forward and how much he seemed cast down with the thought of returning, endeavoured what he could to prevail with the other officers to march and attack the Duke of Cumberland. But they were all unanimous for the retreat. The Prince indeed was much to be sympathized with. His looks declared his concern. He thought had he gained another victory, which he imagined would be as easy as Gladsmuir [Prestonpans], all would have been over. It

was hard to be so near London and yet obliged to return. However, after some time and some strong expressions he said that
since he found it was the general opinion he would follow it,
and desired everything should be ordered accordingly. It was
desired that no man should mention what had passed, for it
might be of very bad consequence had the thing taken air and
the Duke of Cumberland might have been apprised of it.*

It was not easy to keep matters secret. A Derby gentleman, who
had waited upon the Duke of Perth, was in an adjoining room and
heard voices raised in anger, and the moody looks of the Councillors
when they returned to their lodgings for dinner caused their hosts
to surmise that something was seriously amiss. Lord George,
Keppoch, Lochiel and Sir Thomas Sheridan were in a room in
Exeter House discussing the situation half an hour after the meeting
when Sir John Macdonald burst in upon them shouting : " What
is this ? You are going to fly without seeing the enemy ? What !
a Macdonald turn his back ! What ! a Cameron turn his back !
Go with me. I'll lead you." Keppoch, who detested the old man,
asked him : " Who said we were going to fly ? Who informed you
of such lies ? " " I know very well. I have very good intelligence.
I know who proposed it. For shame ! "† retorted Sir John, who
had evidently received a lurid account of the Council meeting from
his friend O'Sullivan.

Without so much as casting a glance upon Lord George, whose
presence he ignored, Macdonald addressed himself in a more sober
fashion to Lochiel : " It is absurd to think of making such a long
retreat with an undisciplined army like ours in the face of regular
troops in their own country. If we are to perish 'tis better to do so
with our faces to London than to Scotland." Lochiel answered
him with his customary gentleness : " If you knew all, you would
agree with us,"‡ he said. Their angry visitor, however, would wait
to hear no more, and left the room.

When he referred to the incident later Lord George remarked
ironically : " This gentleman was old and had dined heartily, for

* The Account of the Council Meeting at Derby is given verbatim from
Lord George's Unpublished Notes, one page of which is missing. Sentences
and paragraphs in square brackets are taken from his other account in
' Marches of the Highland Army.'
† Lord George's ' Marches.'
‡ ' Memoirs of Sir John Macdonald.'

he was much subject to the bottle. He liked his quartets and entertainment better in England than in Scotland and would rather have been taken prisoner than return, for he thought as he was in the French service he did not run the same risk as others did."*

While the vital Council was taking place Broughton had come into the room, unaware, so he said, that a meeting was in progress. He offered to leave, but was called back by the Prince, who saw in him a potential ally. For on this occasion Charles lacked the open support of O'Sullivan, who from the first had maintained that five thousand men were not sufficient to conquer England. While the army lay at Manchester he had even advocated a retreat, since " according to all the rules of war and prudence it was the only party [course] to be taken."†

Unfortunately for the Prince's hopes the little Secretary was no warrior. He seemed, so Lord George noted, " as much persuaded of the necessity of the measure as any person present."‡ But once out of the Council Chamber he told his master that he " had only expressed himself so because he knew it was vain to expect an army to fight when the officers were against it." To reinstate themselves in royal favour now that they saw that " the retreat would certainly be put into execution,"§ both he and Sheridan pretended that that was their only reason for having agreed to it. This plan seems also to have been adopted by O'Sullivan. He may even have gone further ; for a usually well-informed Government spy heard of his being much in favour of continuing the march to London. To placate their irate master Broughton now began to urge an advance, and " endeavoured all he could in the afternoon to bring some of the officers to his opinion. He spoke to Lochiel, Cluny, and Keppoch on the subject. But they all told him it would be betraying the Cause and utter ruin to the Prince and his whole army."‖

The reason given by the ingenious young man for this *volte-face* was, says Lord George, " that by endeavouring to bring the Prince by degrees to what was for the good of the service it was proper to

* Lord George's ' Marches.'
† O'Sullivan.
‡ Lord George's ' Marches.'
§ Ibid.
‖ Ibid.

LORD NAIRNE

From the portrait by Jeremiah Davison at Blair Castle

LOCHIEL

From a portrait in the West Highland Museum, Fort William

Copyright : C. ROGER

[*Facing p.* 113

seem to be of his opinion for a little time, and so convince him by degrees."* Maxwell of Kirkconnel wrote more pointedly :

> From this time the Secretary ceased to be in odour of sanctity with those not highly prejudiced in his favour. The little knave appeared plainly in his conduct on this occasion. He argued strenuously for the retreat because he thought it the only prudent measure, till he found it was carried by a great majority, and would certainly take place, and then he condemned it to make his court to the Prince to whom it was very disagreeable, and lay the odium upon other people, particularly Lord George whom he endeavoured to blacken on every occasion. Some people will wonder that this barefaced conduct did not open the Prince's eyes as to the baseness of Murray's heart ; but if we consider that Murray was in the highest degree of favour, the steps by which he rose to it, and the arts he used to maintain himself and exclude everybody that could come in competition with him, he will easily conceive how he got the better of any suspicions his behaviour might have created at this time.

The Prince had separate interviews with some of his adherents, hoping to bring them to his own way of thinking. He succeeded only with the Duke of Atholl, and perhaps with Perth, who at the Council had suggested turning aside to join their friends in Wales —a proposal supported by Sir William Gordon of Park and opposed by everyone else on account of the danger of being penned in the Principality and prevented from joining the forces in Scotland. Duke William and Lord Nairne had heard nothing of a morning Council—possibly because as devout Episcopalians they had gone to the special service held in All Saints' Church.† The insinuations of his enemies that Lord George had so arranged matters that only

* Lord George's Unpublished Notes.
Lord Elcho bear out this testimony. He later wrote :
On one occasion I asked the Secretary Murray why he had always been of the same opinion as the Prince against that of the whole army and on points, too, whereon he himself knew that his advice was not founded on reason. He told me that the Prince had very little genius and that he could not endure anyone differing from his opinion, that to govern him one must always appear always of the same mind as himself, since he very often came to think differently ; that without himself, the Prince would have fallen into the hands of the Irish, that I had seen (during an illness Murray had) he was ruled by Mr Hay, who, I must know, was a man of very poor calibre. In a word the Secretary spoke of the Prince with much contempt.

† Now Derby Cathedral. A plaque commemorates the service held there by the Prince's followers on 5th December 1745.

H

his own supporters were present is refuted by his casual mention that Menzies of Shian, who commanded a battalion of the Atholl Brigade and of whom he thought highly, had not been told of the meeting. Lord George's account runs thus :

The Prince appeared much more against the retreat towards the evening and reasoned with several upon it. The Duke of Atholl, who had not been present in the morning, was easily persuaded to be for pushing forward. He had no fear himself and believed the justness of the Cause would carry all before it. He was sent in the evening to his brother who had with him at the time Lord Elcho, Colonel Menzies, and the two majors of the other Atholl Regiments who were three good officers as any in the army.* But Lord George had not mentioned to these gentlemen the resolution to return. The Duke of Atholl in the presence of these gentlemen and Colonel Warren who was his aide-de-camp [said] that he was surprised to hear that a resolution had been proposed, and even agreed upon, to return without fighting the enemy. He said a good deal upon the subject. He had no notion of danger ; for if there was ever a man without fear he was certainly so. As he was honest and upright, he could not be persuaded but the English and even their Army would declare for us in so just a Cause. His brother told him that had he been present in the forenoon he would have heard the reasons that obliged them to come to that resolution, and he thought them unanswerable. He then recapitulated what had been said, and added some others. As the three officers of the Atholl Brigade were in his presence he entreated the Duke would ask what they thought of the matter. Indeed these gentlemen expressed their astonishment that there was not some assurances from the London Ministry, or army, for otherways they could not imagine that anybody would have advised His Royal Highness to have advanced as far as they had done. . . .†

[The Duke of Atholl . . . seemed much for going forwards. In the evening when this was understood by the rest of the officers, they told His Royal Highness that they valued their lives as little as brave men ought to do, and if he inclined to go forward they would do their duty to the last, but desired that those who advised His Royal Highness to go forward would sign their opinion, which would be a great satisfaction to them. This

---

* The officers were : Colonel John Menzies, the younger, of Shian, who, as his Chief Sir Robert Menzies was a cripple, led out 300 of his clan who formed the third battalion of the Atholl Brigade ; James Robertson of Blairfettie, Major in Lord George's battalion ; David Steuart of Kynachan, Major in Lord Nairne's battalion.

† Lord George's Unpublished Notes.

put a stop to all underhand dealings, and the Duke of Atholl
when he heard others upon the subject was fully satisfied as to
the necessity of the measure.]*

The Council ended, the Prince's officers retired to their lodgings
to get what sleep they could before the next day's early start. In
the darkness that preceded the dawn they stumbled out into the
streets to find their way to their various regiments. For them the
coming day brought no prospect of gladness although their faces
were set for home. As Sir Thomas Sheridan (now " a drooping
old man,"† according to the evidence of a lurking spy) emerged
from the doorway of Exeter House, he exclaimed prophetically:
" All is over. We shall never come this way again."

* Lord George's ' Marches.'
† Evidence of Bradlaugh, the spy.

CHAPTER VIII

THE RETREAT

IN their accounts of the retreat from Derby, novelists and even serious historians have much to say about the frustration of the Prince, though to judge from Lord George's and Lord Elcho's accounts of previous stormy meetings he had had fair warning of what must ultimately happen. Vivid descriptions have also been given of the loud lamentations of the Highland soldiers, who, knowing nothing of the true situation of affairs, were reluctant to turn back in the hour of seeming triumph, and gazed hopefully at every weather-vane they passed hoping that an east wind would waft to Scotland's shores that mythical invasion force which they were turning back to meet. But only those who had actually taken part in the campaign described the unenviable position of the leading Jacobite officers. Lord Elcho's account is rarely quoted :

> The inferior officers of the Prince's army were much surprised when they found the army moving back and imagined some bad news had been received. But when they were told everything and found the army had marched so far into England without the least invitation from any Englishman of distinction they blamed their superiors much for carrying them so far. They had all along imagined they were marching to join the English and were acting in concert with them.

A general outcry arose among the Scots when their expected English allies failed to rally to the Prince. Kirkconnel wrote :

> I cannot join in the cry against them no more than I can condemn abundance of his friends in Scotland who did not join him. I have told elsewhere upon what a slender foundation this expedition was undertaken. Murray had imposed upon the Prince and hurried him into it without concerting anything with England. . . . It's true the English have in former times taken arms with less encouragement and less provocation than they met with of late, but in those days the common people of England were accustomed to arms, and the insurgents were as good soldiers as any that could be brought against them. Under the Hanoverian Government the people had been disarmed and overawed by armies of well disciplined troops. . . . An insurrection was

almost impossible without being previously concerted. Before they could guess what was the Prince's plan, the Militia was armed in every county for the service of the Established Government, all passes guarded, and suspected persons narrowly watched; by this means an insurrection would be crushed before it was well begun. As for these counties through which the Prince's army passed, there was certainly too little pains taken.

However, the main business was to march the army safely back to Scotland. In this extremely hazardous task Lord George was severely handicapped by lack of co-operation from the Prince, who was slow now in " leaving his quarters so that tho' the rest of the army were on the march, the rear could not move till he went."* Against the advice of his Lieutenant-General he decided to rest a day at Manchester—which was precisely what " Geordie's Laddie " was hoping he would do. The town was in an uproar, and the once friendly mob was inclined to attack the Prince's men, so he sent O'Sullivan to waken Lord George at two o'clock next morning with orders to resume the march that day. The people in the adjacent countryside were equally hostile. Lord Elcho, whose Life Guards usually rode ahead of the army, wrote :

They were quite prepared in case the army had been beat to have knocked on the head all that would have escaped from the battle. Whenever any of the men straggled or strayed behind they either murdered them or sent them to the Duke, and all the way from Carlisle to Derby all the men that were left sick in towns upon the road were either killed or after [being] very much abused sent to jails. . . . John Roy Stewart's and Ogilvy's Regiments, who made the rear-guard coming out of Manchester, were fired upon by the mob, who followed them. But whenever they faced about the mob always run away.

The Prince, who loved to contradict Lord George Murray, wished to stay some days at Manchester, knowing nothing at all of the country roads. If he had followed his own opinion, he would have been caught between two fires, and would never have got back to Scotland. . . . He said to my Lord George Murray that he made him march too quickly before his enemy.†

It was late before the army got under way, and the rear-guard had to stumble into Wigan by the light of lanterns. On reaching Preston the next evening Lord George found that the Duke of Perth had been sent to Scotland without being able to wait to take such

* Lord George's ' Marches.'
† Lord Elcho's Journal.

letters and messages as Lord George might wish to send to the Generals there, or to his wife. As it happened it was as well that he did not send any. He had warned Perth that " if he did not take a strong escort he might be stopped."* But the Duke was now in such a wretched state of health that he was obliged to travel in his coach with Lady Ogilvy and Mrs Murray, for it was thought better to send them out of danger. At Kendal the coach was attacked by the mob, who stole the Duke's mail-bag and killed one of his servants and an Hussar in his escort. The country people were so menacing in every place through which the party passed that they were subsequently obliged to rejoin the army.

The Duke had, in fact, been sent to bring reinforcements to the Prince, who announced that " he was resolved to retire no further till he met them, and then march directly to London, be the consequences what they would." Lord George viewed this decision with dismay :

> If they made any considerable stop and gave time to the different bodies of the enemy's troops to join they would neither be in a capacity to give them battle, nor would they be able to make their retreat without the loss of many of their men, if not the whole army. However since he [Lord George] found the Prince much dissatisfied with him (in particular for the retreat from Derby) he thought it best to let the advice of continuing the retreat as at first agreed upon come from those about him, who he was confident (whatever they might say in private to His Royal Highness against the retreat) yet in their hearts they not only approved of it, but knew there was no possibility to save the Prince's army otherways.
>
> Such is the misfortune of Princes ! Most of those who approach them choose rather to flatter them and approve of anything they see they are bent upon than to risk losing their favour by opposing their opinions, however ruinous it may be to their master's honour and interest.†

Luckily the Prince's cherished companions were not prepared to run the risk of allowing Marshal Wade to march by a straight and easy road to Penrith to block their way to the Border. Since " the misfortune that had befallen to his father's loyal subjects there would be a bad omen,"‡ they persuaded their master to march from

---

* Lord George's Unpublished Notes.
† Ibid.
‡ Ibid.

Preston to Lancaster. There he again persisted in wasting a precious
day. His folly was apparent to his followers.

> This halt was unnecessary, and perhaps imprudent; it was
> represented to the Prince that if Wade's army had taken the road
> to Lancaster it would have time to come up, and he might be
> forced into a battle, which ought to be avoided until he was
> reinforced. But the Prince was inflexible on this point. He
> would show the world he was retiring and not flying. . . .
> He had the highest opinion of the bravery of his own men,
> and a despicable opinion of his enemies. He had hitherto had
> reason for both, and was confirmed in these notions by some of
> those that were nearest his person. These sycophants, more
> intent upon securing his favours than promoting his interest,
> were eternally saying whatever they thought would please, and
> never hazarded a disagreeable truth.*

Lord Elcho takes up the story :

> An hour after the rear of the army left the town [Preston] General
> Oglethorpe took possession of it, and the Duke of Cumberland
> came to Wigan. At supper at Lancaster the Prince talked much
> about retiring so fast before the son of a Usurper, and that he
> would stay at Lancaster. The principal officers, who were not
> at all against fighting when it was reasonable, met and agreed
> since Wade's army could not now get betwixt them and Scotland
> that they would remain and fight the Duke at Lancaster, which
> at the same time would show them whether it was great stoutness
> or contradiction that made the Prince and his Irish favourites for
> stopping in every town.

Actually on his arrival at Lancaster the Prince had sent Ker of
Graden to reconnoitre the land and to report if he found suitable
terrain for a battlefield. Lord George had called at Headquarters
that evening—" the first thing he always did on coming in to report
how all fared."† But he heard nothing about the meditated battle
until he was roused at dawn and told to go with O'Sullivan to select a
battlefield. The Quartermaster-General's choice fell upon a stretch
of flat ground near the road along which the enemy would approach.
Lord George and Lochiel, whom he insisted should come with
them, preferred a hill to the right. This the Irishman retorted
might be " very fit for Highlanders, if Cumberland was obliging
enough to come there. But it was against all rules of war to go two
miles from the high road and leave the enemy to take possession of

* Chevalier Johnstone.
† Lord George's Unpublished Notes.

the town and cut off all communications and retreat."* Lord
George, however, told his master somewhat gloomily on his return
that he had found " a very proper place for a field of battle . . . if
they were not overpowered by numbers, which he expected to be
the case if the enemy's different bodies should join."† As Charles
could not risk offending two of the most important men in his army
by waiving their advice in favour of O'Sullivan's, he decided not to
fight at all, but to continue the march.

The Prince, nevertheless, was no diplomat. To the last he
persisted in sending messages to Lord George by the detested
O'Sullivan, whose muddle-headedness and forgetfulness was known
to drive his Lordship to the verge of distraction. Even when sent
to choose a camp site these two irreconcilables had never been
known to agree. Neither was Lord George a courtier. Like his
eldest brother he had always hated courts. And now worn out
with the fatigues he endured, the sleepless nights, and his sense of
overwhelming responsibility for the safety of the Prince and the
entire army, he lived in such a state of nervous tension that he
occasionally broke into the " violent sallies " of which Kirkconnel
wrote.

As they left the town next day he said to the Prince : " As Your
Royal Highness is always for battles, be the circumstances what
they may, I now offer you one in three hours from this time with
the army of Wade which is only about three miles from us."‡

This was something of an exaggeration. Two green-clad Rangers
(a company which General Oglethorpe had been recruiting for
service in Georgia, but now used against the Scots) had been
captured by a Jacobite patrol and volunteered the welcome information that Wade was well in the rear, although he had sent his Horse
ahead. Kirkconnel wrote of this day's march :

> The rear of his army had hardly got out of Lancaster when
> some of the enemy's Horse entered it. They followed for two
> or three miles, appeared frequently in small parties, but attempted
> nothing. . . . It was to be apprehended that the Cavalry might
> harass and retard the march of the Prince's army as to give the
> Infantry time to come up. Lord George Murray represented
> these dangers and proposed to avoid them by sacrificing the

* O'Sullivan.
† Lord George's Unpublished Notes.
‡ Chevalier Johnstone.

cannon and all the heavy baggage to the safety of the men which was now at stake.

There is no doubt that Lord George placed a higher value upon human life than did his royal master, who, reared in the traditions of other days when men had freely fought and bled for his forebears, failed to realise the change that had come over men's outlook, and which had had so strong a bearing upon his officers' decision to retreat from Derby. On the other hand, the Prince put a strangely childish value upon the wretched pieces of artillery which had been dragged with such labour along the road from Edinburgh, and which proved so much more of a hindrance than a help to the Jacobites throughout their march. "Not a single piece of cannon or a single carriage must be left. I would rather fight both armies than give such an argument to fear and weakness," Charles exclaimed vehemently.

That evening he held a levee at his Headquarters in Strickland-gate. Few but his officers were present. His only real friends in Kendal were the poor and needy, who had been filled with joy and gratitude at the sight of the gold and silver coins which his officers, attending Sunday service in the Parish Church on their way south, had placed in the pewter alms plate. O'Sullivan, who " had got some mountain Malaga which he seemed very fond of,"* asked Lord George to have a glass or two of it, but he either disregarded or forgot his guest's urgent request that men should be kept at work all night transferring baggage and ammunition from heavy waggons to light carts similar to those that had borne it southward to Preston, where better roads had permitted the use of more capacious vehicles. The heavy waggons could not traverse the steep road over Shap Fell by which the Jacobites must march, as the country people had been " digging holes and throwing down big stones from the walls upon the high road."† Lord George's further instructions that two days' rations should be provided to last his men until they reached Penrith, had also been disregarded.

Mr O'Sullivan who was to give the orders sat at table with His Royal Highness till near eleven at night so that most of the majors and other officers were retired before orders were given

* Lord George's ' Marches.'
† Local tradition.

out. It was next morning before they got them. Many of the men returned to the town after they had marched to get provisions. The people in the town shut all their doors lest the stragglers should plunder.*

They had reason to fear the Highlanders, who, burning to avenge the death of the Hussar and the Duke of Perth's servant, " behaved very rudely, exacting contributions, plundering houses, and stripping people of their clothes."† Lord George himself had good reason to be incensed against the people of Kendal, for some of his servants having entered the town the previous evening " before there was a sufficient number to protect them, four of his horse were taken away and never heard of more."‡ Nevertheless he strove to hinder disorders, and was on this account delayed for two hours in setting out upon his march. As the rear-guard filed along the road they caught sight of a parson who, with five friends, was hiding behind a wall counting their numbers. The Highlanders fired upon the party, and pursued them as they ran for their lives until they eventually found sanctuary in a very dirty pigeon-cote.

Lord Ogilvy's Regiment, which had been in the van of the army on the entry to Derby and was noted for its superior discipline, had been detailed to remain with Lord George during the early stages of the retreat in addition to the regiment delegated for rear-guard duty for the day. Tall, blue-eyed, auburn-haired Lord Ogilvy (known as *le Bel Ecossais* during his brief term of service in France), " gay of spirit, light of heart, yet firm steadfast and resolute of purpose,"§ was a good man to have at hand in times of hazard, although he resented being encumbered with the baggage as much as did Lord George. The commanders of other regiments, knowing the difficulties and dangers with which the Lieutenant-General was beset, had often remained with him to offer what assistance they could. But on leaving Kendal Lord George found himself alone with the Glengarry Regiment, whose turn it was that day to march in the rear on what proved to be the worst stage of the retreat.

Lord George's Notes contain a detailed description of the difficulties his men encountered on their march :

* Lord George's Unpublished Notes.
† Local tradition.
‡ Ibid.
§ ' The House of Airlie,' by Rev. James Wilson.

By the time they had marched three miles they got stopped at a water where the four-wheel carriages could not be got through, there being a narrow turn and a steep ascent of a hill. Everybody, officers as well as common men, put their hands to the work. Some of the Manchester gentlemen went into the water up to the middle to push the wheels. It was an excessive rain all day. In this way was the rear employed till a good time after nightfall. They got two or three of these waggons up to the top, more with the force of hands than by the horses—tho' there were nine or eleven put to one at a time.

There was a good farm about a quarter of a mile off the road where Lord George Murray went with the Glengarry Regiment and got them all under cover in the barns, byres, and stables. He placed a guard of fifty men at a small house on the waterside where one of the [ammunition] waggons was still standing loaded. The men were extremely wet and could get but very few fires in these byres and barns. Everything was done that was possible. Many of them were brought into the farmhouse to dry themselves, tho' it was full of officers. All the milk, and cheese, and meal that was in the house was bought for them. Notwithstanding the badness of the night the people of the house sent to a place half a mile off for more cheese as they were promised a penny a pound more than usual. In short before midnight they had all got plenty, and as much cheese as would make them a good meal next day. The men were in very good spirits.

[As soon as day began to break we got all the small carts that had timber wheels, or wheels of one piece of wood (as none other could be had), and sent even two miles off the road and got some. We unloaded the waggons and put the things into those small carts. . . . It was the heaviness of the waggons, and their being so unwieldy and of vast length that had been their stop, and not what was in them. Two of the smallest carts contained all that was in the best loaded waggons ; and we had left above a dozen fine box carts at Preston that would have done more than all the business.] In one waggon was only four barrels. When looked into it was found that two of them was powder and two were filled with biscuit which had come all the way from Edinburgh, and travelled to Derby and back again. It was designed to feed the men upon the Borders where it was imagined there might be occasion for it, and at the time of the Siege of Carlisle. But by unaccountable neglect they had carried several barrels instead of gunpowder all along.

The march of the rear continued without any stoppage for three miles. But at that place there was a large water which by reason of the heavy rains was almost impassable. There was a bridge, but too narrow for the carriages. The night before a cannon had fallen over that bridge. Several carriages were left there, so that Cluny Macpherson with his battalion, who were next in the rear immediately before the Glengarry Regiment, had stayed there all night. But they were gone before Lord George Murray came there. Several carts with cannon-ball were at that place, and the hill they were to mount was by much the steepest of any upon the whole road. There was no possibility to carry all the carts with the cannon-ball up this hill, especially as the horse were very bad.

The Prince had sent that day from near to Penrith an aide-de-camp to Lord George Murray to tell that he must by no means leave anything behind, and that he would rather return than that one cannon-ball should be left. He made answer to the aide-de-camp that when he had undertaken at Derby to be always in the rear and make the retreat he had expressly told he could not be answerable for any of the carriages and baggage. He was promised that he would not have any embarrass about it, but that it should be always in the front and proper persons to take care of it, notwithstanding of which he had more fatigue with other people's charge than with his own. However he bid the aide-de-camp tell His Royal Highness that everything possible should be done, and that he would do all that man could do. He also told his apprehensions that by all the intelligence he could get he expected to be attacked that night or next day. At least he hoped they would send some Horse that he might employ them in going to the rising grounds so as to see any enemy before they came close upon them.

After this he promised any of the men that would carry a cannon-ball sixpence for each the length of Shap, which was but four or five miles. There was about two hundred carried this way, the men tying them up in the corner of their plaids. Take all things together this was a hard day for the rear.*

It was while crossing a " bridge without ledgelets " a cart and four horses toppled into the stream below ; they were got out with great difficulty, " but the horses so spoiled they were fit for nothing. Owing to the breakdown of carts they were obliged to throw a great deal of powder into a large pool to dampnify it so as to be no use to the enemy."† So wrote Lochgarry, who in the absence of his nephew Angus Og commanded the followers of his brother-in-law Glengarry, between whose family and that of the Dukes of Atholl a close friendship existed. Lord George indeed had every reason

---

* Lord George's Unpublished Notes. Supplemented by extracts from ' Marches of the Highland Army ' (in square brackets).

† Lochgarry's Account. Lockhart Papers.

to be pleased with the splendid conduct of these men, " usually
reckoned not the most patient,"* but who had uncomplainingly
carried out duties which Highlanders considered beneath them, and
who, as matters fell out, were destined to remain unrelieved for three
days in the rear. They would not have done what they had for
any man on earth but himself, and were ready to stand by him to
the last drop of their blood, they told their General, who had never
been better pleased with men in all his life. " You will have much
honour in what you have done," he assured them. " I hope there is
no great danger, for the badness of the weather and the roads will
retard the enemy. We can always outmarch the Foot, and the
Horse will not venture except in a great body. I hope we will
join the rest of our friends before any great numbers can come near.
At any rate I will share your fate, and encourage you as best I can."†

They reached Shap an hour after nightfall, and found no welcome
awaiting them there. The inn was bad. The Prince and his party
had been overcharged by its avaricious proprietors, and such food
as had been set before their royal guest had all been consumed.
Scarcely a scrap of anything edible was left in the village ; but the
biscuits which had made so long a journey from Edinburgh, and
the cheese which Lord George had purchased and which " the
Glengarry Regiment had brought from their last quarters was of
great use."‡ Their habit was to cut a slice from a round cheese,
toast it at the fire on the point of a claymore, and then place it
between two hunks of bread.

Charles's addiction to laying burdens on the person whom he
blamed for the retreat now seemed to outweigh his concern for the
safety of his baggage and artillery, or for the lives of Lochgarry's
300 followers. On reaching Shap Lord George found to his dismay
that he was to be burdened still further with the care of the cannon,
most of which were reposing forlornly in the village street. Instead
of the Cavalry he had asked for, he found only a battalion of 200
foot-soldiers who if sent up the hills to scout ran a much greater risk
than horsemen of being shot down or captured by the enemy's
Horse. Their commander, Colonel John Roy Stewart, was a
favourite of the Prince and no friend to Lord George and his

* Lord George's ' Marches.'
† Lord George's Unpublished Notes.
‡ Ibid.

brother, and he caused them a good deal of trouble throughout the campaign. On the present occasion he was notably unhelpful; for his suggestion was to make a bonfire of all the baggage. The Duke of Perth who, hunted and harried by the militia, had now returned to the army, had more understanding of Lord George's problems, since he himself had been incommoded by the " damned cannon " and "accursed equipage " during the greater part of the march from Edinburgh to Derby. On his own initiative he sent back some of his men to assist Lord George in his difficulties.

Lord George left an account of the exciting happenings of the next few hours :

> Next morning Lord George had all in motion before break of day, but some of the small carts being overloaded there was continually some of them giving way. Having had the precaution of sending to places a little off the road more small ones with great difficulty were got, so that the march continued for about four miles without anything remarkable—only that small parties of Horse were observed upon the heights towards the right and left, which was believed to be only Militia. But some who appeared in the rear was thought to be advance scouts of the enemy, accounts of which he sent to the Prince. [He] told how much he was encumbered with the cannon and baggage so that by reason of the badness of the roads he could only advance very slowly. He chose forty of the cleverest men to whom he gave some gratification, and divided them so as some went to the heights on the right and left and some kept a quarter of a mile behind to observe those parties that appeared. The men performed what was desired of them to admiration and were almost as swift as the horse, so that they effectually kept anything from approaching within a mile of the main body. They sent their swiftest footmen to give account of the least thing they perceived.
>
> In this way it continued till they came near a village called Strickland about five miles from Shap. Here a body of Horse appeared and formed upon the road leading to Penrith. They seemed to be about two hundred, and at first everybody took them for the Horse of the Prince's army. But when they blew their trumpets it was soon perceived to be the enemy. The Glengarry men immediately threw their plaids and ran across hedges with incredible quickness and without any order, upon which the Horse went off at the top gallop. There were but three or four shot after them, and one of them was killed. After the men returned Lord George Murray told them the error they had committed. They promised to be more observant for the

future, and indeed their behaviour afterwards that same day showed that they could keep their resolution.*

Lord George was extremely incensed by the officious conduct of an unattached Irish officer who without consulting him had taken upon himself to send the Glengarry men rushing up a hill upon an unknown number of the enemy. Providentially these Government scouts proved to be as lacking in courage as in initiative; for, as Lochgarry observed, if the enemy " had had the least thought or judgment they might have made themselves master of all the baggage and cannon. For if they had had the precaution to have thrown down the two stone walls on the sides of the highway near the village it would not have been possible for the baggage, &c., to have passed." Even without such impediments, the lane leading into Clifton was so narrow that it was difficult for anyone on foot to pass the carts, and when two broke down a block was caused. Substitutes were procured and loaded; and at length the detested baggage train pursued its way to Penrith escorted by Captain Johnstone's company.

John Roy Stewart's Regiment remained at Lowther Bridge while Lord George led the Glengarry men into the policies of Lowther Hall. He hoped that in the park he would come upon and deal with the Light Horse that had hung upon his left all day. A few horsemen were to be seen far to the south near the Hall. But only two were caught. These were " a running footman of the Duke of Cumberland and another person clothed in green who appeared to be an officer, and who informed that the Duke of Cumberland was within a mile with about 4,000 Horse—Dragoons, besides Light Horse and Militia."†

Lord George must have guessed this to be an exaggeration; for the two most unreliable Dragoon regiments that had wrought such havoc trampling upon the Foot in their precipitous flight at Preston-pans, had been sent by the east coast to Edinburgh. He despatched Colonel Stewart with the prisoners to Penrith while he himself remained at Clifton, which was a strong-post, until he received orders from his royal commander. The Colonel put the case to the Prince strongly, and said that if Lord George's men " were

* Lord George's Unpublished Notes.
† Account of Captain John Macpherson of Strathmashie. ' Lyon in Mourning.'

not speedily succoured they would all be destroyed."*   " But at
Penrith they had taken a notion it was only Militia that pursued the
rear-guard," consequently the Prince would not spare any of his
men whom he was proposing to review before setting out for Carlisle.
" As there was formerly a contradiction to make the army halt when
it was necessary to march, so now there was one to march and shun
fighting when there could never be a better opportunity for it,"
recorded Elcho. But he had no patience with the moods of his
royal leader, who throughout the retreat " appeared to be very
much out of humour."

One of the Hussars next galloped up crying out : " If the rear
is not reinforced it will infallibly be cut to pieces," whereupon the
Macphersons ran off to Clifton " like hounds, thinking it was so
late there would be no ploy till morning " unless they bestirred
themselves.†   Perth, hardly fit to be in the saddle, let alone engage
in battle, rode with them, bringing along Ardshiel and his men.
Instead of the Militiamen he expected to see, he found two lines of
Cumberland's Cavalry drawn up on the open moor within cannon-
shot of Clifton. He waited only to confer with Lord George, who
just then emerged from the park.

" I'll immediately ride back and get out the rest of our army,"
he said. " As the grounds where you are drawing up are strong,
I don't doubt you can maintain the post till others join you." " I
only desire a thousand more men," Lord George assured him.
" Then I could not only maintain the post I have, but could send half
my men through the enclosures on my right so as to flank the enemy
on that side. If they attack from the other side and but twenty of
their Horse are killed it will make such an embarrass in the lane
that it will put them all into confusion, and choke up the only road
they have to retreat—except the Appleby road. That might be also
secured, which would give us an advantage. Perhaps we should not
meet with the like again."‡

The Duke then wheeled about and returned to Penrith, accompanied by an Englishman who had been with the rear throughout the
retreat, knew the country well, and promised to lead the army along
a side route by which they could fall upon the flank of the Govern-

---

* Lord George's ' Marches.'
† Strathmashie's Account. ' Lyon in Mourning.'
‡ Lord George's ' Marches.'

JAMES, DUKE OF PERTH

From a miniature in the West Highland Museum, Fort William

Copyright : C. ROGER

[Facing p. 128

WILLIAM, MARQUIS OF TULLIBARDINE
"*Duke William*"

Aged 22. From a miniature at Blair Castle
Artist unknown

[Facing p. 129

ment forces. Lord George left an account of the discussion which ensued with John Roy Stewart who had also returned from Penrith :

> The officers who were with me agreed in my opinion that to retreat when the enemy were within less than musket-shot would be very dangerous and we would probably be destroyed before we came up with the rest of our army. We had nothing left for it but a brisk attack. . . . I shewed Colonel Stewart my situation with that of the enemy. They were by this time popping shots at us. From it was a very narrow road and very high walls so that I could not line them to secure my retreat. Probably my men would fall into confusion in the dark and the enemy must destroy a great many. I was confident I could dislodge them from where they were as they had not, by all I could judge, dismounted above five hundred. Their great body was on horseback at some distance. Cluny and he owned that what I proposed was the only prudent way ; so we agreed not to mention his message from the Prince. Colonel Roy Stewart was close with me after he returned from Penrith. Glenbucket, who was very infirm, stayed at the end of the village on horseback. He told me he was sorry he was not able to go with me. He entreated me to be very cautious for if any misfortune happened I would be blamed.*

This doughty veteran of Dundee's campaign, who though a Lowlander looked the personification of an ancient Highland Chief with his flowing white locks and beard, must have felt a sharp pang of regret that his own fighting days were over as he watched tall, stalwart Lord George and the stockily built but sturdy Chief of the Macphersons march their men back through Clifton.

Lord George then ordered 1,000 of them to march and counter-march in the village to give the impression that the greater part of the Jacobite army was positioned there. This illusion was fostered by the gathering dusk, in which the Highlanders, creeping to their post in blue bonnets and dark plaids, were less conspicuous than the Dragoons with their laced hats and light buff belts. He was careful to place the Macdonalds to the right, and Cluny and Ardshiel's men to the left of the main road, both parties well screened by the hedges. John Roy's men were posted farther back along the road closer to the village, a position vacated by Pitsligo's Horse, who had been sent to reinforce him earlier in the afternoon, but had unaccountably returned to Penrith while he was in Lowther Park. After ordering

---

* Lord George's ' Marches.'

I

the Glengarry officers to advance as soon as they saw him do so, Lord George had to retrace his steps and cross the road at the end of the village as the enemy had got between the Highland lines. This was greatly to the satisfaction of Lord George, who had purposely allowed these dismounted men to " advance among the lanes and hedges till they could not be supported by their friends on horseback."*

A transient gleam of moonlight showed Lord George that only a hedge separated them from Cluny's men, with whom he advanced with the greatest caution until they were close against the hedge. "Bullets were going thick enough"† now, for another company of dismounted Dragoons had opened fire upon them. " What the devil is this ? " exclaimed Cluny, who, as he later confessed, began to consider the situation " extremely delicate, the numbers vastly unequal, and the attack very dangerous."‡ His commander asked his opinion about making a bold onslaught upon the dismounted Cavalrymen. " I will attack them with all my heart if you order me," the young Chief answered. " I do order it then. We have nothing for it but going down upon them sword in hand before they have time to charge," said Lord George. "We may be attacked when getting through the hedge. If this happens I'll attack on the right of your regiment and do you the same on the left of it. We'll advance so if you approve of it." " I'm very ready to attack when your Lordship pleases," replied Cluny.

They broke through the hedge with the help of their dirks, " the prickles being very uneasy to the loose-tailed lads," records John Macpherson of Strathmashie. Once through, Lord George drew his sword, and shouting " CLAYMORE ! " charged ahead with Cluny and his clansmen, who made their attack with " great spirit and keenness."§ After discharging one round of fire upon their adversaries, the men threw down their firearms and attacked sword in hand as their General ordered them to do. This, says Strathmashie, " was readily done, and then we indeed fell pell-mell upon them. But the poor swords suffered much as there were no less than fourteen of them broke on the Dragoons' skull-caps (which

* Lord George's ' Marches.'
† Ibid.
‡ Cluny's Account. Appendix, ' Waverley.'
§ Strathmashie's Account.

they all had) before a better way of doing their business was found out." Colonel Honeywood, the commander of Bland's Dragoons, who had only just recovered from wounds received at Dettingen, was again struck down. Cluny came away with his sword, and his followers secured fifty fine weapons from their defeated enemies.

Bland's Dragoons had broken and fled in confusion; and other companies were driven out of the lane with great slaughter. Many were killed in the ditch dividing the enclosures from the open moor. Their more fortunate comrades ran until they reached the main body of the army drawn up round the Duke of Cumberland, who had not participated in the attack.

"The Glengarry Macdonalds, who were placed behind a stone park dyke, continued to gall the enemy's flank with their fire, since they could not get at them with their swords . . . and . . . would have done greater execution on the enemy had not night prevented them." So wrote their commander Lochgarry, and Cluny, describing the "precipitation and confusion" of the Dragoons' flight, added: "If the Prince had been provided in a sufficient number of Cavalry to have taken advantage of the disorder, it is beyond question that the Duke of Cumberland and the bulk of his Cavalry had been taken prisoners!" "Our brave Highland lads, when it came to action, did their parts most manfully, our General and Colonel charged and acted with conduct, prudence, valour, and resolution," comments Strathmashie, who was equally exultant about the outcome of the Macphersons' first encounter with Government troops.

As it was, over forty of Cumberland's men were killed or wounded, while the Jacobites lost only one Hussar, captured before the engagement, and twelve of Cluny's men who disobeyed orders not to cross the last ditch. Five of them were killed; the remainder were sent to York and sold into slavery after recovering from their wounds.

Lord George gave an account of the close of proceedings on that memorable day on which the Glengarry and Appin men and the Macphersons had so distinguished themselves:

> It was now about an hour after sunset, pretty cloudy, but the moon which was in its second quarter from time to time broke out and gave good light. But this did not continue above two

minutes at a time. . . . I had given orders that our men should not pass the bottom ditch to go up the muir, for they would have been exposed to the fire of the Glengarry Regiment that could not distinguish them from the enemy. We had no more firing after this so we returned to our first post. We had now done what we proposed. Being sure of no more trouble I ordered the retreat, first Roy Stewart's, then Appin, Cluny, and the Glengarry men. It was half an hour after the skirmish before we went off [at six o'clock]. I was the last man myself. The Atholl Brigade [commanded by Lord Nairne] had come the length of a bridge being within half a mile of Clifton, hearing of my being in sight of the enemy, and there waited for orders. Had the rest of the army come out and followed the plan that was proposed they would have been upon the flank of the Dragoons that were on horseback by the time we attacked the others. The officers that were with me, as well as the men, behaved to my wish. . . . Glenbucket gave me his targe.* It was convex and covered with a plate of metal which was painted. The paint was cleared in two or three places with the enemy's bullets. Indeed they were so thick about me that I felt them hot about my head and I thought some of them went through my hair which was about two inches long.†

It was lucky I made that stand at Clifton, for otherwise the enemy would have been at our heels and come straight to Penrith, where after refreshing themselves two or three hours they might have come up with us before we got to Carlisle.

I have been the more particular about this little skirmish because I observed it was very indifferently related in the English newspapers—as if we had been beat from our post at Clifton ; whereas I was there about half an hour after the enemy were gone. I heard they retired a good many miles for their quarters, and I am persuaded they were as weary of the day's fatigue as we could be.‡

---

* John Gordon of Glenbucket was the father-in-law of Lochgarry, and a veteran of Dundee and Mar's campaigns. He had been bedridden for two years, but he had felt a new life welling up within him on hearing of the landing of the Prince, whom he at once rode off to meet. But he was " a very old man, much crouched," and unfit for active service, and he was obliged to travel to and from Derby in the Prince's coach with Lord Pitsligo, who though the commander of a Cavalry regiment was so stiff that he had the greatest difficulty in mounting a horse. The aged Robertson of Struan, after having had the pleasure of watching the Battle of Prestonpans, had been sent back to Perthshire in the coach taken from the defeated Cope.

† Lord George had lost his wig and bonnet in the engagement when he charged through the hedge to the attack.

‡ Lord George's ' Marches.'

So ended this brief but well planned and well fought rear-guard action—memorable in history as the last battle to be fought on English soil. Lord George was luckier than even he had supposed; for it was only because General Oglethorpe providentially overslept in his comfortable bed at Orton Vicarage that his strong detached column did not reach Lowther Bridge in time to intercept the Jacobite rear-guard before the Duke of Perth arrived to reinforce it.

The Prince, "well pleased with what had happened,"* was leaving Penrith as the victors entered the town. There they stayed a little time to refresh themselves, for " some of them had occasion for it,"† remarked Lord George. After toiling heavily laden over the hills for two days, and then fighting a battle, his weary men were now confronted with the prospect of an eighteen-mile night march to Carlisle. Lord George wrote:

> When we came to Carlisle, where we halted next day, I was clear for evacuating it, but it seems another resolution was taken, and I was ordered to speak with some of the officers that were appointed to stay. The Duke of Perth was very unwilling to leave any of his men; as indeed it was no wonder. In the Prince's presence he asked me why so many of the Atholl people were not desired to stay. I told him if His Royal Highness would order me I would stay with the Atholl Brigade, though I knew my fate; for so soon as they could bring cannon from White-haven I was sure it was not tenable. We might have blown up part of the Castle, and at any rate whenever we were in a condition to return, Carlisle could not do us hurt. We could come in by Brampton which was nearer and had not the river Eden to pass. The country was open to us there and in many other places. As for our military stores, what was not easy carried along with us could be thrown into the river. Once we were upon the Scots side we were in no danger of being followed. The grounds were so strong, and Dragoons could not subsist, except they brought everything necessary along with them, which must be a work of time. I do not know who advised leaving a garrison at Carlisle. I had been so much fatigued for some days before that I was little at the Prince's quarters that day, but I found he was determined on the thing.‡

A garrison of three hundred men was left in Carlisle. Kirk-connel regarded this as " the worst resolution the Prince had taken

* Lord George's ' Marches.'
† Ibid.
‡ Ibid.

hitherto." Other Memoir writers also believed that the place
" could not hold out for more than four hours against a cannonade
from a few field-pieces."* O'Sullivan, in his Narrative, tried to
find an excuse for the bad advice he had given his master :

> Some people were for leaving no garrison at all, which would
> be the most unreasonable thing in the world, for we had several
> rivers to pass and were not sure to find them fordable. If they
> were not, Cumberland could not pass the river that runs by
> Carlisle either. He could not pass by the bridge being under the
> lash of the Castle, so that he'd be obliged to pass by Brampton
> which would always give us two days march of 'um. So in all
> respects it was better to sacrifice a party than the whole, as is
> practised on like occasions. . . . It was Mr Brown and Max-
> field's opinion (who served both of them twenty years in France),
> as well as Geoghagan's and Townley's, that Cumberland could
> not take the Castle with the cannon he had, and the season we
> were in, in a country where his Cavalry could not subsist eight
> days.

By taking the advice of his Irish officers the Prince allowed all
his English followers and many Scots to be sacrificed, as well as
ten of the thirteen cannon upon which he had set such store and
which Lord George's men had dragged with such difficulty from
Derby. As Lord George foresaw, heavy guns were brought from
Whitehaven, and within ten days of the Jacobites' departure the
garrison was obliged to surrender, for the Prince was in no position
to redeem his rash promise to return to their relief. The English
and Scottish officers captured at Carlisle died on the gallows ; the
private men were sentenced to seven years in the Plantations. The
Irish officers surrendered themselves as prisoners of war, except for
Brown and Maxfield who took care to slip away from the fortalice
before its surrender.

The main Jacobite army crossed the Esk in safety to their native
land. They had made a march that was an epic in the military history
of the period. Lord George had exploited to the full the mobility
of Highland troops, and had outmarched, outmanoeuvred and out-
witted the commanders of two British armies. In the two earlier

* Chevalier Johnstone.

Jacobite Risings there had been no General capable of making the most of the fine fighting qualities of the Gaels and their natural aptitude for guerilla warfare. There had been no swift swoops down to the Lowlands, and the English Generals, used only to the slow-motion tactics of the day, were in 1745 unprepared for and baffled by the lightning tactics that their formidable adversary employed.

" I don't know who has the command of these people's affairs in the military, but this I can assert that they have not committed one mistake since they came into the kingdom," wrote Lord Cobham when describing the insurgents' march into the heart of England. Modern writers endorse his verdict. As one of them says : " Lord George may be fairly described as a strategical genius. He dodged and outmanœuvred the English Generals on every occasion, marching up and down the country from Edinburgh to Derby with an absurdly inferior force, giving battle only when he chose. This undoubtedly marks him out as a strategist who might have done great things on a larger scale."

A contemporary Whig commented on the moderation with which the invaders " conducted themselves in a country abounding with plunder. No violence was offered ; no outrage committed ; and they were effectually restrained from the exercise of rapine. Notwithstanding the excessive cold, the hunger, the fatigue to which they have been exposed, they left behind no sick, and lost very few stragglers ; but retired with deliberation and carried off their cannon in the face of the enemy."

Discipline is hard to maintain during a retreat. It was the more necessary for the invaders, since to straggle meant death. Militiamen, afraid of a band of armed men, were ready enough to shoot solitary rebels, and some Highlanders were murdered in cold blood by country people. It speaks much for Lord George's iron discipline that, during his memorable march of 240 miles from Carlisle to Derby and back, he lost only forty men—including those killed or captured at Clifton. He lost, in fact, fewer men than Wade during his unlucky five days' march from Newcastle to Hexham and back again. With the notable exception of French-born Jean

Ligonier, the commanders of the British army of that day took little interest in the health and welfare of their soldiers, whom they considered the scum of the earth. But Lord George regarded them as a Chief regards his clansmen. He had guarded their health and sustained their morale, and after all the long and weary marches they had undertaken he had brought them back to their own country in fine fettle.

CHAPTER IX

FALKIRK

LORD GEORGE wrote a brief account of what took place after crossing the Border :

> No concert had been taken what route we were next to follow. His Royal Highness in the presence of some of the officers desired to know my opinion, which I gave. I should march with six battalions that night to Ecclefechan. Next day for Moffat, and then halt a day, and after making a feint towards the Edinburgh road, turn off to Douglas, then to Hamilton and Glasgow. His Royal Highness would go with the clans and most of the Horse that night to Annan, next day to Dumfries . . . and be at Glasgow a day after us. This was immediately agreed to. . . .
>
> Those who went by Ecclefechan had a very bad march, mostly through mossy ground, and our guides led us off the road. It was very late before we got to our quarters, and we were pretty much fatigued. I had contracted a violent cold and cough. The day we left Kendal I had stood several hours in heavy rain, and not having stript for some nights made me feel the effects of it the more. I had wade several waters and often been mid-thigh deep in moss. But when I got myself washed with warm water and oatmeal and water—what Highlanders call a brochin—in bed at Ecclefechan I was next day almost cured. We halted a day at Moffat. It was Sunday, and having Episcopal Ministers along with us, we had sermon in different parts of the town where our men all attended.*

From Moffat Lord George sent an express to Lord John Drummond—the first intimation the commander of the new French levies received that the Highland army had returned to Scotland. The Water of Douglas was high and difficult to negotiate ; and at Douglas Castle, where Lord George had that summer been the honoured guest of the Duke of Douglas, he was now refused admittance by the Duke's servants. They opened the doors readily enough the next night when the Prince arrived with his superior force and his three Swedish cannon brought from Carlisle. It was while at Hamilton Palace that Lord George heard that the Earls of

* Lord George's ' Marches.'

Glencairn and Home had marched away from Glasgow with the newly raised West Country Militia. Lord George entered the city on Christmas Day, as did Lord Elcho, who had been sent forward by the Prince. Charles himself arrived there the following afternoon with his weary men. Since leaving Edinburgh they had marched nearly five hundred and eighty miles. Their clothes and brogues were in a dilapidated state, so the Prince ordered the magistrates of this Whig city to provide 12,000 shirts, 6,000 cloth coats, 6,000 pairs of stockings, 6,000 pairs of shoes for them. Lord George, who lodged in the Stockwell near the Prince's Headquarters in the Trongate, supervised the distribution of this new clothing. He wrote:

> I had endeavoured to get linen and cloth distributed amongst the men which had been furnished by the town of Glasgow. After His Royal Highness consented it should be divided, some people advised him not to do it. They were much in the wrong. If good usage would not keep them nothing would ; and those who were determined to go home for a few days would not be kept for so small matters. I was very much vexed at this as it had very bad effects."*

Since the return to Scotland 500 men had deserted and only sixty recruits had come forward to augment the Jacobite forces which were reviewed on Glasgow Green on 2nd January. The day after this review the Prince advanced to Stirling by Kilsyth, and Lord George with the six Highland battalions marched to Cumbernauld that night. He then hurried on to meet Lord John Drummond who had only succeeded in bringing over 780 men—namely, his own somewhat " weak and badly organized "† regiment, the Royal Scots, fifty piquets from each of the six regiments of the Irish Brigade, and a hundred of FitzJames's troopers. Most of their chargers had been lost on the voyage, and they could not readily be replaced in a country " ill furnished with horses and harness."‡ English warships had captured three of his transports, forced others back to port, and prevented the remainder of the promised 10,000 men from venturing to sea. Lord George entertained the gravest doubts that further reinforcements would arrive in time to save the situation.

Lord John had made transport difficulties his excuse for failing

---

* Lord George's ' Marches.'
† O'Sullivan.
‡ Kirkconnel.

to join the Prince in England. As the Castle garrison had broken an arch of Stirling Bridge, guns would have to be sent across the Fords of Frew on floats, and those at a greater distance brought up by boat from Cambus. Lord George rode there with Lord John as it seemed the best place for embarking the cannon.

Lord George had much sympathy for the harassed young man so long absent from his own country, and wrote :

> He had much trouble and difficulty bringing up the cannon. Some came by the Frews, and others by Alloa. But there was so small a guard with those at Alloa that Lochiel's Regiment, which was now about seven hundred strong (being joined by his recruits) was obliged to be sent there. We had intelligence of many regular troops being shipped to land on that side, so the cannon would have been in great danger had he not gone over as he did with his regiment. They had not sent enough men to Alloa from Perth, and it was by much the nearest road for the cannon to get over the Forth. I luckily got a vessel that was lying off Airth, the tide before the frigates came up, which served for transporting many of our cannon and stores to a place near Polmaise. We got three of our own cannon placed at Elphinstone to keep off the frigates. I was obliged to have strong guards relieved there every day, as well as at Airth. The frigates, so soon as the spring tide served, came up. There was a good deal of firing from them and from our battery for two days. But they could make nothing of it, and were obliged to fall down the Forth again. I believe they lost some men. We had none killed or wounded.*

Lord George was stationed on outpost duty at Falkirk with five Highland battalions. Two were " very thin," he records. " The duty was hard, having many guards to furnish, and we were but a day's march from Edinburgh where the enemy were turning very strong."† Throughout the bitter winter days and nights his piquets were obliged to remain on duty far longer than would have been the case had not the Prince, many miles behind the lines, persisted in keeping the Atholl Brigade as his guard at Bannockburn House. Sir John Macdonald, his unamiability much increased by the rheumatic pains he suffered as a result of the persistent downpour during the retreat, had evidently not missed this opportunity of hinting that from Falkirk Lord George might easily lead them over

* Lord George's ' Marches.'
† Ibid.

to the enemy. " Scarce any of them ever got thanks for venturing life and fortune, and even the gallows," for the Cause, Lord George had written to William, and the Athollmen seem to be " not thought equally good with other men."* Stung by slights, weary of inactivity and of their apparently useless victories, they were taking themselves off to their homes. The Brigade was now reduced to two-thirds of its former strength—a contingency that would not have occurred had the Athollmen been left under Lord George's eye.

Several of Lord George's associates of early days had come over with the French troops, including the Old Lochiel, who, far from being dead as Lord George had supposed, had returned to Scotland at the age of eighty to offer his services to the Prince. Charles gave him a nominal command at Perth, but treated him with less honour than his devotion and his sacrifices for the House of Stuart deserved.

On 9th January the overworked commander of the Jacobite army received a letter which had the same effect on him " as good rest after excessive fatigue." It was the first he had received from his " Dearest Life " since leaving Edinburgh in October. Lest his reply should fall into enemy hands he wrote to her in an ambiguous fashion :

> For news I can write none that is certain. A good part of the army lies here, and I know not how soon they may attack or be attacked. For my part I am prepared for the worst, and have been so for a long time. I asked Lord George if he had any word. He bid me assure you of his best wishes. He has a load of affairs upon his hands. He says he approves much of the setting of the Milton in the way proposed as well as Marie's Croft and the rest. The people might get any reasonable security of labouring them three years. He expresses great anxiety to see you, but does not believe it possible—at least till affairs be more settled. He could not leave his post at present were it to save his friend's life. . . . Once more he recommends to you that evenness of temper, contentedness, and resignation to whatever may happen. The only true philosophy that he has endeavoured to practise—especially of late. He thinks that as soon as your condition of health will allow you should either have it in your power to remove to Arnhall or Glencarse till you fix on some town where you can be most to your liking. He would recommend

* Lord George's letter to Duke William from Carlisle. Jacobite Memoirs.

Glasgow. There are very good people there, tho' their principles may differ from that his Lordship has possessed. He thinks that in certain events (for it is only on that supposition he recommends all this) you will think yourself easier where you have fewest acquaintances. . . .*

At four o'clock on the morning of 13th January Lord George with his five battalions marched from Falkirk to Linlithgow to forestall the Government commander General Hawley, who was expected to occupy the town that night. On the way the Highlanders were joined by Lord Elcho's Life Guards and Lord Pitsligo's Horse, which Lord George had ordered to meet him.

Inishewen, who had evidently heard Lord George's trustworthiness questioned, wrote :

> Previous to the Battle of Falkirk Lord George marched from that town before daylight to Linlithgow to carry off all the provisions and forage which General Hawley had ordered. Hawley's advance guard unexpectedly met ours at the east end of Linlithgow, upon which they retired. Immediately we marched out of the town to meet Hawley. He had retreated. Imagining he had gone to Edinburgh we returned to Linlithgow to execute our first design. But Hawley marching to Bathgate, Lord George ordered the bagpipes to play and to march slowly through the town to make a feint to meet General Hawley till our men were out of the houses. Making a front of our rear we retreated to Falkirk, the enemy pursuing us to the Bridge of Linlithgow. If Lord George had been so inclined, it was easy for him without suspicion to have frustrated the whole of the Prince's views.†

Lord George longed to attack Hawley's Dragoons, four Infantry regiments and Militia which had come so close that the Jacobites and Government men were able to hurl abuse at one another. " It was too great a venture to have attacked them, since it was risking the whole Cause, tho' we had the fairest prospect imaginable to have cut them off. Lochiel's Regiment, which should also have been with us, had, to my great concern, been ordered over to Alloa two days before. Had that not happened . . . nothing would have prevented us from attacking them."‡

After making what Lord Elcho describes as a masterly retreat

* Unpublished letter at Blair Castle.
† Inishewen's ' Vindication.'
‡ Lord George's ' Battle of Falkirk.'

from Linlithgow, Lord George marched to Bannockburn and billeted his men in the villages round about Stirling, which had surrendered to the Prince on 8th January. His quarters were bad ; as were provisions. It was a hard matter to find accommodation anywhere ; for, as Kirkconnel wrote :

> By this time most of the reinforcements were arrived from the North, or so near that they could not fail of being up before an engagement should happen. They looked mighty well, and were very hearty. The Macdonalds, Camerons, and Stewarts were almost double the number that had been in England. Lord Ogilvy had got a second battalion much stronger than the first. It was commanded by Sir James Kinloch, Lt. Colonel. The Frasers, MacIntoshes, and Farquharsons were reckoned three hundred men each. The Irish piquets, and a part of Lord John Drummond's regiment, were already at Stirling : the rest of the regiment, and Lord Lewis Gordon's [800] men, were within a day's march. The Earl of Cromartie, and his son Lord Macleod, were at Alloa, at the head of their men [200]. In fine, all were at hand in high spirits, and expressed the greatest ardour at the prospect of a battle. The Prince employed the 15th in choosing a field of battle [Plean Muir], and the 16th in reviewing his army. That evening he got advice that Hawley had advanced to Falkirk, and had encamped his whole army betwixt the town and the river Carron.

The Highlanders were in such a fighting mood, and so impatient of being paraded without apparent reason, that some of them told their officers that, if disappointed again, they would engage the enemy without a commander. The Prince was now at the head of 9,000 men, the same number that Hawley was reputed to command. Lord George was therefore all for taking the initiative and launching an attack upon the Government forces before they were augmented by the arrival of Cumberland, or the 5,000 Hessians now on their way to Scotland to replace the Dutchmen, immobilised since the landing of French soldiers in Britain.

In his 'Battle of Falkirk' Lord George gives a full account of what happened on that memorable 17th January :

> The officers being called into His Royal Highness's presence I observed how difficult it was to bring our men together from so many different cantonments for several miles around, and that we found it was always midday before we could be assembled. Whereas the enemy, being encamped, had nothing to do but to strike their tents. As they had carriages for them they could

march by break of day, and so be in the heart of our quarters before we could make head against them—there being but four miles from a great part of our cantonments and their camp. In which case I was afraid we would be in great confusion and probably not be able to make a stand on that side of Stirling. I said that by holding [going to the west] above the Torwood, we would gain the Hill of Falkirk as soon as them, as it was a thing they did not expect. I knew the ground well, and thought there was no difficulty of taking it before they could.

This was approved of by everybody, and His Royal Highness was much pleased with the design. I then asked if I should march off at the head of the two lines in the manner they were then drawn up, which the Prince agreed to. It was done accordingly, for there was not a moment to be lost, it being then betwixt twelve and one. After I had marched about half a mile Mr O'Sullivan came up to me and told me he had been talking with the Prince, and that it was not thought advisable to pass a water [Carron] in sight of an enemy. Therefore it was best delaying it till night, and then we could do it unperceived. This surprised me. I told him that we would be all past the water in less than a quarter of an hour, and the place where we were to pass was two full miles from the enemy. I did not halt; and he went back to His Royal Highness, who was riding betwixt the two lines.

Hawley's men at Falkirk were preparing dinner when a countryman ran into the camp exclaiming : " Gentlemen, what are you about ? The Highlanders will be immediately upon you ! " " Seize that rascal. He is spreading a false alarm ! "* cried some of the officers, who only awoke to the danger when two of their number attached to Howard's Regiment climbed a tree and saw through a telescope that the Jacobite Cavalry were indeed in motion. Colonel Howard then rode off to Callander House, which Hawley, who was sixty-seven and fond of his creature comforts, had made his Headquarters. Seated by a roaring fire, enjoying the food and wine with which he was plied, the General was much annoyed by this interruption to his pleasant tête-à-tête with his once unwilling hostess Lady Kilmarnock, who now used every wile to detain her unwelcome guest. The General had declared that with two regiments of Dragoons he would drive the rebels from one end of the kingdom to the other. " Having come to drive the ' wretched rabble ' from Stirling, he never thought they would attack him at Falkirk."* Still fuddled by the quantity of wine he had drunk, he contented

* Chambers's ' History of the Rebellion of 1745.'

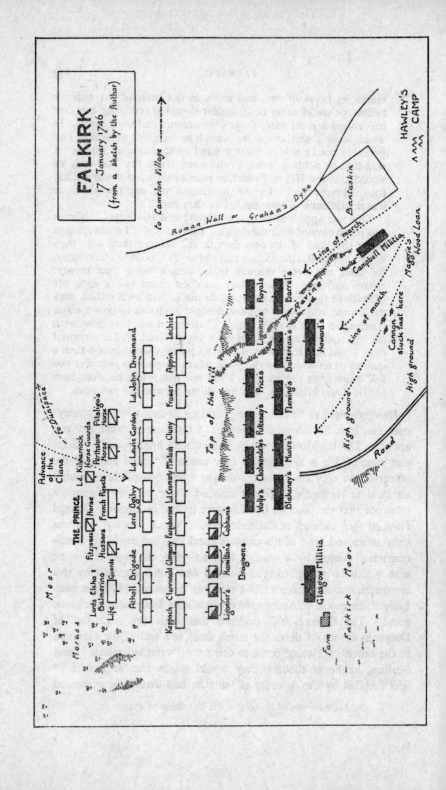

FALKIRK
17 January 1746
(from a sketch by the Author)

to Camelon Village

Roman Wall or Graham's Dyke

HAWLEY'S CAMP

Bantaskin

Line of march

Campbell Militia

Ravine

Royals

Barrels

Ligonars

Howard's

Line of march

Prices

Batterau's

Cannon stuck fast here

Maggie's Wood Loan

High ground

Flaming's

Pulteney's

Cholmondely's

Munro's

High ground

Top of the hill

Wolfe's

Blakeney's

Road

Lochiel

Appin

Fraser

Ld. John Drummond

Cluny

Ld Cromarty M'kash

Ld. Lewis Gordon

Lord Ogilvy

Farquharson

Clanronald Glengary

Keppoch

Ligonier's Hamilton's Cobham's

Dragoons

Farm

Glasgow Militia

Falkirk Moor

Advance of the Clans

to Dunipace

THE PRINCE

Ld. Kilmarnock Horse Guards

Fitzjames Horse

Perthshire Horse

Pitsligo's Horse

Lords Elcho & Balmerino

Hussaars

French Piquets

Life Guards

Atholl Brigade

Moor

Morass

himself with sending the Colonel back to the camp with orders that the men might put on their accoutrements, but there was no need to get under arms.

As nothing further could be done in their commander's absence, the soldiers had begun their dinner when some well-mounted volunteers, having posted themselves by the Carron, brought word that the Highlanders were only two miles away and were preparing to ford the river and outflank the army on the left. A scene of wild confusion ensued as Hawley's men formed up in front of the camp. Officers shouted contradictory orders, and the private men loudly voiced their suspicions that their unloved commander had sold them to the enemy. Half an hour was wasted in this manner before the General, hatless, breathless, and with the white hair of his periwig waving wildly in the wind, galloped into the camp roaring out orders to his Dragoons to ride up the rough and broken hillside to Falkirk Muir to hold the enemy in check until the Infantry could be brought up. His officers deemed it madness to engage their adversaries on terrain so obviously unsuited for Regular troops. But Hawley believed that the Highlanders would be swept from the field by Cavalry as easily as at Sheriffmuir, failing to recollect that the marshy ground had then been frozen. But now, Maggie's Wood Loan, leading up the Hill of Falkirk, was inches deep in mud. His ten cannon stuck fast in the hollow at the foot of it, and the disaffected local carters cut the traces and made off with the horses—a providential circumstance for the Prince, whose artillery was brought up by Farquharson of Monaltrie's 300 men after the fight was over.

So far all had gone according to plan with the Jacobites. Lord John Drummond had been ordered to make a feint by leading his own regiment, the Irish Piquets, and most of the Horse along the road from Stirling to Edinburgh, which was plainly discernible from Hawley's camp until it led through the middle of a large wood. As they passed from view " they had the art to light fires and leave their great white Standard flying on the other side of the Torwood where it was supposed they were encamping."* A great display of banners caused this column to be mistaken for the main army; and the enemy were further puzzled by seeing a body of men (probably Colonel Stewart's Edinburgh Regiment) marching back towards Stirling. The Castle had not surrendered, and it was

---

* Fortescue's ' History of the British Army.' Letter contained in it.

K

thought to be unsafe to leave less than 1,200 men in Stirling in case the garrison should make a sally.

Since Hawley had not troubled to send out patrols that morning none knew that the Prince's and Lord George's columns had marched by fields and byways to the west of the Torwood till they reached Dunipace House. That devoted Jacobite, Sir Archibald Primrose, led them to the Steps of Dunipace, a little to the west of his home where the Carron, usually difficult to cross at this season, was fordable. Undeterred by " bad sloughs and morasses " the Jacobites quickly gained the " rough and ridgy " stretch of ground known as Falkirk Muir. There the columns stretched out in two parallel lines two hundred paces apart. Lord George's, which was to form the right wing of the army, marched along the southern edge of the muir ; Keppoch's Regiment, now over 450 strong, led the van. He was followed by Clanranald, and the two battalions of Glengarry men, each comprising 600 men, commanded by Angus Og and Lochgarry. All were in the same order in which they had been drawn up on Plean Muir that morning. The post of honour on the extreme right of the front line was, however, secured by a small company of Glencairnaig's MacGregors, who outstripped the Macdonalds in the race to the summit of the hill. They reached it soon after the Dragoons, who had come up from Falkirk alongside the wall of the Bantaskin enclosures.

> The sight of the enemy gave fresh spirits to the Highlanders, and it was hardly possible to restrain their ardour. But they still kept their ranks, and marched up in the finest order imaginable, though at a prodigious rate. When they were within musket shot of the enemy, the Dragoons made some feints towards the Macdonalds, who were opposite to them, to draw off their fire, or at least retard their march ; but finding it was to no purpose, they made a motion to the left, as intending to flank them. The Highlanders eluded that motion by a similar one. They stretched a little to the right, where they found a morass, which secured them on that side.*

On coming up the hill the Macdonalds faced Ligonier's, Cobham's, and Hamilton's Dragoon Regiments, comprised of 1,300 men, and under the command of Colonel Francois Ligonier,† a brother of

---

* Kirkconnel.

† Formerly commanded by Colonel Gardiner. Colonel Ligonier, who had been ill with a quinsy, died a few days after the battle as the result of the soaking he then received. His brother Jean had commanded the Infantry Regiment which still bore his name.

the famous General. Brigadier Cholmondely, who was just opposite
Lord George, commanded the left wing ; but found himself without
any regular Infantry battalions, for the six front-line Infantry regiments took up their position farther to the right than was intended.
This caused the fatal outflanking of the left wing of the Prince's
army. As the Hanoverians were baulked on the left by a bog, and
the Jacobites by a ravine, the right wing of each army stretched some
distance beyond the left of the other. The ground, which was
very uneven, fell sharply away at either end of the long Jacobite
front line, which was 4,000 strong. It was thus impossible for those
on each extremity to see what was happening at the other end.
Moreover, the sky, which had been unusually clear, suddenly dark-
ened, a gale arose, and the rain came lashing down in torrents.
It was, as an early chronicler states, " exceedingly disturbing to the
eyesight." It beat straight in the faces of Hawley's Infantrymen,
who, impeded by their stiff uniforms and heavy accoutrements, and
hardly able to see where they were going, struggled up the steep
hillside upon which they were obliged to take up a most disadvantageous stand. The six regiments of the second line huddled
in behind those of the first, with the result that only the Cavalry
squadron near the centre could count on any support from the
Foot. As Lord George readily admitted in his subsequent account
of the action :

> The Highland army had all the advantages that nature or art
> could give them. Their right wing, which consisted of the
> Macdonalds in the front line, and the Athollmen in the second
> line, was a full quarter of an hour in sight of the enemy's Horse,
> and within musket shot. They advanced very slowly, both that
> they might keep their ranks (which they did perfectly well), and
> to give time to the left to come up and form, for from the time
> they had passed the Water of Carron at Dunipace, which was in
> sight of the enemy, till they had taken possession of the ground
> they intended, they had marched very quick to prevent the enemy
> gaining the advantage of the ground and wind. But so soon as
> they got possession of the field they advanced in line of battle,
> foot by foot, till they were within pistol shot of the enemy's
> Horse. . . . All this was executed with as much exactness as
> was possible, and as sometimes one part of the line was farther
> advanced than the rest they halted till the others came equal with
> them.

> Upon the left Lochiel's battalion, who were upon the extremity
> of the line, were outflanked by three battalions of the enemy.
> This might have been easily remedied had two or three battalions

of the second line been extended on that wing. But as each
Colonel commanded only their own regiments, they gave no orders
to any but their own men ; for Highlanders do not willingly
obey the Chiefs of another. The great loss was that there was no
superior officer upon that wing.

[Had Mr O'Sullivan been riding alongst the lines as an
Adjutant-General should before the action, and acquainted the
Prince that the enemy outflanked us on the left by three regiments,
it would have been the easiest thing in nature to have remedied
it by bringing up as many from our second line, or *corps de
reserve*, to have faced these. In which case not one of their
Foot could have escaped.] But that gentleman had certainly no
knowledge in these affairs ; nor was he ever seen to do anything
in the time of action.*

" Mr O'Sullivan " had instead been pestering Lord George with
unsolicited advice. He had pointed out the danger to be apprehended from some stone dykes on the right, and advised Lord George
to march on, which he did. He then recommended bringing up
the Atholl Brigade from the second line (where the so-called Lowland Regiments were usually placed to support the Highland shock
troops), to cover the right of the first line. He was apparently as
unaware of the bog into which they would have floundered as of the
state of mind into which the Macdonalds would have been thrown
had the Athollmen advanced to that coveted post. Lord George,
knowing both these facts, curtly dismissed the Quartermaster-
General, who rode off to give orders to the Colonels and Majors
of the seven other clan regiments drawn up in the front line. One
of Lochiel's officers, Daniel Cameron, warned him of the outflanking
enemy regiments posted on the far side of a little gully running
up to the Jacobite front line. He did so in no measured tone, and
O'Sullivan, who admits in his ' Narrative ' that he " did not like this
reflection," went and saw for himself that Cameron's warning was
justified.

Unfortunately O'Sullivan was inclined neither to confer with his
inferiors, nor to seek out the Prince who, at the urgent request of his
officers, had remained twenty yards to the rear of the second line.
Instead, he sent his young secretary Charles Corn, who was always
at his heels, to bring up Lord Ogilvy's Regiment to take the post

* Lord George's ' Battle of Falkirk.' Passages from ' Marches ' in
parenthesis. The Whig historian Home, who was present at the battle,
bears witness that O'Sullivan " kept aloof till the end of the action."

on the left on the second line immediately behind the Camerons. If he had had the inspiration to send them across the level ground to march along the far side of the ravine, this fine regiment, consisting of two battalions of well-disciplined men, would probably have routed Ligonier's and Price's Infantrymen (not yet joined by Barrel's Grenadiers) with as much ease as the men of the first line swept away the other regiments opposed to them.

During the fifteen minutes when all this was taking place, Lord George was standing in front of Keppoch's men, claymore in hand and targe on arm. At his side were John Roy Stewart, Oliphant of Gask, and Anderson of Whitburgh—that invaluable young man who had guided him through the swamp to Cope's army at Prestonpans, and whom he frequently kept beside him in times of danger. He and Colonel Stewart, the only officers on horseback, had been sent to reconnoitre, and had just returned with confirmation of Lord George's surmise that there were no Foot stationed behind the Horse. He was determined to keep his eager men in line until the left wing was fully formed. He ordered Keppoch's men to stand fast. The command was transmitted to the two other regiments, and they all " reserved their fire as resolutely as . . . the steadiest troops in Europe."[*] Lord George put " his wig in his pocket, and scrogging [pulling] down his bonnet gave orders not to fire until the Dragoons had fired first."[†]

Darkness was already setting in on that stormy winter's afternoon, and the Jacobite second line was barely in position when shortly after four o'clock Hawley ordered the Dragoons to advance. They made a fine show as they " came on at a great trot as boldly as any troops in the world." When " Lord George presented his piece, which was the signal,"[‡] Keppoch's men began the fire which ran down the whole Jacobite line—the Macdonalds aiming with such precision and at so close a range that quite eighty saddles were emptied. Then, throwing down their guns, they charged valiantly upon the oncoming horsemen. Ligonier's Irishmen turned and bolted, as they had bolted under their late commander Colonel Gardiner. So likewise did Hamilton's; and, as at Prestonpans, they crashed in among their own Infantry, trampling upon and killing many of their

* Lochgarry. Lockhart Papers.
† Inishewen's ' Vindication.'
‡ Chevalier Johnstone.

comrades, and bearing a company of Glasgow Militiamen away with them on their flight.

" The Highlanders did not neglect the advantage they had obtained, but pursued them keenly with their swords, running as fast as horses, and not allowing them a moment's time to recover from their fright."* Some unfortunate horsemen had turned to the left and floundered into the bog where, as one Highlander put it, they were cut to pieces as easily as a slice of meat. Cobham's Dragoons swerved to the right and ran the gauntlet of a devastating fire poured upon them from the centre and left of the Jacobite front line. They raced madly away between the two armies until their course was deflected by the gully that ran up towards the left wing. One small company under brave Colonel Whitney pierced the Highland lines, nearly causing the death of Young Clanranald, who lay pinned under a dead charger. His clansmen and the Athollmen, by stabbing the horses and dragging or hacking down their riders, soon dispersed them.

> It was a fine beginning. But the first success had like to have cost very dear, for the left of the Prince's army having spent their fire upon the Dragoons, found the enemy's Foot before them, and by this time the rain, which had begun with the battle, was become so violent that it was impossible for the Highlanders, who do not use cartridges, to load again. Nevertheless they drew their broadswords, and went on with abundance of resolution. They received the fire of those that were opposite them, and attacking them sword in hand, forced them immediately to give way.†

" There was no possibility of making the Macdonalds keep their ranks," Lord George found. " Many of the first line pursued the Horse, and fell in with the Militia." These were 1,800 volunteers from the vicinity of Glasgow, stationed at a farm some distance behind the Dragoons, and they fled for their lives at the sight of Keppoch's men. The 1,200 Campbells, billeted in distant villages, had been detailed to observe the movements of Lord John Drummond (who had remained on the high road while the other columns crossed the Carron). They reached Hawley's camp after he had left it, so they took up a safe position at the lower end of the ravine where, fortunately for themselves, they were not observed by their

---

* Lochgarry's Account. Lockhart Papers.
† Kirkconnel.

hereditary foes. Unnerved by the sight of the fugitive Dragoons ; the Argyllmen fled from the field without firing a shot. John Roy Stewart, a free-lance without a regiment, seems to have made in their direction, but his attention was attracted by the sight of Barrel's Regiment and part of Price's and Ligonier's moving up the hillside down which the Highlanders were still pouring, but safely separated from the main body of them by the gully. Fearing an ambuscade, he called loudly to the oncoming clans to halt. His shouts were, unfortunately, heard. The cry of " Stop ! " flew from rank to rank and the clansmen on the left, galled by this fresh fire on their flank, paused in their onslaught."*

This fatal pause enabled the demoralised men of the nine routed Infantry regiments to make their escape behind the three that stood fast. The declivity hindered the clansmen from charging in their usual whirlwind fashion upon these stubborn adversaries, and wet powder prevented them from returning their devastating fire. Nor were these regiments in danger of being outflanked, for as Lord George observed :

> The second line of the Highlanders left, instead of moving farther to the left, or keeping their line till they should receive orders, crowded in with the first line—at least many of them did —and went down upon the enemy with them. The rest of the second line fell into confusion with their ranks being thinned by those who had run in with the first line. Those that had attacked, seeing the three regiments of the enemy that were upon their left, entire and nothing to oppose them, retired back to the ground they had first been drawn up upon.†

The twenty-year-old Colonels, Lord Lewis Gordon and Lord Ogilvy, posted respectively on the left and centre of the second line, had allowed their followers to get so mixed up with the Highlanders that they never succeeded in finding them again that evening. Behind them the leaderless Royal Scots, believing that the day was lost, took fright and retreated in all haste in the direction of Bannockburn. Their Colonel, Lord John Drummond, had rushed forward to take charge of the left wing, which would have been commanded by his brother, had not the Duke been left in charge of operations against Stirling Castle.

Lord John would have done better had he led his regiment across

* Chevalier Johnstone.
† Lord George's ' Battle of Falkirk.'

the muir and outflanked the three enemy regiments. As it was, he reached the front of his left wing too late to be of much service. So also did the reinforcements brought forward by the Prince. The lie of the land and " the badness and darkness of the weather "* prevented Charles from seeing much from where he and Brigadier Stapleton stood, with O'Sullivan remaining assiduously by their side. The Irish Piquets, Elcho's and Balmerino's Life Guards and the Hussars were on his right, and Kilmarnock's and Pitsligo's Horse on his left; for the Jacobite's horses, " worn out and ill cared for, were in a very bad state,"† and not fit to sustain the shock of the enemy's charge. When at length the Prince marched forward with this *corps de reserve*, which Lord George sent word should be brought up to support the left wing, he was in some danger of being killed or captured. Hawley had been " huddled off the field " by his terror-stricken troops, who were " running off by forties and fifties to the right and left."‡ But his second-in-command General Huske, and Brigadier Cholmondely, had succeeded in rallying Cobham's Dragoons. These Cavalrymen, who had fought well enough in Flanders, now showed an inclination to dash in upon the Prince's newly-formed wing. The Prince's Irish Piquets, however, advanced boldly upon them and caused them to retire. They did so in an orderly fashion, joining up with the three Infantry regiments to form an effective rear-guard. Barrel's Grenadiers even contrived to rescue one of Hawley's three small cannon, and some Dragoons' horses were caught and yoked to the other two.

Lord George, unable to rally the Macdonalds, hurried back to take command of the Atholl Brigade, which had been the only second line regiment to remain in place, and now stood isolated on top of the hill. On his way he picked up some of Keppoch and Glencairnaig's men, who rearmed themselves with muskets that lay strewn about the field. He was greatly concerned to see three unbroken enemy regiments. He longed to attack them, but feared that by doing so he " would be risking all the advantages gained." As he continues in his subsequent account of the action :

> The Atholl Brigade kept their ranks. They were the right of
> the second line. But they were not above six hundred men,

---

* ' Memoirs of Sir John Macdonald.'
† Chevalier Johnstone.
‡ Lord George's ' Battle of Falkirk.'

many of them having gone off after their return from England.
. . . Colonel Ker came with the French Piquets, and Lord John
Drummond came alongst with them and joined me when I was
a good way down the hill. But the enemy went off with so
much precipitation and hurry that it was not possible to overtake
them. . . .

Some of the officers upon the left . . . blamed me for not
being on horseback, because if I had, and had come up to
them as they were engaging, they said I would have remedied
the disorders that happened, by our line not being supplied
with men to face the enemy on our left. My answer to this
was that I had no particular charge. I had asked twice that
morning who were to command in the different stations, and His
Royal Highness went and talked of it to some others; but I
got no answer. . . . Two of His Royal Highness's aides-de-
camp came up to me just before the engagement. But they had
dismounted, so they were of no use but as single men. I had
nobody but Colonel Ker and another aide-de-camp to carry all
the orders that it was necessary for me to give upon the wing I
was on. . . . Most of the general officers were with His Royal
Highness in the time of the action, and they had the opportunity
to see and advise what was proper to be done. . . .

Our pressing forward and going into Falkirk was owing to my
being pretty positive about it.

Many of the Prince's officers wished to retreat to Dunipace
where the men might be under cover—" it being a prodigious rain "*
—instead of driving the enemy out of Falkirk. Their men, who
" had been under arms and in motion from seven o'clock in the
morning, were all wet to the skin, and nothing but wet ground to
lie upon." But Lord George said firmly : " If we do not go at
once the enemy must have time to line the houses and clean their
guns so as to make it impossible to get in. Therefore there's not a
moment to be lost. I'll either lie in the town or in Paradise," he
added, quoting Count Mercy's words at the Battle of Parma.

They were standing at the foot of the hill by Hawley's seven
large embedded guns when the Prince came up. He approved of
the attempt to enter the town, but he was advised to remain
in a house on the hillside until it was cleared of the foe. The Master
of Strathallan and his cousin Laurence Oliphant of Gask went
forward disguised as countrymen, and later returned to report that
Hawley had arrived at his camp without having lost many men on

* Lord George's ' Battle of Falkirk.'

his retreat.   He had not, however, remained in such a dangerous vicinity.   After ordering the burning of his tents (many of them were too wet to catch fire) he marched eastward towards Linlithgow. Three detachments of the Jacobite army then entered the town. That marching in by Robert's Wynd was led by Lord George, the other two by Lord John and Lochiel, both slightly wounded, the one in the arm, the other in the foot.   Lord John had had his horse shot under him and had taken two prisoners with his own hand.

A few redcoats were straggling in the streets when the Jacobites entered the town.   Lord Elcho records :

> Lord George immediately dispatched a party and took pos-
> session of their camp and all their baggage.   But as the troops
> had greatly suffered by the badness of the weather it was not
> possible to pursue them to Linlithgow.   However a body of
> Horse was ordered to go along the Linlithgow road to pick up
> stragglers.   The completeness of the victory was known only to
> that half of the army that was at Falkirk that night, for the other
> half that took up their quarters in the villages betwixt the field
> of battle and Stirling knew nothing of the matter until next
> morning.

The people of Falkirk were friendly to the Jacobites owing to the influence and popularity of Lord Kilmarnock.   At the Prince's bidding the Earl rode off across the policies of Callander House till he came close to the Linlithgow road which, as far as he could see in the darkness, was congested with Government troops.   Officers and men, Horse and Foot, were mingled together in indescribable con-fusion, struggling through the torrential rain as if the devil himself had been at their heels.   Next day they continued their flight to Edinburgh, where their enraged General strung up his own cowardly soldiers on the gibbets that had been erected for the Jacobite pris-oners he had expected to capture.*

Lord Kilmarnock returned with the gratifying news of the spectacle he had witnessed, and shortly before eight o'clock the Prince was conducted to his lodgings by torchlight, although the streets were then lit up by the conflagration at the camp which the Highlanders had pillaged.   Many of them remained on the field till late at night stripping the dead, whose naked bodies, discernible through next morning's mist and rain, resembled at a distance a flock of sheep lying on the hillside.   Captain Johnstone and his

* Four were hanged in one day.

company, sent out about seven o'clock to bring in the captured
cannon, had the disagreeable experience of stumbling over the
bodies of the unburied dead, and of standing guard over the embedded
guns throughout that wet and bitter night.

The Jacobite casualties were 32 killed and 122 wounded. Seven
officers lost their lives, among them Keppoch's brother, and the
only prisoner was his nephew and Major the gallant and chivalrous
Macdonald of Tiendrish. Hawley was computed to have lost 400
dead, as well as many badly wounded men left upon the field. He,
however, sent in his official returns as 280 killed, wounded, and
missing, in what he and his officers chose to describe as a " little
brush " or skirmish in which premature darkness had deprived them
of a complete victory. But as Strathmashie wrote when commenting upon the favourable reports given by Government commanders of their encounters with the Prince's men : " They have
their own way of telling stories." Some Jacobite Memoir writers
boast of 700 prisoners—numbers augmented by the thoroughness
with which Lord Elcho scoured the country next morning to hunt
out stragglers. Three hundred is the number given by Lord
George, who made it his business to send a list of them to Hawley
in order to relieve the minds of the relatives of the missing men,
most of whom were volunteers, including quite a number of ministers
and Hawley's captured hangmen. The hangmen were allowed to
give their parole, as it was thought their word would be as good
as that of English officers, who broke theirs so lightly.

Although delighted with the conduct of his Athollmen who had
" behaved admirably well,"* Lord George was disappointed that
the Government forces escaped destruction. As he wrote in his
account of the battle :

> One vast loss was that not a pair of pipes could be got. The
> pipers whenever a battle begins give their pipes to their boys,
> who take care of themselves. And the pipers, who are commonly
> as good men as any, charge with the rest. This, though it may
> appear trifling, was the reason why the Macdonalds and others
> had not rallied from the first. Excepting the piquets and the
> Athollmen, none of the other corps were together when they
> entered the town. But there were several of the officers, such as
> Keppoch, Glengarry's son, Lochiel, Ardshiel, Lord Ogilvy, and
> Colonel Roy Stewart. . . .

> * ' Atholl Chronicles.'

Had the Macdonalds on the right either not broken their ranks, or rallied soon after, they with the Athollmen would have cut the whole enemy's Foot to pieces, for they were close to them, and must have driven them down the hill before them. And by speed of foot, not a man of them could have got off from them.

Had there been any officer on the left to have ordered two or three battalions from the second line, or reserve, to have faced the enemy that outflanked them, they would have had a complete victory.

O'Sullivan's comment, on the other hand, was mainly directed against Lord George :

If the Highlanders would but let themselves be governed, they would have done wonders, or rather if Lord George did not oppose everything that was proposed to him almost, the Prince would still be in Scotland or the King perhaps restored.

He also asserted that the Athollmen were always kept well out of harm's way by their commander, and had therefore suffered no casualties throughout the expedition. Sir John Macdonald went even further and accused Lord George of " purposely stopping the Highlanders from pursuing the enemy and completing their destruction."* The old man's words sank deep into the hearts of the Macdonalds who had resented the attempts to check their pursuit of the foe. They knew no other mode of warfare, for only such experienced officers as Lord George and Keppoch (who maintained some hold over his own men) realised the futility of pursuing fugitive Militiamen when regular troops remained to be routed. Even Lochgarry wrote with great bitterness that his men " were much surprised to find themselves stopped by generals and officers who with difficulty restrained them with their drawn swords and cocked pistols, conjuring them to return to their ground."

Elsewhere the Lieutenant-General's praises were loudly sung. It was said : " If Lord George could have been everywhere the affairs would have been finished."† Robert Mercer wrote that he had " gained fresh laurels,"‡ and the Marquis D'Eguilles described how he had " fought like a lion at the head of his Highlanders."§ The Ambassador's eulogies were so displeasing to the Prince that,

---

* ' Memoirs of Sir John Macdonald.'
† ' Atholl Chronicles.'
‡ Ibid.
§ The Marquis D'Eguilles' Dispatch.

as a counter-blast, he directed Sir Thomas to write to the French Ministry recommending the interests of his " dear O'Sullivan." Charles pointed out the zeal he had shown, the exertions he had made, and how greatly he had distinguished himself everywhere.

" It is not an easy task to describe a battle,"* Lord George had declared. Nevertheless he sent two accounts of the engagement to Duke William, who, though crippled with sciatica, had obeyed his injunction to hasten to Blair to beat up reinforcements—for desertion among the Athollmen caused deep concern to both brothers. On 22nd January Lord George was able to send his wife a longer letter, in which he referred to the tragic shooting of Angus Og Macdonell which was to have repercussions that nobody could have foreseen :

> When I have a moment of time I can never employ it so agreeably to myself as writing to my Dear Friend.
>
> We hear from Edinburgh by severals come from it this day that our enemies are in the greatest confusion, and quarrelling amongst themselves, holding court martials to try their officers to throw the blame off the commanders. . . .
>
> A most unfortunate accident happened here two days after the action ; Colonel Angus Macdonell, Glengarry's son, who was a modest, brave, and advisable lad, was mortally wounded by an accidental shot of a miserable fellow of Clanranald Regiment out of a window upon the street, of which he died this day, vastly regretted. It is more loss to us than all we suffered at the battle.
>
> The accounts sent to France put me quite out of countenance. My name is almost in every paragraph. The French Minister and the Irish officers make true French compliments.
>
> One thing I can say. There was not a moment lost. No time for consultation, but the disposition made without hesitation, and the attack in the same manner. To tell the truth I had little assistance, for the time would not allow it. I can say another thing that since I joined I never disobliged any person except by telling my mind too frankly and sometimes with some warmth, but that only when the service required it. I believe my opinion was mostly found right in the long run, and always approved of by the officers that are regarded and of the most weight. . . .
>
> If I be in love with life it is only owing to my love of my dear Amilie, and nothing else. Otherways I should not wish to survive a defeat. Adieu. My blessing to your young folk.
>
> After reading over my letter I'm displeased to have said so much upon my own subject, and I would have burnt it but had not time to write another. Farewell.†

* Lord George's ' Battle of Falkirk.'
† ' Atholl Chronicles.'

CHAPTER X

RETREAT TO THE HIGHLANDS

BLINDING rain on the 18th, which kept Adjutant-General O'Sullivan indoors all day, prevented the immediate pursuit of the Government forces. Everyone then expected that it would begin next morning. After Prestonpans the Prince at the head of a mere handful of men had longed to pursue Cope to England. But after Falkirk he perversely refused to push on to the capital to complete the destruction of Hawley's already disorganised forces—now no larger than his own.

In Lord George, as a later historian pointed out, the Prince had a General with whom none could vie " in planning a campaign, providing against disasters, or improving a victory."* But instead of being permitted to improve that of Falkirk, he was left there to grapple with the problem of sparing guards for various outposts from the inadequate number of men he was allowed to have with him. Charles himself returned on the 19th to Bannockburn House ; to the company of his host Sir Hugh Patterson's niece Clementina Walkinshaw, and his sorry band of unofficial councillors.

And off to France with tidings of victory sped another of the Prince's Irish envoys. Elcho said :

> It would have been better for his Cause had he sent some of the Scots gentlemen who had taken arms for him, for as a party concerned they would have let the Court of France know the true state of his affairs and perhaps have procured him more assistance, as it was not that Court's interest that the war should soon end. But those gentlemen that he sent, as they were in the French service, they told the French Ministers what they thought would be most agreeable to them, in order to get what they wanted which was preferment and pensions.
> The true state of his affairs was never known at Versailles.†

Ignatius Michael Brown, in spite of the rough manners which so offended the extremely polished and cultured young Lord Elcho, was no exception to the general rule. He stretched the long bow so

* Lord Mahon's ' History of the Rebellion of 1745.'
† Lord Elcho's ' Journal ' and ' Narrative.'

far as to inform the French Court that Charles was at the head of
17,000 to 18,000 men, and that at Falkirk only 7,000 Highlanders
took part, defeating 15,000 of the Hanoverian troops ; he also added
that 2,400 of the Duke of Argyll's followers had deserted to Charles.*
Sir Thomas Sheridan sent similar statements to the Pope and to the
Kings of France and Spain. Captain Brown's eloquence won him
a colonelcy in the French army ; but it brought no reinforcements
to the Jacobites. Foreign troops seemed little needed ; and thereafter no worthwhile help was ever sent from France.

James Johnstone, who, like other young officers, longed to deal
the enemy a smashing blow, wrote angrily :

> We ought to have pursued the English with the rapidity of a
> torrent, in order to prevent them from recovering from their
> fright. We should have kept continually at their heels ; we
> should never have relaxed until they were no longer in a con-
> dition to rally. . . .
>
> The Prince received news from Edinburgh every moment with
> details of the consternation and panic terror of the English in
> their flight. He was informed that . . . there were not four
> thousand present in Edinburgh. . . . Friends exhorted him to
> repair in all haste to the capital to disperse the wrecks of the
> English army and resume possession of that city. This in the
> opinion of everyone was the only sensible course the Prince
> could adopt. . . . But with fatal blindness, instead of pursuing
> a vanquished and routed enemy, the Prince resolved to continue
> the Siege of Stirling Castle. This determination was the result
> of a consultation with M. Mirabelle, the senseless individual who
> promised to reduce it in the course of forty-eight hours. . . .
> The absurd wish to possess an insignificant castle which could
> be of no use to us produced a series of effects which ruined the
> Prince's enterprise and brought a great many of his partisans to
> the scaffold.

Unfortunately for the Jacobites, Hawley's defeat in no way
altered brave old General Blakeney's resolve to hold out in Stirling
Castle. Owing to Charles's neglect to tell the French what cannon
were needed to reduce the stronghold, the wrong types had been
sent over with Lord John. And with the cannon had come an
equally diminutive and useless French engineer named Mirabel de
Gordon, who was the laughing-stock of the whole Scottish army.
The Prince, however, fell completely under his sway, for he was
too unversed in military matters to perceive any flaw in the plans of

* ' Memoirs du Duc de Luynes.'

this latest protégé. Lord George knew well enough that the new arrival was " too volatile " to be of any use at all. Even O'Sullivan, disliking the Frenchman almost as much as he disliked the Scots, describes him thus :

> A headstrong fellow that would have his own way and follow no man's advice. . . . He . . . had chosen such bad ground full of stones and very little earth, that the trenches could hardly be perfected anywhere, and his battery was so ill made and so ill placed that it could not resist. . . . There were no siege guns . . . and no labourers. The Highlanders would not undertake this work for fear of derogating from noble birth of which they were so proud, and the Lowlanders were too lazy to work in the trenches. There were thus only the soldiers from France ; and they worked even better than could have been expected.

In spite of the promises of " Monsieur Admirable " to reduce the fortress in a few days' time, " the siege went heavily." The Chiefs, except for Lochiel, were all at Falkirk. They were thus completely cut off from intercourse with their royal commander, who contented himself with sending an aide-de-camp over now and then with a polite note to his Lieutenant-General. But army business could not be satisfactorily dealt with in this haphazard fashion. Any proposals made by Lord George would automatically be denounced by his enemies, who had their master more entirely in their own hands than at any other time during the campaign. As Lord George wrote in his ' Marches of the Highland Army ' :

> I was indeed very cautious in offering my opinion, except at a Council of War, or when most of the principal officers were met together in His Royal Highness's presence. I thought it both safest and best that anything of great consequence should be agreed so as the fitness and objections to any measure might be duly considered. Then, even if things did not succeed, there was at least the satisfaction that what was done was for the best— and with the concurrence of the principal officers. I was much for having more frequent Councils of War ; and this I had pressed as hard as I could.

But at Derby the bitterly disappointed Prince had declared : " I will hold no more Councils since I am accountable to no one except God and my father, and will therefore no longer ask or accept advice."* The Chiefs petitioned that more Councils should be

* Elcho.

held. But their plea was disregarded, and Charles continued to manage his affairs " in a hidden way " by Sheridan, O'Sullivan, Broughton, and the Assistant Secretary, Hay. The Scots having been deprived of King and Court for close on a hundred and fifty years, had received the heir of the old royal line with the delight and affection with which a childless woman would have welcomed a longed-for child. Had he lived in ruder times his favourites might have dangled over the Forth as the obnoxious associates of his ancestor James III. had dangled from Lauder Bridge. But Lord George Murray was not destined to play the part of a second Archibald Bell-the-Cat. Instead, a week or so before the battle his long-suffering fellow officers had requested him to draw up a Petition for the convening of Councils.

Highlanders were leaving the ranks daily. The new regiments, comprising many conscripts, were not as staunch as the old. The men were nearer to their homes, and had returned there with their booty. In order to ascertain the number of deserters Lord George reviewed the army on the Field of Bannockburn. The Prince was absent, detained indoors by a cold, and attended by his Clementina. But on recovering from his indisposition he was seized with a desire to march upon his foes, who showed no sign of obligingly coming to engage him, as he hoped, upon this auspicious battleground. He has been described as a wishful thinker. But at times he appeared not to think at all. Though Hawley had by now been given ample time to reorganise his shattered army, and Cumberland was bringing up fresh troops from England, the Prince was " in the highest spirits to think that he was to have to do with the Duke," who was advancing upon Edinburgh. But the Highland Chiefs believed that they had too few men at Falkirk to risk a clash with Government troops. As Lord George wrote :

> The best of the Highland officers . . . were absolutely con-
> vinced that except they could attack the enemy at very considerable
> advantage, either by surprise or by some strong situation of
> ground, or a narrow pass, they could not expect any great success,
> especially if their numbers were no ways equal. A body of regular
> troops was absolutely necessary to support them when they should
> at any time go in sword in hand. They were sensible that without
> more leisure and time than they could expect to have to discipline
> their own men, it would not be possible to make them keep their
> ranks, or rally soon enough upon any sudden emergency. Any

L

small number of the enemy, either keeping in a body when they were in confusion, or rallying soon, would deprive them of a victory—even after they had done their best.*

Many Highland and Lowland officers now felt that the Prince had no other recourse than to withdraw to the fastnesses of the North. Lord Elcho thought favourably of such a plan, and wrote :

> I have heard my Lord George Murray (who did me the honour to make me his friend) say sometimes that if the Prince would have been willing to be guided by him he would have been able to maintain the war in Scotland for several years and possibly to oblige the Crown to come to terms, because the war rendered it necessary that the English troops should be occupied elsewhere.
> There were those at hand to tell him [the Prince] that from the discourses of Lord Elcho, friend of Lord George Murray, many wished to hold their Prince in the same state of dependence as their ancestors had held Charles II.

The Prince, however, held very different views. He sent his Secretary to Falkirk with a paper containing his suggestions for a battle. Lord George " made several corrections with his own hand," but with slight modifications embodied most of his leader's proposals in a fresh plan which he himself drew out and sent next day to Bannockburn House. It was probably carried there by O'Sullivan, who had come to Falkirk to inform Lord George that a retreat " would discourage the men " ; but that if he kept his ground " it would encourage the whole army and discourage the enemy, not yet cured of panic."† On finding that all the Chiefs still wished to retreat, he urged them to go no farther than that field " where Robert de Bruce gained victory over the English."

In private life Lord George made it a rule to let anything " uncouth " heard in one ear go out at the other. " If we swallow the cow we must not stick at the tail,"‡ was a proverb he was fond of quoting. He had swallowed more insults from the Prince's favourites than he would have done from any man not a servant of the King, who considered quarrels among his adherents most detrimental to his affairs. He kept his temper under control this day, so that the Irishmen transmuted the General's civility in greeting him and going to see him off when he mounted his horse

---

* Lord George's ' Battle of Falkirk.'
† O'Sullivan.
‡ Unpublished letter at Blair Castle.

into signs of respect and friendship. He left Falkirk " as satisfied of his reception and of having gained upon Lord George as if he had gained a battle. When things were represented to Lord George in a right light he understood reason. He is a very useful man. He begins to have an influence with the Chiefs."* So said O'Sullivan to his guileless master, who, believing everything this favoured servant told him, went off to bed in a very happy frame of mind.

But that same evening—29th January—news reached Falkirk that Cumberland was hourly expected in Edinburgh and was likely to advance from there with three new regiments besides those that had been in the late battle. His army would then be about 10,000 strong —almost double that of the Jacobites, who believed that nearly a third of their men had deserted. The Chiefs now openly discussed the advisability of withdrawal to the Highlands. As Lord George wrote : " In less than two hours after they first talked of this matter the officers at Falkirk drew up their opinion and signed it and sent it to His Royal Highness. I was told I was mostly blamed for it. I really cannot tell who first spoke of it ; but this I am sure, every one of us was unanimously of the same opinion."†

So a messenger sped that night to Bannockburn with a packet which also contained a note from Lord George to Broughton's brother-in-law John Hay of Restalrig, a middle-aged Writer to the Signet who formed one of the ever-increasing band of watch-dogs placed by the Secretary around his royal master. " Take the most prudent method to lay it before His Royal Highness without loss of time," Lord George wrote. " We are sensible it will be very un-pleasant : but in the name of God what can we do ? "‡

Consternation reigned in Bannockburn House when Hay showed the letter to Broughton, who came into O'Sullivan's room in great perturbation. Fearful of the Prince's wrath, they waived the Lieutenant-General's injunctions and decided not to wake him. " This will make him mad. He'll see plainly it is a cabal and that Lord George has blinded all these people,"§ exclaimed the agitated Secretary. O'Sullivan suggested that, this being the case, Mr Murray had better ride forthwith to Falkirk to see if he could

* O'Sullivan.
† Lord George's ' Marches.'
‡ Blaikie's Itinerary.
§ O'Sullivan.

prevail upon his Lordship " not to cross the Forth."* Broughton rode out on that cold winter's night upon a mission that proved as fruitless as O'Sullivan's. The Chiefs were adamant in their decision to retreat.

The Secretary's prophecy about the Prince's reaction to the Chief's proposals was correct. Next morning when Mr Hay nervously presented the fateful document the Prince appeared to be utterly stunned on reading it. " He struck his head against the wall till he staggered, and exclaimed most violently against Lord George Murray. His words were : " Good God ! have I lived to see this? "† Old Sir Thomas Sheridan was at once sent off to Falkirk with his master's written remonstrances and objections to a withdrawal. Neither his reasonings, nor the propositions put forward by his worried emissary, altered the resolution of the Chiefs. Keppoch and Cluny went to Bannockburn House to interview their offended young commander, who later admitted to having shown them something of his " despotic temper."‡ But rather surprisingly Sheridan became convinced of the necessity for retreating. Charles was still so much under his old tutor's influence that soon after the Chiefs left him he wrote a second letter to his leading officers giving his reluctant consent to the withdrawal northward ; but adding that he " washed his hands of the consequences."§

Meanwhile Lord George, in no happier frame of mind, had been writing to his wife at Tullibardine :

> I have all along had but faint hopes of success, as we have had the worst regulations in all parts of our conduct. You know in part, but not wholly, what a burden I have upon my hands. Often I was resolved to demit and retire into some corner of the earth, if I could not find an occasion for falling in the field, which was what I most wanted, as I imagined to myself by that means to save my family from forfeitry. But I must resign myself to Providence. . . .
>
> I expect in two or three days we may have another battle, which will assuredly be more decisive than the first, tho' a more real Victory cannot be obtained. . . .
>
> Once more remember the virtue I have most recommended to you—Fortitude. With the possession of that and those you have,

* O'Sullivan.
† Hay's Statement. ' Home's History.' Appendix.
‡ The Prince's letter to the Chiefs.
§ Ibid.

nothing can hurt or discompose you. Let everything be done for the best, and then, happen what will, our mind will be at ease.

I am persuaded the French will now attempt a landing in England. But will it come in time ?*

He kept the letter open, and before leaving Falkirk he had time to add a lengthy postscript telling her of the intended retreat :

I shall now tell you our situation is changed since what I wrote yesterday. Our men are impatient to be home, and numbers have left us. So we are in an absolute necessity to retire north-wards, and the season hinders the taking of Stirling Castle.

I expect to see you, were it for a moment, in a few days. We will be able to make a stand (with those who will abide with us for a winter campaign) towards the confines of Atholl, on this side of that country, and are positive in a little time to bring a much greater army out of the Highlands than ever. Duke Cumberland came about three this morning to Edr. Adieu.

John MacAllister is not only a thief, but has run off. My Secretary is a little picaro, at least I believe so.

I have once more had it in my power to do essential service, which you will know more of at meeting. Take care of yourself, and be in good spirits. All may yet be well. Farewell.

A note appended to his letter reveals how the strain was telling even upon his iron frame :

What would I not give for a little rest ? I have heard of a person being turned into a post-horse (by those who believe in transmigration) as the worst change that could happen. If I continue much longer in the way of life I am in now a post-horse would be an ease to me.†

" Duke Cumberland," who had arrived in Edinburgh in company with Duke James, spent only thirty hours in the capital. On the morning of 31st January he set out for Linlithgow. Jacobite scouts brought timely word of his approach, and just after sunset Lord George marched his Highlanders " in perfect good order . . . to Bannockburn." At Bannockburn House a cold welcome was accorded the Lieutenant-General, who " received very cavalier-like all the Prince said to him "—or so at least thought O'Sullivan. After supper a consultation was held about the retreat. The forces from Falkirk and Bannockburn were to be drawn up in line of battle at nine o'clock next morning in a field to the east of the village of St

* ' Atholl Chronicles.'
† Ibid.

Ninians. There Lord George was to select a hundred picked men from each regiment to form a strong rear-guard. The thousand men at Stirling were to be in readiness between nine and ten ; but they were not to vacate the town until further orders. The Athollmen were all there, for despite Lord George's vigorous protests they had been annexed for the blockade of the Castle. This was the third occasion on which they had been impressed to assist at a siege.

The informal meeting lasted until nearly one o'clock. Lord George was about to leave for his quarters at Easter Green Yards Farm, when O'Sullivan begged him to step into Broughton's room "where they could regulate all for the march in a moment."* Lord George, who had "several other things to order," retorted that he was quite capable of making the retreat by himself. He had already sent detachments of Cavalry to patrol the Edinburgh road to prevent a surprise attack and to give the impression that Falkirk was still occupied.

On his way to the farm, a mile distant from Bannockburn, he met two troops of Horse Guards who had been on continuous patrol duty for forty-eight hours. It was so important to prevent the enemy from receiving information of the Jacobites' movements, that he was obliged to order the weary troopers out again to the Bridge of Carron. But he sent Colonel Ker with a dozen bottles of brandy to cheer them and the other patrols at Callander House and Torwood during their chilly patrol.

At daybreak that same morning the tireless General repaired to Wester Green Yards where he found to his extreme annoyance that "very bad care had been taken to put things in order for the retreat."† Horses and carts had been "ordered in from all quarters on the pretext of carrying the field artillery and ammunition towards Edinburgh, whither it was given out the army was to march instantly." But "the country people were resty on this occasion —perhaps they read in the countenances of those that gave the orders the true meaning of them."‡ The strong draught horses and two hundred carts which Lord George had requisitioned "were mostly let slip away." Since there were not enough horses left to drag one in six of the waggons loaded with linen and cloth, shoes

* O'Sullivan.
† Lord George's ' Retreat from Falkirk.'
‡ Kirkconnel.

and bonnets, Lord George ordered a Mr Jackson, who was in charge of these goods, " to give a piece of cloth or linen to any man that would carry it."* To Lord George's amazement few Highlanders availed themselves of this offer, and he began to suspect that something was amiss.

His suspicions were heightened when a loud detonation was heard, which he mistook for a burst of gunfire from the Castle batteries directed upon troops leaving at an earlier hour than was intended. But the explosion proved to be of quite another nature. It was occasioned by the accidental blowing up of St Ninian's Church. Charles, finding himself without sufficient transport to carry away fifty barrels of gunpowder and other goods stored there, had directed that twenty civilians should carry all barrels that could not be loaded onto the carts to some open ground behind the church and the powder scattered or exploded to save it from falling into Cumberland's hands. A pamphleteer gives a good account of the tragedy that followed :

> The morning the rebels went away they were busy executing the above orders, and had called in, not only twenty people, but any they could get for the greater expedition. But those unfortunate people, by virtue of the New Doctrine that had been preached up to them for some time past, thought it no crime to rob Highlanders ; and instead of helping to carry things out of the church were taken up with opening barrels and sacks, filling their pockets, and hiding parcels of powder under most of the seats of the church for the better conveying away after the rebels were gone. So that, by the barrels being opened in this manner, the frequent carriages out to the carts and horses occasioned, of course, a train from the church door to the places where they stood. One of the sentinels seeing the people employed in pocketing instead of working, fired his piece to threaten them, tho' levelling at a distance from them. But unfortunately the colfing fell into the train, which fired all the way to the door of the church, and there communicated itself to the different parcels of powder which were hid under the seats, and occasioned that melancholy accident. Nobody will, I imagine, think that the sentinel knew the consequence of what he did, otherways he would have been more on his guard in an experiment where he must undoubtedly suffer. Nor can any reasonable person suppose that, had it been a premeditated thing, they would have taken so bad measures as to involve four of their own people in the ruin.†

* Lord George's ' Retreat from Falkirk.'
† Ibid.

The sentinel, a comrade, and two sick Highlanders left in the hut received no hurt when the church blew up. One man who was blown two hundred yards had a narrow escape. Beneath the debris were found the bodies of two of the Minister's servants, who had been scurrying backwards and forwards casting bundles of loot into their master's garden. The Minister's outhouses and several nearby dwellings were in ruins, and the Manse was only saved from a like fate because it was protected by the detached steeple which withstood the shock of the explosion. The Prince " with his Secretary and all his Counsellors about him " had left the vicinity only eight minutes earlier. Lochiel, suffering from his wound, narrowly escaped injury from falling stones, and Broughton's handsome wife, who was driving in the same chaise, was thrown out and lay senseless on the road until picked up by some of the villagers.

O'Sullivan, a late riser (he was once pulled out of bed by the Prince himself), often sat late over his wine while Chiefs and officers yawned in an anteroom awaiting orders. But orders had never before been reversed after issue. On this occasion after the officers left Headquarters the time of departure had evidently been put forward by two hours. No notification of the change was sent to Lord George, and on reaching the proposed rendezvous he gazed upon a scene of indescribable confusion :

> At a distance the scattered men [were] all running off as if an enemy were in pursuit of them. . . . There was none belonging to the army at St Ninians. But the ruins of the church were to be seen and many country people gathered about the place, for it was an hour and a half after it was blown up. . . . It was by no means a retreat, but a flight. The men were going off like so many sheep scattered upon the side of a hill, or like a broken and flying army after a defeat and hot pursuit.*

Colonel Ker had returned from visiting the patrols on the Carron with the reassuring news that the enemy had not as yet come to Falkirk. Lord George bid him ride ahead and convey this news to the Prince. He himself galloped off in another direction intent on halting what regiments he could. He overtook the Glengarry men on some rising ground crowned with fir-trees near St Ninian's. But many of the Clansmen had returned to their homes after the tragic death of the nineteen-year-old son of their Chief. The second battalion of the regiment was composed chiefly of men not of

* Lord George's ' Retreat from Falkirk.'

Macdonald blood; and the whole regiment was in a demoralised state. On this occasion the Glengarry men were of no help to Lord George, who wrote in his account of the retreat :

> The Glengarry Regiment . . . halted but would not . . . return back the length of Green Yards where they were assured they would each get a piece of cloth. They said it was not right for them to stay so long after the rest of the army, because a body of horse might get in betwixt them and their friends, and so they might be cut off.
>
> . . . Those in Stirling marched all in the utmost confusion and . . . did not place a guard at the port of Stirling by which they were to retreat so that the very townspeople shut the gate and kept in severals of the army who had not been apprised of the retreat. . . . Nor was there a guard placed at the river Forth below Stirling where several boats were kept for a free passage, so that people were also taken at that place. . . . All the cannon except the four largest which were ordered to be nailed up [could] have been saved, for they might have had the whole day without the least hurry or confusion. The fine brass eight-pounders (which are nine-pounders English) were left after being brought over the Forth.

Three other regiments refused to halt; and Colonel Ker was equally unsuccessful in his attempt to assemble 1,200 men with whose help Lord George had hoped to make the further stages of the " retreat with a good grace," and prevent the garrison from sallying out of the Castle until all stragglers were clear of the town. He would then have drawn up his rear-guard by Stirling Bridge and done his utmost to prevent Blakeney's men from mending the broken arch preparatory to pursuing the Prince and his followers. Having had to go miles out of their way to cross the Forth by the Frews, the Jacobites might well have been overtaken if repairs to the bridge had been effected quickly.

Colonel Ker had told the Prince that patrols were still at Larbert. Charles thereupon sent aides-de-camp to call them off; but to ensure that no further mistakes were made, Lord George ordered the Colonel to go there himself. Ker told him that near Stirling he had fallen in with Lord John's Regiment which " had been ordered to stay in town till the cannon were nailed or carried off."*

* This is confirmed by Rev. John Cameron in his Account printed in ' The Lyon in Mourning.' The evening before Mr O'Sullivan wrote from Bannockburn to Lord John Drummond ordering him to leave Stirling and cross the Forth by break of day, which order his Lordship obeyed, and by five in the morning marched.

He was also told that O'Sullivan had sent orders to the forces at
Stirling to march precisely at six o'clock that morning. The men
there, knowing nothing of their leaders' decision to retreat north-
wards, naturally supposed that an overwhelming force of Hanoverians
was hard upon their heels. They were already thoroughly dispirited
after witnessing the demolition of Monsieur Mirabel's earthworks
and batteries, which had taken three weeks and cost so many lives
to erect; for General Blakeney (who had only permitted their
completion in order to keep the Prince from attacking Hawley) had
pounded them to pieces after half an hour's bombardment. Panic
started among the Irish Piquets, who had lost a sixth of their number
during the siege, and spread through the besieging army. The four
Generals, Perth, Lord John, Glenbucket and Stapleton, were so
occupied in attempting to check the men already in flight that they
neglected to wake and warn others. Lady Ogilvy woke to find the
town almost denuded of her friends. Her coach had fallen into
the enemy's hands and she was forced to make her escape as best
she could.

So small was his escort that Lord George himself was fortunate
to evade capture by the Castle garrison. " In a concern not to be
expressed," he pushed forward along the road to the Fords of
Frew—a road bad enough at all times and now congested with
carriages and baggage wains. Soon he came upon " Mr O'Sullivan,
who was at a bridge with two or three pieces of cannon to which
were yoked a parcel of poor country garron." Lord George knew
well that any of the officers would have lent their horses to draw
the guns, which could then have all been rescued, had O'Sullivan
and others in charge of their transport kept their heads. He confessed to losing his temper, which he vented with full force upon the
Irishman. " Who advised this flight ? " he demanded angrily.
" I cannot tell," replied O'Sullivan. " Why did they not tell me
if there was any alteration in the resolution that was taken about one
o'clock this morning ? " pursued his Lordship. " It was the hurry
we were in," was the excuse put forward by the Irishman, one of
whose most infuriating qualities was his inability to realise, or rather
admit, the dangerous consequences of his frequent lapses of memory.
Lord George then directed his gaze towards the group of men
struggling to extricate the cannon. " Zounds, sir ! What is this
for ? What are you doing here ? " " You see, my Lord, what I

am doing," replied the Quartermaster-General. Then placing his
hand upon Lord George's arm, he added, " Would you have me
abandon these two pieces of cannon ? We have abandoned too much
already." " Ay, by Gad ! and you'll abandon more," said Lord
George. " I believe so, my Lord, if we go on at this rate," retorted
O'Sullivan, who had also lost his temper. " You know very well
the Prince was never for this retreat. You know very well who is
the author of it, and if you had not sent us a sentence of death
signed by you and all the Chiefs the Prince would never have consented to it. It is very ill of you to speak so high and make people
believe to the contrary."*

According to O'Sullivan's account Lord George then " began to
bluster and curse all those that were about the Prince . . . crying
very high before the men " until Lochgarry took him by the arm,
and drawing him apart, persuaded him to go to Mr Moir's house
at Leckie, where they had dined on the march south. There Lord
George encountered his royal leader, and told him " before all the
company that it was a most shameful flight, and that they were a
parcel of villains that advised him to it." He spoke as if he had had
no share in it himself, wrote O'Sullivan, who was apparently
incapable of distinguishing between the strategic retreat Lord George
had envisaged and this hasty ill-considered flight.

After the Prince departed Lord George stayed to refresh himself.
On regaining the road he found the stout Quartermaster-General
(who had had no dinner) still struggling with the field-pieces ; for
methods applied with success to Continental serfs procured him
little help in transport difficulties from the independent Gaels.
Lord George rode up to him and spoke to him as if nothing had
happened between them, telling him somewhat dampingly that
he would never get the cannon out of the deep hole. He also asked
for his former quarters at Dunblane to be prepared. The fact that
he never occupied them, " but went off to Tullibardine without
saying a word to anyone,"† was an added grievance to the Quartermaster-General, who mendaciously alleged that his Lordship had
been late in leaving Easter Green Yards because he had been
picking out cloth and linen with which to clothe his own household.
After the trials of the last few hours even a brief respite at his

* Conversation taken from O'Sullivan's ' Narrative.'
† O'Sullivan.

home meant much to the sorely-tried commander of the Jacobite army. He had longed to see his wife and the infant daughter, Kathy, born to her on 23rd January. He found his Amalie well on the way to recovery, and heard with pride how ably Amie had shouldered the family responsibilities and had carried on a correspondence with her Uncle William, who evidently thought the world of her.

Next day he rode to Crieff, where the Duke of Perth's authority sufficed to keep order, though the inhabitants bore deadly hatred to the Jacobites ever since Mar burned their town in the hope of checking Argyll's advance. They probably feared a repetition of the outrage when a Highlander was heard to remark : " She would be a braw toon gin she had anither sing. She'd be the better of her brent." Fine new houses now lined the street along which Lord George passed on his way to Fairnton where the Prince was staying with Perth's uncle. Old Lord John Drummond had been one of the signatories of the Jacobite pact of 1741 ; but he was now too old to take the field. A fine type of old-time Catholic gentleman, who never turned a beggar from his door, he welcomed former comrades-in-arms who now sought his hospitality. But sour looks were cast by the Prince's entourage upon Lord George, who to O'Sullivan's amazement came into the Prince's presence " boldly, as if he had never misbehaved." He was yet more astonished that the Prince, who had been so much upset by his General's " disrespectful and impertinent manner," received him " as usual and began to treat of matters as if nothing hard had passed between them."*

A review at Crieff showed that only 1,000 men had deserted, instead of 3,000 as had been supposed.†

> Highlanders indulged their restless disposition and sauntered about the villages in the neighbourhood of their quarters and abundance of them had been several days absent from their colours. Their principal officers knowing for certain that some were gone home apprehended that was the case with all that were not to be found in their respective quarters : but all the stragglers had got to Crieff and appeared at the review there.

So wrote Kirkconnel, who added that shady persons who administered the Prince's funds, suspecting " the opportunity would not last long, made the most of it and filled their pockets." This could be done by making false muster-rolls. On the present occasion more

* O'Sullivan.

† The review was held on the site of the present Cattle Market.

men were set down as being on the Perth road than was actually the case—a trick which Lord George seems to have suspected.

The Council of War convened at the Drummond Arms at Crieff threatened to be a stormy gathering. All realised that the debacle at Stirling had dealt a heavy blow to the prestige of the Jacobite army. Lochiel, usually " a man of few words," had much to say upon the subject ; and Elcho, whose troop, unnotified of the withdrawal, had narrowly escaped capture, was simmering with indignation. " There never was a retreat that resembled so much a flight," he declared. The principal officers were determined to brook no further prevarication, but to have a full and frank discussion about the many unfortunate events that had recently taken place, and to find out who had suggested the alteration of the hour of rendezvous. After Lord George had left Bannockburn House several Chiefs had been summoned to the Prince, who " spoke feelingly to them," but could only prevail upon them to wait till ten o'clock next morning to assess the real strength of the army. Elcho was inclined to lay the blame on Charles, for he suspected that " orders that had been agreed upon between him and Lord George were changed afterwards by him and his favourites Sir Thomas, Messrs Murray and Hay. . . . Any wrong step that was taken could never be laid at the charge of the principal officers of the Prince's army, as orders always came from his Quarters, and he never consulted any of them."

Kirkconnel and Johnstone raged with equal vehemence about the " little people " with little dirty views who hung about the Prince, and whose " baseness of soul corresponded to the obscurity of their birth." Any one of these might be a paid informer who " out of sinistrous views "* gave him bad advice—thus accounting for the persistency with which he had played into his enemies' hands since the reversal of his fortunes at Derby. It was freely said that the detested little French engineer had been bribed to keep the Jacobites dallying at Stirling to suit the convenience of Cumberland and Hawley. Queer stories were also in circulation about O'Sullivan, who was suspected of being a disguised priest, he having been trained as one in Rome.†

* Lord George's ' Retreat from Falkirk.'

† On falling from the Prince's favour O'Sullivan subsequently mended his fortunes by marrying a not very young spinster with an ample dowry. They had one son, John, whose descendants asserted that Charles had conferred the Dukedom of Munster upon their ancestor.

In his subsequent Narrative of the campaign the Quartermaster-General gave a vivid description of this long-deferred Council meeting, at which, if his words can be relied upon, the Lieutenant-General held the field. " Lord George," he wrote, " would suffer nobody to speak but those he named—one to give his opinion and his reason, another his opinion without any reasons. If the Prince offered to speak he threatened to go off, and told the Prince he must not speak until every man had given his opinion. Lord Lewis Gordon asked him if he was mad, and if the Prince was not master to speak when he thought fit ? "

The youthful Lord Lewis, who had left the army at Edinburgh to raise the Duke of Gordon's men, had not suffered such trials as the officers who had accompanied their master to England. His protests did not deflect Lord George from his purpose : " Will your Royal Highness name who gave this pernicious advice ? " he demanded. " I am afraid we have been betrayed, for it is worth the Government at London's while to give a hundred thousand pound to any who would have given such advice and got it followed." . . . O'Sullivan roundly swore he was not responsible. The Prince declined naming anybody " and took it upon himself. So there was no more to be said."

Charles had now learned the unpalatable truth that he had an army he could " not command any further than their chief officers please."* He was in the unenviable position of those who listen to malicious gossip of underlings bent upon maligning anyone who might lessen their own influence. He mistrusted, but dared not dismiss, the commander of his army in whom the Chiefs placed such confidence. He must not run the risk of their deserting him now that they were nearing their own territories, for there had been trouble enough with the Glengarry men. Nor had a competent commander been sent from overseas to supersede Lord George. His favourites told him that " the ignorance of Lord John Drummond in the art of war astounded everyone,"† and Walter Stapleton who had fought at Glenshiel, was a new-made Brigadier and his abilities as a commander were as yet unknown.

Colonel Warren, the Irishman who acted as aide-de-camp to

* Charles's letter to the Chiefs at Falkirk.
† O'Sullivan.

the Prince and Lord George, and equerry to Duke William, wrote
in eulogistic strains to King James of the patience with which the
Prince bore the trials that beset him after the retreat from Stirling.
But his patience was not in evidence at this meeting ; and he refused
Lord George's offer to make a stand in Atholl. Lord George then
proposed that the Prince should march with the main army by Wade-
bridge over the Tay and then by the hill road to Inverness, while
he himself led a column there by the east coast. Lord John said
that he "was very willing to go by the coast if Lord George did." The
majority of the Councillors voted for this plan ; for the Chiefs were
all anxious to go north by the quickest route to round up clansmen
who had slipped away to their homes. But the Prince stubbornly
declared his wish to lead them by the coast, and to hold the ports,
as he expected daily succour from France. His Lieutenant-General,
with vivid recollections of Mar's retreat through these towns,
declared them to be untenable. For the sake of maintaining harmony
Lochiel at length yielded to his master's wishes. But his nephew,
Cluny, who like Lord Ogilvy and most of the other officers was in
great " concern for the ugly look of the Prince's affairs,"* stoutly
declared that it was necessary to pass through his own country to
collect his men. He left the room in a blazing rage. Outside the
house he encountered Broughton. Cluny told him that " it was
surprising the Prince should be positive in a thing so contrary to
his interests."† The Secretary, realising the gravity of the situation,
sent to Sir Thomas to entreat their master to reverse his decision,
which he did. " There had never been such heats and animosities
as at this meeting," comments Kirkconnel. However, after a
great deal of wrangling and altercation, the question was put
to the vote and carried by a great majority that the Horse
and Low Country regiments should march towards Inverness
along the coast, while the Prince with the clans took the Highland road.

Lord George led his contingent to Perth late that evening, the
Prince remaining at Fairnton to cover his march and to allow
him time to send ahead the cannon needed for the reduction of

---

* Lord Ogilvy to Lady Ogilvy.
† Strathmashie's Account, ' Lyon in Mourning.'

Inverness, Fort William, and Fort Augustus. The 'London Gazette' gives a detailed account of the arrival of the insurgent army at Perth :

> They were entering the town in straggling parties on horseback from nine in the morning of the 2nd till seven at night. Then Lord Lewis Gordon, Lord Ogilvy, and Sir James Kinloch's men came in a body, as did the French Piquets about nine. These last consisted of not above 100 men, and the whole amounted to about 1,500. About 200 stragglers followed on the 3rd. The same day came in from Crieff 140 men commanded by Mr Robertson of Faskally and Blairfettie and having with them seven pieces of brass cannon and four covered waggons. Nineteen carts with ammunition had come in the day before. The persons of the greatest distinction that came to Perth were the French Ambassador, the Earl of Kilmarnock, the Lords Pitsligo, Elcho, and Ogilvy, Lord George Murray and John Drummond, Sir John Maclean and his brother, Brigadier Stapleton, Majors Nairn and Kennedy, and Mr Mitchell.

The reporter was a little confused about the importance of these various personages, " Mr Mitchell " being in point of fact the Prince's Italian valet Michele Vezzosi. But the account shows that there were fewer troops in the town than anyone (except the makers of the false returns) supposed. Lord Ogilvy wished to take Lady Ogilvy (who was not only his " fondest wife " but his " 'listed soldier "* and had accompanied him on the march to Derby) back to safety at his home. He therefore suddenly asked for leave to take his Regiment north by way of Cortachy. " Unaffected and human, good humoured, gay of spirit, light of heart,"† Lord Ogilvy was a general favourite with everybody in the Jacobite army. Lord George readily granted him and his followers seven days' leave ; for it was obvious that " as they were to pass so near their own country there would be no hindering them—so the sooner they went the sooner they would [re]join."‡

Lord George was thus obliged to send back word to Fairnton that he was left with insufficient men to spare an escort for the guns. Broughton was despatched to Perth, where he engaged a Quaker (of all people) to convey them as far as Blair. But still there were

---

* Lord Ogilvy to Lady Ogilvy.
† ' The House of Airlie,' by Rev. James Wilson.
‡ Lord George's ' Marches.'

LORD ELCHO

From the portrait by John Alexander at Wemyss Castle

[Facing p. 176

LORD OGILVY

From the portrait by Allan Ramsay at Winton House

not enough men available to form an adequate escort. O'Sullivan, who had also gone to Perth but returned to Fairnton, relates :

> Lord George . . . left the cannon and ammunition in the middle of the street without breaking carriages, nailing them, or destroying the ammunition which could have been thrown into the river. Notwithstanding all that Stapleton and other French officers could tell him [he] went off as if the enemy was all at his heels. There never was such a retreat seen, as those that were with him say. No orders given.

This statement is a tissue of falsehoods. The cannon and ammunition which O'Sullivan saw in the street were taken to Dunkeld and Blair by Lord Lewis, who bore thither fourteen out of the nineteen carts of ammunition, four great waggons, and seventeen small cannon, including those which James Robertson of Faskally and the men of Lord George's own regiment had dragged with such difficulty from Stirling. Lord George took two eight-pounders as far as Montrose, where he had them placed aboard a ship which eventually took them to Inverness—a hazardous journey and slow, for the vessel had to hide in various coves to avoid British frigates. Sir Thomas, writing from " Le Chateau de Blair d' Atholl," says that all the cannon left at Perth were rendered " *hors de service*," a statement borne out by Lord Elcho and by the ' Scots Magazine,' which said : " At Perth the rebels left thirteen pieces of iron cannon, about eight and twelve-pounders, nailed up ; and threw into the river a quantity of cannon-balls, and fourteen swivel-guns that formerly belonged to the *Hazard* sloop." These guns were fished out of the Tay by Cumberland's men, and some, if not all, of the spiked pieces were used for mooring boats along the shore.*

A groundless rumour arose that Lord John Drummond intended to blow up a quantity of gunpowder kept in a cellar beneath the Tolbooth, destroying the building and all the naval and military prisoners immured there. Lord George, who " had feelings of humanity and a regard for the town," agreed to sell the powder to a man he knew called John Anderson, whom he could trust to keep it out of Government hands. He guarded against such an accident as that which had occurred at St Ninians. He also liberated the prisoners, advising them to keep out of the way of any of his soldiers who might pass through the town after he left it.

* Five of them remained there for over a hundred years.

M

The French Ambassador, detesting the discomfort of this winter campaign, drove off in a coach with Lord Kilmarnock and Macleod of Raasay under Lord Lewis's escort to enjoy Duke William's hospitality at Blair Castle. Lord George allowed Lord Nairne to take the second battalion of the Atholl Brigade by the same route in order that his cousin should be able to spend a little time at his own home. He himself made no long stay in Perth but crossed the Tay about noon on 4th February *en route* for Coupar Angus accompanied by Lord John Drummond and Lords Strathallan, Pitsligo, Balmerino, and Elcho. Lord George fared badly at the inn where he passed the night and had a dispute with his landlady " over her bill which was extravagant,"* and included fodder for a dozen horses which had not been stabled there. The men who went by Blairgowrie had better entertainment. They made short work of a fine dinner of beef and greens which local curlers had ordered at Eppie Clarke's inn at Hill of Blair.

At Montrose some of the men who had come from France loitered behind to give themselves up, as some of their comrades had done at Stirling. At Aberdeen, Lord George had trouble with Lord John, a hot-tempered young man who, bred abroad and ignorant of the customs of his own country, threatened to hang some Presbyterian Ministers who had caused offence. But while there the Jacobites heard with joy that " many carriages of arms and military stores had come in a Spanish ship to Peterhead, and that many ordered at Eppie Clarke's inn at Hill of Blair.

These much-needed munitions were convoyed with great difficulty to Aberdeen by valiant Lord Pitsligo, who, though sixty-seven and sadly troubled with rheumatism and asthma, never spared himself in his efforts to aid the Cause throughout that bitter winter campaign. A " vast storm of snow " swept down upon the retreating Jacobites as they left Aberdeen after a two days' halt, impeded now with three hundred cumbrous carts and waggons. The storm was vividly described by Captain Daniels, whom the Duke of Perth had recruited at Preston, and who was probably the only Englishman to accompany the army to the Highlands :

> It blew, snowed, hailed, and froze to such a degree that few pictures ever represented winter with all its icicles about it better than many of us did that day ; for here men were covered with

* Lord George's ' Marches.'
† Ibid.

icicles hanging at their eyebrows and beard; and an entire cold-
ness seizing all their limbs. It may be wondered at how so many
could bear up against the storm, a severe contrary wind driving
snow and little cutting hail bitterly down our faces in such a
manner that it was impossible to see ten yards before us. And
very easy it now was to lose our companions, the road being bad,
and leading over large commons [moors] and paths being immediately filled up with drifted snow.*

Horses were almost girth-deep in snow, and conditions were
much as Lord George remembered them thirty years before when
Mar's defeated army had marched along the same road. But after
many days of " inconceivable fatigue and trouble "† the weary
troops reached Elgin—the " Canaan of the North." There they were
joined by John Gordon of Avuchie—loyal and " very upright man,"
who, after fighting as a boy at Sheriffmuir, had served in the Russian
army. He had with him six hundred Deeside men whom he and
Lord George's intrepid cousin " Colonel Anne " Mackintosh had
succeeded in raising. Lord Ogilvy also rejoined, but with a sadly
depleted regiment, for many of his men had refused to leave their
homes after their brief spell of leave. He had left his young and
lovely wife at his father's home at Cortachy until he saw " how the
bowls rolled." Although he believed that the weather would have
killed his " angel in one day " had he brought her farther, he lived in
constant apprehension of a former " formidable rival " replacing
him in her affections. In such a love-sick state he must have been
more of a trial than a help to his commander. Lord George, however,
was understanding with his young officers and got on well with
them. But his detailed orders irritated some of the older and more
experienced men. Lord Balmerino, who was " of a warm disposition
and blunt deportment," was driven frantic by them during this
march. " Let us do what we are ordered. It is vain to dispute,"
he told his fellow officers. " A time will come when I shall see
things righted at Lord George's cost and mine. But at present he
is my superior, and we must obey for the good of the Prince."‡

* Captain Daniel's Progress. Blaikie's ' Origins of the 'Forty-Five.'
† Lord George's ' Marches.'
‡ Captain Daniel's Progress.

CHAPTER XI

THE SIEGE OF BLAIR CASTLE

LORD GEORGE left his men at Elgin and rode ahead to join the Prince and to learn how it had fared with the main army in their march over the hills. He went straight to Headquarters to report upon his own progress and to lay before Charles the scheme that he and Lord Pitsligo had devised for buying meal from the coastal districts. Many officers at the Headquarters were lamenting that Lord Loudoun's Government Militiamen slipped away from Inverness just before their own arrival*—a thing that would not have happened, they told Lord George, if he had been at hand. Lord Cromartie, sent to pursue the Earl, " was doing no good, and the men had not much confidence in him."† Lord Kilmarnock was appointed to supersede him ; but to pacify the Chiefs he was now asked to stand aside in favour of Lord George.

Lord George set out for Tain, but learned that Loudoun had crossed into Sutherland two days earlier. The Jacobite officers agreed that it would be useless to march after him by the head of the Firth ; for should he recross by boat to Easter Ross, they would be cut off from the Prince, who would need their help if Cumberland advanced upon him. So Lord George ordered boats to be collected to convey the Jacobites to Dornoch. While this was being done he withdrew his forces to Dingwall to disguise his intentions. He himself returned to Inverness, leaving the conduct of the expedition to the Duke of Perth, who had resumed his command as Lieutenant-General since the return to Scotland, where his appointment was not against the laws of the land. As Lord George lamented :

> It was one of the best laid plans that could well be. Boats were got on the coast and sent to Tain, undiscovered. . . . By carelessness the men who had the charge of the boats did not keep them afloat, so they lost a tide ; but next morning it proved so foggy that they got over the firth undiscovered. They came up

---

* The Earl of Loudoun, who commanded the Government's Highland Militia Forces, had retreated to the North by Kessock Ferry.

† Lord George's ' Marches.'

at first with about two hundred of Earl Loudoun's men commanded by his major. Instead of attacking them immediately—in which case they must have laid down their arms and surrendered—they parleyed with them and many messages went back and forwards. This took two hours' time ; and then they surrendered. I was told the Duke of Perth was advised in this by Mr O'Sullivan, which lost him so much time, during which Lord Loudoun and most of his men with the [Lord] President went off.*

Lord George next planned to dislodge the Government forces from various houses in Atholl which they had turned into forts and blockhouses, and so tempt Cumberland to return from Aberdeen to aid his threatened Perthshire troops. The Prince did not relish the proposal. His army was already widely scattered ; for Keppoch and Lochiel, whose country was ravaged by the Fort William garrison, had been granted permission to besiege that stronghold. Lord George had not liked to thwart the project of these tried and trusted friends, although he and Brigadier Stapleton had no hopes of success. He was, however, allowed to put his own scheme into execution, and wrote :

I was ordered at that very time to go to Atholl. There was about three hundred of the Argyllshire Highlanders at several posts in that country, and it was apprehended their numbers would increase. It was given out that General Campbell was coming from Argyllshire with one thousand more. Then the Hessians were to march from Perth and join them, as also the garrisons of Blair and Castle Menzies, and to march towards Badenoch. By choosing a strong camp they might harass us much on that side, especially their Highlanders. At the same time the Duke of Cumberland was to march from Aberdeen. I was, therefore, to surprise those Highlanders, and, if possible, to be master of Blair Castle, where there was three hundred regular troops.†

On 12th March Lord George set out for Rothiemurchus, where he had been befriended by the father of the present Laird when on his way to the coast after the disaster at Glenshiel. Lord Nairne's battalion was quartered on the Spey to keep the Grants in order, and with them he set forth to capture Castle Grant—and possibly the owner's Whig son, Ludovic Grant, who, however, was away with Cumberland. But alarmed by a false report that they were

* Lord George's ' Marches.'
† Ibid.

to be beleaguered by 1,600 men with great 9-pounder cannon, his retainers hurriedly surrendered the Castle.

Lord George then wheeled over the hills to Dalwhinnie. Shian, posted at Ruthven with the Menzies and Campbells from Glen Lyon and Cluny, left with his 300 clansmen to guard his own country, joined him in Badenoch. Lord George had sent ahead instructions to guard all passes into Atholl to prevent intelligence from getting through to the enemy—a precaution that contributed much to the success of this miniature campaign. At the head of 700 men he covered thirty miles of stiff country in a day and a night. After battling through a heavy storm he came to Dalnacardoch. Here he explained to his officers his plan of campaign—hitherto divulged only to Cluny. The whole force was divided into thirty small companies consisting of an equal number of their respective followers. Each company was to attack one of the thirty houses and inns in Atholl now occupied as Government outposts. Wherever practicable each attacking force was to be commanded by the owner of the house. All posts were to be attacked before daybreak—as nearly as possible at the same time. A guinea was promised to any man who surprised a sentinel on guard.

Determined to drive the detested Campbell Militiamen from Atholl, Lord George's followers carried out what has been described as " a perfect execution of a complicated piece of military service."* The plan had been well and carefully devised by their commander. It owed its success to the good training of his men and his insistence upon discipline as well as to the skill and courage of the Highlanders themselves. All the houses, and the inn at Bridge of Tilt (which was garrisoned by Regular soldiers), were captured between two and five o'clock the following morning. They fell without a blow having been struck or a scratch received by any of the attackers, although they were fired briskly upon at Kynachan and a few other outposts.†

Some of the ladies and elderly gentlemen in beleaguered Atholl had been keeping their friends in Inverness informed of all that was taking place in their homes. Thus one Atholl laird was able to walk straight into a room where the enemy's arms were stacked and seize them before the soldiers in the house and outbuildings awoke. An officer who had his pistol under his pillow tried to

* ' Sketches of the Highlands,' by General Stewart of Garth.
† Strathmashie's Account, ' Lyon in Mourning.'

seize it, and was shot dead. The only other casualty was at Kynachan, where a drummer's daughter was accidentally killed while peering through a window. The seizure of this important post at Tummel Bridge, garrisoned by a hundred Argyll Militiamen, was entrusted to Charles Stewart of Bohally, formerly a gentleman soldier in the Black Watch. Like a knight-errant of old, young Stewart came to the rescue of his cousin and sweetheart, Kynachan's sister, who, with her sister-in-law and infant nieces, was living very uncomfortably in a house filled to overflowing with their hereditary enemies. The commander, Captain Campbell of Knockbuy, was absent that night at Taybridge. He afterwards received a severe reprimand for neglect of duty, especially as all his letters fell into Jacobite hands, including the order from Cumberland stating that no quarter must be given to rebels.

The Bunrannoch garrison were too drunk after a funeral wake to offer resistance. But a sergeant of Lord Loudoun's Regiment made his escape without clothes or arms to Taymouth Castle where the Bunrannoch commander, Campbell of Glenure, was spending a convivial evening. Lady Blairfettie had sent a herd-lad to Inverness to tell her husband how Campbell officers had forced her to wait upon them, and had kept her and her ailing children short of food. Blairfettie longed to carry out reprisals. But his wife, thankful for the restoration of her husband and her liberty, begged that her persecutors might be spared—a generous gesture which did not save her from insult or her home from plunder when the Jacobite Cause lay in ruins.

Many houses had already suffered severe depredations. Cumberland had given Sir Andrew Agnew, the commander at Blair Castle, a free hand to burn and destroy the homes of the disaffected, but this last measure had not been put into execution on account of Duke James's sensible reminder that such houses would be of greater use as outposts than as ruins. Lady Lude, as might have been expected from a daughter of militant old Lady Nairne, was in a far less charitable frame of mind than gentle Lady Blairfettie. Filled with indignation, she recounted to her rescuers how the men of the 21st Regiment [Royal Scots Fusiliers] quartered upon her had broken to pieces doors, windows and furniture, and even torn up floors for firewood. She herself had been carried off as a prisoner to Blair Castle, but was liberated the same evening. The Highlanders vowed vengeance upon Sir Andrew for permitting such misdeeds, as they drank her health in brandy which she had concealed from her unwelcome guests. Gay and sprightly, she danced reels with them to celebrate her liberation. At her subsequent trial all these proceedings were reported by the captain of the Bridge of Tilt garrison, who now stood by, a morose spectator of the joyful scene.

The garrisons in the small barracks at Coshieville and the inn at Blair had time to retire, respectively, to Castle Menzies and Blair Castle. Sir Andrew Agnew was thus warned of the danger that threatened his own garrison.

Lord George and Cluny awaited the return of their followers at Bridge of Bruar. When enough had come in they marched forthwith to Blair, where they found soldiers under arms all round the Castle, clearly hoping to tempt the Jacobites to attack them before their numbers were doubled. But Lord George was not to be drawn. He merely placed guards so as to prevent the soldiers from carrying any further supplies into the stronghold. The sick had already been gathered in from the old stables, recently converted into an infirmary. So, too, had most of the horses. One wretched Highland garron, newly purchased by Captain Wentworth of Barrel's Regiment, was trapped in the lower part of the Cummings Tower without forage or water—a circumstance which greatly distressed some of the young English officers, who on several occasions risked their lives creeping out to procure a little fresh grass for their own mounts.

Sir Andrew drew his men into the Castle, and made preparations for a siege. One piquet company under the command of a subaltern was fired upon by the Highlanders and narrowly escaped capture. So rapidly did the Jacobites now approach, that another young officer and twenty-five men were marooned on the top of Duke James's new wing, where the walls had been carried only a few feet above the roughly floored third storey. Though supplied with food and water, they remained unrelieved throughout the siege. They were not only exposed night and day to the bitter cold, but also to the stones and insults which the besiegers flung up at them. Many disrespectful remarks were made about their old commander, Sir Andrew.

Such were the stories circulated in the village about the eccentricities and volcanic temper of this Border baronet, that not one of Lord George's valiant officers, usually so ready to volunteer for any dangerous enterprise, seemed eager to carry to him the summons to surrender. It was then that Molly, the pert and pretty serving-maid from MacGlashen's inn, where Lord George set up his Head-quarters, stepped forward and expressed her willingness to place the summons in the hands of one of his officers. Waving the important document above her head, she skipped nimbly across the park to the window in the low stone passage of the Castle, where she had been accustomed to make assignments with the gay young gentlemen of the garrison. Three or four of them were waiting there to receive her. "Lord George Murray with a thousand soldiers and his cannon will batter down, or burn the Castle and destroy the whole garrison, unless his terms are instantly accepted,"* she informed them breathlessly. This announcement was received with hoots of derision. Only one of her hearers, an intoxicated lieutenant, took the matter seriously. The awful prospect of facing such an untimely end seemed far more dreadful to him than that of facing his commander, to whom he offered to deliver the summons. The fact that this order to "Sir Andrew Agnew, Bart., commanding the troops of the Elector of Hanover,"† to surrender forthwith was written on a dirty sheet of paper, increased the wrath of the recipient. He roared out orders that it was to be sent back forthwith. Impre-cations against Lord George, threats to shoot his messengers through the head, and other alarming words came floating down the stairway, and caused poor Molly to take to her heels. The Jacobite com-manders, who were standing in the churchyard awaiting her return, were immensely diverted.

By nine o'clock, 17th March, the Castle of Blair was completely invested. But the Jacobites contented themselves with parading about at a distance to observe from which side it could best be attacked. At the suggestion of the Laird of Balnacree women and children in plaids mingled with the men on distant hillsides to give the impression that their numbers were greater than was actually the case. By evening two cannon, laboriously hauled from Inverness by way of Ruthven, were set up on rising ground near the church. O'Sullivan, enjoying a blissful period of rest and ease in Inverness, and overlooking the wildness of the country that lay between Spey-

* 'The Siege of Blair Castle,' by Captain Robert Melville of Strathkinnes. Printed in 'The Siege of Blair Castle,' by the seventh Duke of Atholl.
† 'Atholl Chronicles.'

side and Atholl, blamed Lord George for not having dragged the cannon captured at Castle Grant to Blair. O'Sullivan could have persuaded his master to send men for such a duty, but Lord Nairne, the commander of the Castle, had none to spare, for his had been sent back there with the 300 prisoners, who needed careful guarding in a hostile country.

The following morning, Tuesday, 18th March, the siege began in earnest, and Lord George accorded his elated cousin Lady Lude the honour of firing the first shot. But although the besiegers " fired briskly " the results were disappointing, for the four-pounder cannon allocated to Lord George made no impression upon the seven-foot-thick walls of Blair Castle. One of the cannon would not even remain in position, despite the ministrations of the local blacksmith and two inexperienced French engineers. Little damage was done beyond the smashing of windows, letting fresh air into rooms where, since the occupation of the fortress, men had been huddled together " breathing in the most nasty scents."* But the cold from which they now suffered was even harder to endure, for they had very little firewood in spite of the wholesale cutting down of Duke James's treasured trees. His Grace, who had visited his once proud home a week earlier, had found it so befouled and verminous, and his policies in such a " deplorable condition,"† that he felt it would be a long time before he fancied living there again.

Gazing upon the besiegers from the shattered windows the redoubtable Sir Andrew exclaimed ironically : " My Lord is playing ball against the walls of Blair Castle ! Is the loon clean daft knocking down his brother's house ? " Noting that the shots were directed upon a certain window on the staircase, he went to investigate matters. His wrath knew no bounds when he discovered that some wag had purloined one of his old uniform coats, stuffed it with straw, and stuck it up, spyglass in hand, as if reconnoitring the enemy. " Let the loon that set it up just go up himself and take it down,"‡ he roared, and under heavy fire the crestfallen practical joker had to do so.

Although Cumberland had issued instructions that any man who

* Rae's ' History of the Rebellion of 1745.'
† ' Atholl Chronicles.'
‡ ' The Siege of Blair Castle.'

did not do his utmost to defend the Castle could be put to death without a court martial, he had not expected it to be attacked, and had sent no guns, ammunition, or military stores there. The defenders had only nineteen cartridges apiece, and these were only to be used in an attack. Their spirits were kept up by the merry fiddling of Blind Jack of Knaresborough—truly a jack-of-all-trades —who had been a musician at the Assembly Rooms at Harrogate, and had now enlisted as a fiddler in Colonel Thornton's newly raised Yorkshire Horse.* Nor were they deprived of female society. The young housekeeper, Betty Harrison, and three maids were still in the Castle. But, except for a few delicacies for the officers' table, there was nothing for anyone to eat but cheese and biscuit.

As bread had been sent up every fourth day from Perth, Sir Andrew had not laid in a stock of meal. The indoor well was guarded day and night by a small party of men under a non-commissioned officer. Water could no longer be brought in from the Banvie Burn, or from the curling-pond. Each man was only allowed a pound of biscuit and a bottle of water a day. Sir Andrew hoped the water supply would last for a fortnight. If Lord George's old regiment, the Royals, had not been recalled to Perth a few days before the siege began, provisions would assuredly have been exhausted in a week.

Lord George now attempted to set fire to the roof of the Castle— a work of which, he confessed, he was " by no means fond."† For two days 180 fire-balls, heated in the furness brought from Inverness and erected in the churchyard, clattered down upon the slates. Some plopped on to attic floors. Others, lodged in rafters, merely charred the wood round them. Sir Andrew was seen scurrying hither and thither with a shovel of red-hot ashes in his hand. As a Whig chronicler wrote, " such was the alertness of the garrison that their carpenters were ready to cut the bullets whenever they stuck and throw them out to cool."‡ Most of them were " caught up in an iron ladle from the Duke of Atholl's kitchen and tossed

---

* After taking part in the Battle of Falkirk, Blind Jack Metcalf returned to the town in search of his missing commander and found him hidden in a closet in one of the houses. While there the intrepid fiddler interviewed several leading Jacobite officers, including Lord George, who, struck by the man's courage, entertained him to a glass of wine.

† Lord George's ' Marches.'

‡ Rae's ' History of the Rebellion of 1745.'

into tubs of urine, for better water could not be bestowed in quench-
ing them."*   Lord George had no good word to say about his two
field-pieces :

> The cannon were not only small, but bad. One of them seldom
> hit the Castle, though not half-musket shot from it. We under-
> stood the garrison had not much provisions, and that in a fortnight
> or three weeks they must be obliged to surrender ; and this was
> what I thought best. It had been indeed proposed before I left
> Inverness to make a mine to blow up the Castle ; but I had no
> positive orders to attempt that. I believe it might have been
> done by the old stables under the protection of which the wall
> could have been undermined, if I had been furnished with
> proper workmen. I placed a guard of three hundred men in the
> village of Blair, where I was myself, and another of near the same
> number near the Mains at the new stables. I got a reinforcement
> of four or five hundred men in the country of those who had
> been with us formerly.
>
> I sent a party down to Dunkeld who staid there till the Hessians
> came from Perth, and then they retreated to Pitlochry two miles
> below the Pass of Killiecrankie. We continued in this position
> for a fortnight. We had " picqueting " with the Hussars and some
> of St George's Dragoons for four or five days. They came near
> Pitlochry in the day time and retired at night. I was commonly
> back and forwards twice a day betwixt that and Blair. . . . I was
> well assisted by the officers and men as I could desire, particularly
> Cluny who always kept to the post at the town of Blair. For the
> first seventy hours I did not get four hours' sleep. Much the
> same thing happened to me the last three days of our retreat to
> Carlisle, for besides the marching and fatigues others underwent,
> I had all the orders to give and dispositions to make, and though
> others were relieved and took it in their turns, I had none to
> relieve me. Receiving and dispatching expresses, settling guards
> and sentinels—which at first I always saw done myself till the
> thing went on of course—alarms, gaining intelligence, and other
> necessary duties took up much time. I believe the country
> suffered by our being on this expedition ; but as little as was
> in my power. We were forced to take meal and some sheep,
> for by this time the men had no pay.†

When the siege had been in progress a week the unsatisfactory
cannon were moved under cover of night and mounted two hundred
yards south of the Castle. The garrison were somewhat alarmed at
the prospect of an attack from behind the terrace and sunk fence

* ' The Siege of Blair Castle.'
† Lord George's ' Marches.'

near the pond. Besides cannon-fire " there was a constant fire of
small arms kept up against the windows,"* but no damage was done
beyond a further smashing of glass.

Lord George makes no mention of his own feelings, which must
have been strange indeed as he wandered about the Castle grounds
in the company of men to whose presence the late owner would
have objected so strongly. They certainly afforded a striking
contrast to the favoured English grieve, Nicholas Harrison, and the
gardener, John Wilson, who had formerly accompanied him on such
peregrinations. He would willingly have protected any of James's
servants who had stayed to carry out their duties. But all had taken
refuge in the Castle ; and stout old Harrison must have been
losing weight on a diet so different from that to which he had been
accustomed. Meanwhile his flocks and herds fell a prey to Highlanders bent on procuring something over and above their daily
ration of oatmeal. Cluny, nobly aiding his commander in his
efforts to protect the property, " offered a guinea to anyone who
would inform of a man who shot a deer."†

The Government troops did far more damage than the Jacobites.
When Lord George's father held Blair for George I. his new
trees were sacrificed for firewood. But those planted by his son
James (many of which came from the nurseries at Tullibardine)
were damaged and destroyed out of sheer wantonness. Drunken
officers coming from the inn slashed at and beheaded the Whig
Duke's cherished larch saplings—dealing with them as they would
have liked to deal with rebels.‡ It was painful to Lord George to
see the harm already done to this cradle of his race—the home of
the Stewart Earls of Atholl, on the improvement and modernisation
of which his brother James had spent a fortune. He, too, had taken
an intense interest in all these schemes, making toilsome journeys
into Atholl to see that all was being carried out as his brother wished.
But he had already steeled his heart to demolishing the fine old
Castle to which he himself was the heir, once the garrison surrendered and the valuables and heirlooms could be removed. On
24th March he wrote to William, who, usually so patient and gentle,

* Elcho.
† ' Atholl Chronicles.'
‡ The remaining larches were among the first planted in Scotland, and
in the opinion of the late Duke of Atholl were older than those at Dunkeld.

had been much annoyed that he had not been informed of the expedition to Atholl :

DEAR BROTHER,

I hope you will excuse my not writing to you since we came here for you would hear of everything I wrote to Sir Thomas or Mr Murray, and indeed I have not had one spare moment. Our duty here is constant and fatiguing ; but we grudge nothing that is for His Royal Highness's service and the good of the Cause.

Colonel Mercer with 150 men is at Dunkeld, and secured the boats. But I have ordered him to retire to the Pass if a body of the enemy should come near that place, which they can do by passing the river at Perth. All here desire to make you their compliments.

The people in the Castle have not set out their heads since we came and are living on biscuit and water. If we get the Castle I hope you will excuse our demolishing it.

Duke William began his reply of 26th March without the usual prefix :

BROTHER GEORGE,

Since, contrary to the rules of right reason, you was pleased to tell me a sham story about the expedition to Blair without farther ceremony for me you may do what the gentlemen of the country think fit with the Castle. I am in no concern about it. Our great-great-grandfather, grandfather, and father's pictures will be an irreparable loss on blowing up the house. But there is no comparison to be made with these faint images of our forefathers and the more necessary public service which requires we should sacrifice everything. . . .

At the upper end from the door of the old stable there was formerly a gate which had a portcullis into the Castle. It is half built up and boarded over from the stable side with a hollow large enough to hold a horse at hack and manger. People that know the place imagine it may be much easier dug through than any other part of the wall so as to make a convenient passage into the vaulted room which is called the servants' hall.

Lord George answered this letter on the 29th :

DEAR BROTHER,

I received your letter of the 26th. I'm sorry you seem to think I told you a sham story (as you express) about our expedition here. I told you we were to endeavour to take possession of Castle

Grant and try to hinder that clan taking party against us. This
was done as far as in our power. I also told you if we could
contrive to surprise any of the parties in this country we might
attempt it. But that depended so much upon incidents that my
very hopes could not reach so far as we performed. Secrecy and
expedition was our main point once we resolved upon the thing,
which was not till I met Cluny and Shian in Badenoch. . . .*

Atholl had been cleared of supplies by the armies that had recently
swept through it. Lord George asked that meal might be sent
down for his men. But Murray of Broughton was lying ill at Elgin
of " a languishing disorder which had all the symptoms of a con-
sumption."† He had been succeeded by his brother-in-law John
Hay, and greatly alarmed to hear of the influence he now exercised
over the Prince. Mr Hay displayed reluctance to part with any
of the stores entrusted to his care and William wrote to tell his
brother that his demands were " not well understood [or] much
regarded " by the incompetent staff now at Headquarters. " Was it
not hoped that by this time you have near got the better of these
obstinate intruders into the Castle I should go myself and try if
I could not usefully help towards reducing them to a speedy sur-
rendering of such unfortified old walls,"‡ added the Duke, who
again enclosed an account of the half-forgotten passage.

Lord George had hoped to march upon the Hanoverian troops
at Dunkeld before they were reinforced, " pitch on an advantageous
ground " and fight them. " He urged the Prince much to send him
a reinforcement of 1,000 Highlanders, promising on that condition
to give a good account of the Hessians. But the proposal was over-
ruled, it seems, by those at Inverness, who were quite bent upon
reducing all in the north in order to bring out the clans and leave
no enemy behind."§

The Prince's fear of entrusting his Lieutenant-General with
troops required for any especial enterprise had lost him the chance
of gaining treasure at Liverpool, worthwhile victories at Clifton and
Linlithgow; and he now threw away this opportunity of compelling
Cumberland to withdraw from his menacing position at Aberdeen.
Yet when O'Sullivan had proposed to entice the Duke back to

* Jacobite Correspondence of the Atholl Family.
† ' Genuine Memoirs of John Murray, Esqr.'
‡ Jacobite Correspondence of the Atholl Family.
§ Strathmashie's Account, ' Lyon in Mourning.'

Perth by dislodging his outposts from Dunkeld, Keppoch and Lochiel had been ordered to abandon the Siege of Fort William and march into Atholl under the favourite's command, along with other companies from Inverness and Elgin. That project was, however, abandoned owing to Sir Thomas Sheridan's nervous apprehension that Lord George might be upset by the intervention of O'Sullivan.

Lord George now sent out the Fiery Cross—the last recorded occasion on which that device was used among the hills and glens of Scotland to summon clansmen to battle. Four hundred men, who had left the colours at Stirling, responded to his call—all burning with rage against the Government soldiers who had set fire to or plundered their homes. But the 1,100 Highlanders he now had round him were not enough to hold off the powerful forces assembling at Dunkeld should they march against him in a last-minute effort to save Sir Andrew before hunger compelled him to surrender.

For the defenders of Blair were very near starvation point. On 23rd March two of their number had evaded the sentries and slipped away to Perth to call for troops to raise the siege. Their comrades in the Castle had no means of knowing of their safe arrival there, so on the day that Lord George was writing to Duke William their brother's head gardener John Wilson, " a loyal, stout, sensible man," volunteered to try to bring help from Dunkeld. He was accordingly entrusted with a letter to the Earl of Crawford, commanding the Government forces there. He promised to destroy the missive if captured, and he was allowed to take his choice of the officers' horses. While it was still dark the great door of the Castle was unbarricaded and Wilson slipped out. He had not gone far before he was fired upon by sentries on either side of the lower part of the avenue. The defenders on the roof opened a spirited fire upon these snipers. The horse bolted, and when just out of sight of the men at the Castle windows, threw its rider. As a Highlander was seen astride it next morning Sir Andrew's men supposed that their messenger had been captured. The gardener had, however, escaped on foot. He sped to Dunkeld House, where he found Hussars picketed in the drive, Dragoons in the garden, two battalions of Hessian soldiers in the ornamental wilderness, and a third billeted in the village of Inver.

BLAIR CASTLE, 1736

From a sketch by a Mr Frederick, nephew of the Duchess of Atholl, in the ' History of the Siege of Blair Castle in 1746', privately printed

CULLODEN

*Detail from the ' Battle of Culloden,' ascribed to Morier, at Windsor Castle
Reproduced by gracious permission of Her Majesty The Queen*

(Jacobite prisoners at Southwark were made to pose for the Highland soldiers)

The Minister of Blair, captured at the Struan outpost, had contrived to send Duke James word that he believed the rebels would not again venture as far south as Dunkeld. The Duke was still at Dunkeld House with timid Lord Glenorchy, who was too unnerved to journey on to Taymouth Castle. His other guests were middle-aged Lord Crawford (who later ran away with his lovely sixteen-year-old daughter Lady Jean) and the Prince of Hesse, who had brought over 6,000 of his subjects to fight for his father-in-law George II.—in place of the Dutch, immobilised owing to the landing of French soldiers. These odd-looking new arrivals, proud of their appearance and forever combing their blond locks, were objects of great interest to the inhabitants of Dunkeld. Their accoutrements are described in Dugald Graham's metrical account of the Rising :

> The Hessians were a warlike band,
> Six thousand did their Prince command.
> Their countenance was awful fierce,
> They spoke High Dutch or German Erse.
> Had white buff belts and all blue clothes,
> With a long beard beneath the nose.
> Their Grenadiers had caps of brass.
> Thus ordered were the men of Hesse.

The Hessians proved to be the reverse of " a warlike band." With mule-like obstinacy they refused to enter the Pass of Killie-crankie, which they likened to the Gates of Hell. Country people believed they had been frightened by the ghost of Claverhouse. But their alarm was more likely caused by the stories which the Latin-speaking innkeepers at Dunkeld and Inver told their officers of the fate that befell Mackay's men there. So in spite of the snares he laid for them, on 30th March Lord George caught only one of their number, an Hussar, whose horse was killed under him during the exchange of a few shots between the outposts—the Hessians' only casualty throughout the campaign. Lord George wrote :

> One morning we took one of their Hussars and two or three horses. The men got off, except the Hussar. He was a Swede by birth and spoke very good Latin—was a gentleman, and had formerly been a Lieutenant. As he said he did not expect any quarter (for Hussars seldom gave it) he was surprised when he found himself so well treated. I sent him back to the Prince of Hesse desiring to know if he intended to have a cartel settled ; but I had no answer. The Swede asked me if he must return.

N

I told him, not, except the Prince of Hesse sent him. He went away very well pleased.

The day before we left Blair a considerable body of the Hessians came up the length of the Haugh of Dalshian within two short miles of Pitlochry. The Dragoons and Hussars came forwards, and we retired to the foot of the Pass where we made dispositions to dispute it, and stayed there above six hours till we heard that a great part of them had returned to Dunkeld—others staying about Pitlochry. I had the day before and that day got three expresses to return to Inverness for it was believed the Duke of Cumberland would march there in a day or two. I had that morning ordered off our two pieces of cannon that we might not be impeded in our march. About ten at night I drew off the men in the Pass and came to Blair. As I had left orders all was in readiness, so we marched off about two in the morning.*

So ended the historic fifteen days' Siege of Blair Castle—the last house in Britain to be beleaguered. And thus, as Kirkconnel wrote sympathetically : " Lord George had the mortification to retire from a place that must have fallen in a very few days." Had hostilities continued he might have found himself opposed in battle to Duke James, who was with Lord Crawford that day at Dalshian— his only day of service with the forces. Before leaving Atholl George wrote to him to apologise for the depredations among his sheep and cattle, which, as he pointed out, would not have happened had " Harrison attended to his charge as usual when the Castle was blockaded."† This note, unsigned and undated, was the last he ever sent to his brother. Careful even now in little things, Lord George collected the instruments, bandages, dressings and medicines taken from Hawley at Falkirk but carelessly left by Lord Lewis Gordon at Blair—for the forty-four physicians and surgeons serving in the Jacobite army were woefully short of all such things.

On 2nd April Sir Andrew Agnew's men awoke to find that their adversaries had all " packed off in the night like April Fools." One of the officers, Lieutenant Robert Melville of Strathkinnes, left an interesting account of the siege :

If the rebels could have kept up the close blockade for a short time longer the garrison, after being reduced to eat horse-flesh, must have tried the last resource by an attempt in the night-time to break through the blockade and try to join the King's troops at Castle Menzies. The garrison could then have issued from the

* Lord George's ' Marches.'
† ' Atholl Chronicles.'

Castle only by a door, under the annoyance of an enemy so near;
and must afterwards have been exposed to their attacks from all
sides with very superior numbers during a march of about ten
miles, mostly across a country very mountainous and without
roads. . . .

A week after the commencement of the blockade there was
very distinctly heard such a noise of knocking, seemingly under-
neath the ground of the Castle, as if miners were hard at work
in forming a design to blow it up. . . . But the whole of that
mighty alarm was found to be caused by nothing more than a
soldier cutting a block of wood which lay on a floor in one of
the uppermost rooms.

After the apparently unlucky fate of Wilson no hope of relief
remained, but from the chapter of accidents, especially with the
soldiers who used frequently to say among themselves that Sir
Andrew's good luck would certainly help them out in some way
or other. For they had heard many strange stories about him,
as of his never being sick or wounded, or in any battle that the
English did not win. They were therefore the less surprised
when at break of day on the first [2nd] of April, not a single
Highlander could be seen. Soon after McGlashan's maid Molly,
who had brought down the summons, came to congratulate her
old friends that Lord George and all his men, as she called them,
had gone off in the night to Dalnacardoch and Badenoch; adding
that she believed the Highlanders had been afraid of being
surrounded by Lord Crawford with the King's Black Horse from
Dunkeld. . . .

[Sir Andrew] was purblind and could not have the evidence of
his own eyes, nor would trust to the eyes of others. He positively
ordered that the garrison should be kept shut up till further
orders. Those orders were not given for its releasement until
next morning when an officer having arrived on horseback from
the Earl of Crawford he informed the Commandant that his
Lordship, with some Cavalry, might be expected in an hour, as
accordingly happened. The garrison being drawn out, his
Lordship was received by the Commandant at the head of it with
this compliment: " My Lord, I am very glad to see you, but, by
all that's good, you have been very dilatory, and we can give you
nothing to eat." To which his Lordship answered laughingly,
with his usual good humour: " I assure you, Sir Andrew, I
made all the haste I possibly could, and I hope that you and the
officers will do me the honour to partake with me of such fare
as I can give you." His Lordship did accordingly entertain
afterwards in the summer-house in the garden Sir Andrew and
his officers with a plentiful dinner and very good wines, and
returned in the evening to Dunkeld. . . .

One remarkable incident at the end of the blockade still remains to be told, which is that after Sir Andrew's general jail delivery of the garrison, some officers hastening to see the poor dead horse of Captain Wentworth, it being the 17th day of its confinement, they were precipitately driven out, laughing, to avoid the animal who was wildly staggering about. That fine stout animal, having received the most proper care and best treatment by order of his master, soon became in excellent condition, and, as it is believed, was then sent to England by Captain Wentworth as a present to one of his sisters!

Having despatched the Athollmen to Elchies on Speyside, and left Cluny and his followers in Badenoch, Lord George arrived at Inverness on 3rd April. His first thought, as he records, was to ascertain how the prisoners from Castle Grant were being treated :

I visted the soldiers that were prisoners in the church of Inverness and got relief and assistance sent to the sick. There was one thing like to happen there which I was exceedingly displeased with. An officer of our army got a new corps raised, and they were very ill clothed. What possessed him I cannot tell, but a complaint was brought me that he and his men were stripping the prisoners in the church of their coats to clothe his own men. I immediately went to the Prince, and an order was sent to stop it. Before the order came they had got off most of the coats ; but they were all immediately returned.*

Following the example of their royal leader and his two Lieutenant-Generals, Jacobites of all ranks had hitherto treated their captured adversaries with every mark of consideration. But now, ill-clothed against the winter cold, and their pay in arrears, they began to resent the Prince's extraordinary care for his prisoners. He had, as Kirkconnel says, " a great many of them on his hands towards the end and they were maintained while his own men could hardly find subsistence. So that, if it is possible to err on the side of lenity, several errors of this kind may be justly imputed to him." This tenderness for his enemies bore hard upon his friends when the Cause lay in ashes. Had he followed the advice of his officers and the French Ambassador and shipped to France the sixty-four officers taken at Prestonpans, they would, in all probability, have been exchanged for an equal number of the seventy-five Scottish officers condemned to die upon the scaffold on Tower Hill, or the gallows at Carlisle and Kennington.

* Lord George's ' Marches.'

An intercepted letter to Robertson of Struan shows that " great jealousies prevailed against Lord George " at this time. His enemies had taken advantage of his absence to hint to their master that he had been " too tender " of his brother's house to blow it up, and that he could have taken it had he wished to do so. Even D'Eguilles, who at one time described Lord George as " *Un homme d'un vrai genie, l'âme et le conseil du parti*," evidently believed that Charles's almost childlike fear of betrayal must be based on some certain knowledge of his General's complicity with the enemy.* He now wrote to the French Minister of War D'Argenson that he believed Lord George meant to betray the Prince, who shared D'Eguilles's views and intended to take precautions.

Truly, as even the junior officers in the Jacobite army were now observing, " Irish intriguers and French politics were too much predominent,"† and that the Irish who dominated all his councils were " extremely injurious to the interests of the Prince from the bad advice they gave him."‡   There were, as Lord Elcho says, plenty of people ready to tell the Prince that the commander of his army " by the Prince of Hesse and his brother's means was entirely reconciled with the Government," for as O'Sullivan pointed out, " How could anyone know that it was a cartel he sent ? "§   Charles drank this draught of poison at a gulp. Years later, when brooding over the harm which he believed Lord George had done to the Cause, he wrote :

> He took a Hessian officer [the man was in reality a trooper] and sent him back to the corps without giving notice or asking consent of his chief commander—a thing so contrary to all rules or any military practice that no one that has the least sense can be guilty of—without some private reason of his own.

" Lord George was altogether undeserving of a suspicion. . . . Faithful while suspected, and honest though calumniated, he adhered to the tenor of his principles and continued to serve with zeal and fidelity a master by whom he knew he was not beloved."‖ In his letter (still extant) he had in the Prince Regent's name demanded

* ' Annales de l'Ecole Libre des Sciences Politique.'
† ' Memoirs of Robert Strange.'
‡ ' Memoirs Chevalier Johnstone.'
§ O'Sullivan.
‖ Scott's ' Tales of a Grandfather.'

of the Prince of Hesse a cartel for the exchange of prisoners—a request which the recipient described to his royal brother-in-law as reasonable and just.   Cumberland, furious at seeing his august father referred to as " the Elector of Hanover," refused to consider an exchange.   As a result the Hessian Prince refused to move a foot beyond Pitlochry, declaring that he was " not enough interested in the quarrel between the Houses of Stuart and Hanover " to sacrifice his subjects' lives in " combatting with men driven to despair."*
The British Government was thereby deprived of the services of 6,000 Hessians at the Battle of Culloden—a circumstance probably unrealised by Lord George's contemporaries, and usually overlooked by historians.

  * Lord George's letter to the Prince of Hesse is printed verbatim in the Appendix of Lord Elcho's ' Affairs of Scotland.'

CHAPTER XII

THE NIGHT MARCH TO NAIRN

ON 12th April Cumberland crossed the Spey unopposed. Perth and his brother would willingly have disputed the passage, but the Prince and Lord George considered it useless for them to do so ; for although summonses had been sent for the recall of the armies in the north and west, they could not arrive in time to aid the Duke. Even O'Sullivan, out of sorts and out of spirits, advocated withdrawal to Fort Augustus—for he believed the rumour that the enemy were 18,000 strong. On the 14th it was learned that Cumberland had pitched his camp at Balblair, a little to the west of Nairn and only eight miles from Culloden.

Ordered by Lord George to report upon the country that lay between the opposing armies, Colonel Ker and Major Kennedy reconnoitred some rough ground near Dalcross Castle. They reported that it would be a suitable place on which to make a stand against the enemy. But O'Sullivan, sent there later by his master, condemned this battleground, and selected another a mile to the south-east of Culloden House, where a wide morass would protect the left wing of the Jacobite army.

At dawn on the 15th drums beat, pipes played, and the clansmen were led out on to this new battlefield—about which Lord George had not so much as been consulted. But before the army was drawn up in battle array he insisted, and insisted vigorously, upon having his own men under his personal command in the right wing—an arrangement that caused much murmuring among the Macdonalds, who, restless and discontented since the clan quarrel occasioned by the shooting of Angus Og of Glengarry after the Battle of Falkirk, had deserted in great numbers. With the Glengarry Regiment partly composed of men from other clans, its second battalion awaiting reinforcements, and Keppoch's whole regiment absent, the Macdonalds were not at this stage so strong and reliable a unit as the Atholl Brigade. Lord George had recovered 400 of his deserters, who had not much incentive to return to their own country now that it was again under enemy occupation, and the ladies of Atholl, " more busy in raising men than became their sex . . . had found means to send . . . as good men as were in the country " to augment the three battalions of the Atholl Brigade.* Moreover the happenings at Falkirk, where the Macdonalds had got out of hand and the Athollmen had remained steady, had shown the defects of the old system of placing only purely Highland regiments in the front line to act as shock troops.

The men remained drawn up in order of battle until eleven o'clock, when the Prince " ordered them to refresh themselves by sleep or otherwise."† But they could not even be provided with meal, which they had had to accept instead of pay for several weeks. All the provisions were in Inverness, and Charles's incompetent new Secretary had not assembled any carts to transport them even as far as Culloden—a distance of six miles. John Hay, " one of those silly but noxious creatures by whom from a natural attraction weak princes are usually surrounded,"‡ seems to have been regarded as a sort of Secretary of War " without whose orders a boll of meal or a farthing of money was not to be delivered.§ . . . ' Everything is ordered. Everything will be got,'" he told the unbelieving General, who before the army marched from the town sent his friend Major Kennedy to interview this exasperating bureaucrat :

> Major Kennedy . . . told him that as the enemy was on their march towards them it was more than probable there would be a battle ; and as the event was very uncertain, it was prudent to guard against the worst. They might get the better or be defeated. In this situation he wished he would propose to the Prince his sending a large quantity of provisions then in Inverness to some distance that, in case of the worst, scattered troops might join and have wherewithall to subsist them till rejoined by such as had not returned from their commands they had been out upon. If this was not done all must disperse, the Cause must be given up, and the Prince behoved to be in danger ; for the neighbourhood of that country could not supply the smallest number of men for one week. Mr Hay say nothing nor . . . ever mentioned it to the Prince.‖

* ' History of the Rebellion in the Years 1745 and 1746.'
† Rev. John Cameron's Account, ' Lyon in Mourning.'
‡ Note to the ' Memoirs of the Chevalier de Johnstone.'
§ Lord George's letter to the Prince.
‖ Rev. John Cameron's Account, ' Lyon in Mourning.'

On O'Sullivan's showing the Prince was well aware of the gravity of the food situation, yet he had spent much of the night discussing with his favourite a possible raid on Cumberland's camp at Nairn— instead of devising a more feasible scheme such as sending Cavalry-men to Inverness to bring out sacks of meal. He now walked about the field " cajoling the different Chiefs, and proposed to all of them separately to march off the men towards evening and attack the enemy at daybreak. But finding the bulk of them against the proposal (reckoning it rather too desperate a proposal until they were joined by Keppoch and his men with others that were soon expected), he dropped the project."*

The Duke of Perth and his brother " expressed their dislike of the measure." " Lord George Murray, Lochgarry, with many others . . . were very sensible of the danger should it miscarry."† The officers from France for the most part considered it " a desperate attempt, and if it failed of success would dispirit and disperse " the men. Lochiel wished to wait until they had 1,500 more troops. Others also pointed out :

> A great many of the army had not as yet joined, particularly Keppoch, the Master of Lovat, Cluny, Glengyle, the Mackenzies, and many of the recruits of Glengarry and other regiments, which were all expected in two or three days, and some of them sooner. If they should fail in the attempt and be repulsed, it would not be easy rallying the Highlanders in the dark. If the Duke of Cumberland was alarmed by any of his patrollers, he might have time to put his army in order . . . and place his cannon charged with cartouch shot as he had a mind. His Horse might be all in readiness so as to pursue, if the Highlanders had been beaten off. And lastly, the difficulty of making their retreat with perhaps a good many wounded men whom the Highlanders will never leave, be it possible to bring them off. Add to this, how fatiguing it would be to march backwards and forwards twenty miles and probably be obliged to fight next day. Nor could they make their retreat safe and not be attacked before they joined the rest of the army.‡

Lord George was now much concerned about the terrain on which the Jacobites were supposed to fight. O'Sullivan, convinced that he was an authority on the type of ground best suited to the High-land mode of warfare, had, unfortunately, pitched upon exactly the

* Rev. John Cameron's Account, ' Lyon in Mourning.'
† Lord George's Particular Account.
‡ Ibid.

kind that a commander of regular troops would gladly have chosen. As Lord George wrote :

> I did not like the ground. It was certainly not proper for Highlanders. I proposed that Brigadier Stapleton and Colonel Ker should view the ground on the other side of the Water of Nairn, which they did . . . Mr O'Sullivan had gone to Inverness, so he was not with them when they reconnoitred the ground.
>
> The hill ground on the south side of the Water . . . appeared to be steep and uneven, consequently much properer for Highlanders. The ground they were drawn up upon was a large plain muir ; and though in some places it was interspersed with bogs and deep ground yet for the most part it was a fair field, and good for Horse.
>
> After two or three hours they returned and reported that the ground was rough and rugged, mossy and soft, so that no Horse could be of use there. The ascent from the water side was steep ; and there were (only) two or three places in about three or four miles where Horse could cross, the banks being inaccessible. They could not tell what sort of ground was at a greater distance ; but the country people informed them it was much like the other.
>
> Upon this information [I] proposed that the other side of the Water should be the place for the army to be drawn up in line of battle next day ; but this was not agreed to. It was said it was like shunning the enemy, being a mile further from the muir they were then upon and a greater distance from Inverness, which it was resolved not to abandon, a great deal of baggage and ammunition being left there.
>
> I was convinced there was enough at Inverness which might even have been brought out—part to where we were, and the rest sent towards Loch Moy where our army must have retired.*

But such words of wisdom were lost upon the Prince, who had an amazing capacity for believing that all would turn out exactly as he wished. Having " dispatched messengers on all sides to call his troops that were scattered far and wide, he took it for granted he would be strong enough to venture a battle before the enemy could come up. He did not concert an alternative in case the enemy arrived sooner, or his army was not assembled as soon as expected."†

---

* Compiled and condensed from Lord George's ' Marches,' his letter to Hamilton of Bangour, 1749 (Appendix of ' Home's History '), and his letter of 10th May 1746 printed in ' The Lyon in Mourning ' but often referred to as the ' Particular Account.' This may have been the same description of the happenings on 15th and 16th April which he left at the Scots College in Paris.

† Kirkconnel.

He was still " in a sanguine and exalted frame of mind, and said that he had no doubts of the issue of the approaching conflict with the Duke of Cumberland ; he believed that the English soldiers would with difficulty be got to attack him. He refused to listen to any suggestion of retreating and awaiting reinforcements, and when a rendezvous in the event of defeat was spoken of, he replied that only those who were afraid could doubt of his coming victory."* As Lord Elcho records in his account of the campaign, he had indulged the previous evening " in boasting unworthy of a Prince. As he had consulted only his favourites, everything was in the greatest disorder. The persons capable of serving him were suspected or neglected, and those in whom he placed his trust had not the ability to be useful to him." Kirkconnel endorses this statement :

> Their blunders had never proved so fatal as on the present important occasion. There was at that time a provision of meal in Inverness and salt beef . . . besides other meat. But such had been the negligence of those whose province it was to supply the army that such as had not servants to bring them victuals were in a downright starving condition.

The decision to fight upon a ground where disaster would infallibly overtake the Jacobite forces, the arrival of Keppoch, and the return of Elcho and his scouts with a report that the enemy were quiet in their camp, caused Lord George to feel that almost anything was better than to remain at Culloden. He sought the Prince and expressed his willingness to accede to his wish to attack Cumberland. His plan, however, was for a night attack—not one at dawn, such as Charles had envisaged.

> The Prince assembled all the principal officers and asked them for the first time since Derby what was best to be done. Lord George Murray made a speech, wherein he enlarged upon the advantages Highlanders have by surprising their enemy, and rather attacking in the night than in daylight. For as regular troops depend entirely upon their discipline, and on the contrary the Highlanders having none, the night was the best time to put them most upon an equality. He concluded that his opinion was that they should march at dusk of that evening so that the Duke should not be apprised of it. He should march about the town of Nairn and attack them in their rear with the right wing

* Elcho.

of the first line, while the Duke of Perth with the left should attack them in front, and the Prince should support the Duke of Perth's attack with the second line. Everybody agreed to Lord George's opinion. It was only objected to him that, as he did not propose to march from Culloden until the dusk of the evening, and as Culloden was eight miles from Nairn, it was to be feared the army would not accomplish that march before the daylight. Lord George said he would answer for it.*

The Prince, whose opinion it was too, was charmed at this. . . . Sullivan was called upon to give his opinion, who said he saw nothing but that [which] could promise them a victory. [He] began to enlarge and show the advantage of it—that any troops that are surprised, or attacked before they are formed, are half conquered. That the Horse, which was what he had most to fear, would become useless. Their Artillery the same. They could not fire upon us without destroying their own—especially the way they were camped. [He said] Great care should be taken . . . not . . . to . . . fire upon one another.

As the Horse are camped separately from the Foot (which is not usual) a column should attack the Horse to cut the horses' collars, while the rest should fall upon the tents. Troopers afoot were not dangerous enemies. A regiment of the column . . . should likewise be named to seize upon the *faisseaux d'armes*. . . . If this was conducted well we would find but little or no resistance.†

It was thought the attack might succeed if the camp was reached by one or two in the morning, especially if they were undiscovered, as they had great hopes they might. Having examined the different roads, of which they had perfect intelligence from the MacIntoshes, who lived in those very parts, they found they could keep upon the muir the whole way so as to shun the houses, and be a considerable way from the highroad that leads from Inverness to Nairn. Should they even be beat off without the desired success, they might before daybreak get back the length of Kilravock, which was very strong ground. From thence by a hill they could retire the whole way on the south side of the Water of Nairn till they were joined by their friends whom they expected, and by the stragglers. Nor did they believe the enemy would follow them . . . till it was good daylight so as they could see about them and send out reconnoitring parties to prevent their falling into ambuscades and snares. . . . On the hilly ground . . . their cannon and Horse (in which their superiority consisted) would have been of little use.‡

* Elcho.
† O'Sullivan.
‡ Lord George's Various Accounts.

So the plan was decided upon. The Prince commanded O'Sullivan " to give orders and explain what he said in them. Lord George answered that there was no need of orders. Everybody knew what he was to do. He'd march with the first line, and whom His Royal Highness pleased with the second. The order of battle was sufficient."*

Lord George had laid his plans very thoroughly, and he was careful not to impart them all to the Irishman. There must be no such leakage of information as at Derby. Only senior officers were told of the march, and details were only imparted to the Prince, his Generals, and Anderson of Whitburgh, who with other Life Guardsmen had asked permission to accompany Lord George on foot as volunteers. Elcho's troop had been posted behind the right wing at Falkirk, and in their eager charge forward had nearly lost their horses in a bog. As this had caused ill-natured and wholly unjustified sneers at their expense, they were determined to be in the thick of the fighting on the present occasion.

Charles was delighted at the adoption of his scheme. But as Lord George wrote :

> About seven at night an incident happened which had liked to have stopped their designed attempt ; and upon it many were for giving it up as impracticable. The thing was this. Numbers of men went off to all sides, especially towards Inverness. When the officers who were sent on horseback to bring them back came up with them, they could by no persuasion be induced to return again, giving for answer—they were starving ; and said to the officers they might shoot them if they pleased, but they could not go back till they got meat.
>
> The men had only got that day a biscuit each—and some not even that. It was feared it would prove worse next day, except they could take provisions from the enemy. And they had reason to believe that if the men were allowed to disperse to shift for some meat (which many of them would do if the army continued there all night) that it would be very difficult to assemble them in the event of a sudden alarm.
>
> Even tho' meal should be brought, the men could not make it ready without dispersing for several miles to all the houses round about, which could not be done when the enemy was so near.
>
> His Royal Highness said that whenever the march began the men would be all hearty and that those that had gone off would

---

* O'Sullivan.

return and follow. His Royal Highness had so much confidence in the bravery of his army, he was rather too hazardous, and was for fighting the enemy on all occasions. What he had seen them do, and the justice of his Cause, made him too venturous.

I was with many others for a night attack. But that was only of two evils to choose what we thought the least. We thought that it was better than to fight upon that plain muir. I was for it provided it could be done before two in the morning so as to surprise the enemy. Our reason for being for the attempt was that His Royal Highness had declared the day before he was resolved to attack the enemy without waiting for those who were to join us. The expression was had he but a thousand men he would attack them. It was resolved that day (the fifteenth) not to abandon Inverness (because I suppose so much of the army baggage was there) but to [a]wait the enemy. My opinion and that of the Chiefs (at least those that were present) was to retire to a strong ground, where, if the Duke of Cumberland should attack us, we were persuaded we would have given a good account of him. And if he did not venture to cross the water we proposed to retire farther and draw him up to the mountains where we might attack him in some pass. But the Prince resolved to fight without endeavouring to draw the Duke of Cumberland's army farther from the sea, from whence he got all his provisions, that was brought about in ships which sailed along as his army marched near the shore.

That night when so many of the men went off we altered our thought [and] gave it up as a thing not to be ventured. Then indeed, I do not know of one officer who had been made acquainted with the resolution of surprising the enemy but declared in the strongest terms for laying it aside. Much was spoken by them all for not attempting it then. But His Royal Highness continued bent on the thing, and gave me orders to march.

It was agreed that if we could make the attack by one o'clock in the morning, or at least by two, we might have had great hopes of success ; but no one ever imagined we could attempt it later.

For these reasons the gentlemen seemed to think the night march might be attempted. But most of them thought they were in very bad circumstances at any rate, and no attempt could be more desperate than their present situation.

So wrote Lord George, who fully realised that the Jacobites were between the devil and the deep sea. He found it impossible to share the optimism of his exuberant and wholly inexperienced young commander, who, although a third of his 6,000 men had now gone off, declared : " I have men enough to be at the enemy, who I believe are utterly dispirited and will never stand a brisk attack."

He still persisted in supposing that he had friends within the enemy's camp and hoped that in the dark " some of them would industriously propagate the terror and confusion when they could do it without being discovered." Lord George, remembering that this was Cumberland's twenty-fifth birthday, was quite sure that his officers and men would be in remarkably good spirits that night. His only hope was that they would all be " drunk as beggars."

> It was near eight at night when they moved, which could not be sooner, otherwise they might have been perceived at a considerable distance, and the enemy have got account of their march. Lord George Murray was in the van, Lord John Drummond in the centre, and the Duke of Perth towards the rear, where also the Prince was, having FitzJames's Horse and others with him. Proper directions were given for small parties possessing all the roads, that intelligence might not be carried to the enemy. There were about two officers and thirty men of the Mackintoshes in the front as guides, and some of the same were in the centre and rear, and in other parts, for hindering any of the men from straggling.

Almost as soon as the march began the Prince came up to the head of the leading column, placed an arm round his General's neck, and said : " Lord George, you can't imagine, nor can I express to you, how acknowledging I am of all the services you have rendered me. But this will crown all. You'll restore the King by it. You'll have all the honour and glory of it. It is your work. It is you imagined it, and be assured that the King nor I will ever forget it." . . . Lord George never deigned to answer one word. The Prince continued to walk near him after he quitted his hand for a long time. At last, seeing that Lord George did not speak a word, the Prince took his leave. Lord George took off his bonnet, made a stiff bow, and the Prince went off !*

So the march continued. Poor Lord George had also the undesired company of O'Sullivan, with whom he was more than ever out of patience. Considering himself worn out by the fatigues he had undergone since coming to Scotland, the Irishman had had himself " bled and purged, tho," as he admitted, " it was no proper time for it."† For once Lord George shared his views. But he had been so unsympathetic as to expect the invalid to make two or three orders

* O'Sullivan.
† Ibid.

of battle on the very day he had been bled," and on several succeeding days.   One of these this victim of overwork had spent in bed without giving out any orders, or directing others to do so—a circumstance that occasioned Lord George's subsequent jibe that O'Sullivan had fought the Battle of Culloden in his night-cap.   But he had come on the march accompanied by Sir Thomas Sheridan, a most unsuitable person to venture on the expedition, for he was over seventy, had suffered three strokes, and had not taken part in any battle since the Boyne in 1690.   Lord George curtly requested them not to march with him " as their horses made too much noise."*   So they fell behind, and the aggrieved Quartermaster-General confided to his elderly friend that, although he much approved of the present undertaking, he feared that it was being badly carried out.

It was.   But the fault did not lie with Lord George.   The sturdy Athollmen and Camerons under his command were indeed proving their right to be designated " the Flower of the Highland Troops "† ; for although Lochiel's men had only returned the evening before from their long, fatiguing march from Fort William, they were covering the ground at the rate of two miles an hour, a pace that would bring them to their objective at the prescribed time.   The Prince's own followers were taking twice that time.   Scarcely a mile was covered when the first of about fifty messengers (whose advent delayed and exasperated the General) came up from the rear begging him to halt and allow the second column to catch up with the first. Lord George sent back the messengers with requests that the other commanders would increase their pace.   He merely slackened his own, for as he said afterwards : " A halt in the van occasions a greater one in the rear when the march begins again, whereas by marching slow the rear might have joined without that inconveniency."

Why the Prince wished to slow down is a mystery : probably he had visualised his little army moving forward in battle array, much as Cumberland's did when advancing on Culloden the following morning.   Such a picture could hardly have presented itself to Lord George, who was obliged to lead his men three abreast in one long line, on a track that wound between bog and boulders.   In all probability neither the Prince nor his General had ever made his views clear to the other.   It was afterwards said by his enemies

* O'Sullivan.
† Lord George's letter to Hamilton of Bangour.

that Lord George had "acted contrary to the plan laid down, in filing off in the dark, without giving advice to the second line, by which the Prince's scheme was disconcerted, and the lives of his men endangered . . . and . . . he had, without any necessity, put himself in posts of danger, and therewith prevented the execution of all designs."*

As the Prince was with the first column at the beginning of the march he could have rectified these matters had he chosen to do so. But even had the army marched three columns abreast, as Kirkconnel considered would have been a better plan, the lag would have been the same; for before they were half-way to Balblair a gap half a mile long yawned between the first and second columns. The Prince's Highlanders were capable of marching at the same pace as the men from Atholl and Lochaber, and he would have done better to have hastened onward with the Highland regiments and the Cavalry, leaving behind the Royal Scots and the Irish Piquets, now only a few hundred strong. For they, as Lord George pointed out, had only been brought along to form a *corps de reserve*.

The twenty or thirty Mackintosh officers and men whom, because of their knowledge of the country, he had procured as guides for each column, had not reckoned upon the slow progress of the mercenaries from France who "were not so clever in marching"† as the more lightly accoutred Highlanders. Even the Lowlanders were finding the going extremely difficult. Various Memoir writers left vivid descriptions of their stumbling march "along the foot of a ridge of mountains which fronted the sea but had scarcely ever been trodden by human foot . . . through trackless paths, marshes, and quagmires . . . where men were frequently up to their ankles, and the horses in many cases extricated themselves with difficulty."‡ It was a foggy night and the darkness was so intense that John Daniel, the only Englishman taking part in the expedition, found it impossible to distinguish a white horse from a black one.

Lord George intended to cross the Water of Nairn about two miles short of the town, march along the south bank to avoid Hanoverian outposts, and then recross the river a mile farther on. From the south-east he would then fall upon the flank and rear of

* So-called "Articles of Impeachment" of Lord George Murray.
† Particular Account.
‡ Accounts of Robert Strange, Andrew Lumisden, and John Daniel.
  O

the English Cavalry. The remaining two-thirds of the army were to keep to the north bank until they came almost to the camp. They were then to branch off to the left in a line extending to the sea, and launch a simultaneous attack from the west upon the Infantry. It was an ingenious plan which English officers afterwards asserted would have placed the Government forces in an awkward position; for although Gaelic-speaking spies who had mingled with the Jacobites had brought word of their advance, it was supposed by Cumberland that they were merely on their way to take up a fresh position for the coming battle.

When they had gone about half-way, Lord George ordered Colonel Ker to ride back down the line to tell all officers " to order their men to make the attack sword in hand, which would not alarm the enemy so soon " as if they began the assault by the usual discharge of muskets. On entering the camp they were to overturn all the tents, and wherever a bulge was noticed in the fallen canopy " there to strike and push vigorously."* With the approval of Lochiel he also sent word to the Prince that the men must be assembled " in order of battle as they came up, with a view to presenting a front and attacking the enemy together without confusion." Charles, however, evidently realised that the lagging rear column could not get up in time to co-operate with the vanguard, for he ordered Lord George to fall upon the camp as soon as he reached it with whatever number of men he had.

Lord George commanded less than 1,200 men when he was asked to make this onslaught upon an enemy outnumbering him by almost eight to one. He asked Lochiel to tell their master that he did not think " it proper to continue his march because he could never be strong enough." The Prince exclaimed : " But we are stronger than when we left Culloden ! One cannot imagine what a quantity of men have come in since."† So the Cameron Chief was sent back with an absolute command that the march must continue. On such a dark night it was impossible to see how many men had fallen out. But many could be heard whispering among themselves that it would soon be light, and others were even talking of declining

---

* Lochgarry's Account, Lockhart Papers.

† In the ' Scots Magazine ' it is stated that so many men " had fallen off, thinking they might do so in the night unobserved and hid themselves in the fields," that only 3,000 could now have been with the Prince.

to attack. Lord George's men kept slipping from the ranks and throwing themselves in utter exhaustion upon the ground as they passed along the path through Kilravock Wood. The way was narrow there, on account of a long stone wall that ran beside it, and the men were no longer able to march three abreast. Lochiel returned to report the gravity of the situation to the Prince. " I'll answer for the men ; but I am surprised that you are the man chosen to bring me such a message," retorted the Prince, whose mood had changed at the first hint of opposition to his wishes. There had been no sincerity in the honeyed words he had uttered to Lord George so short a time ago, and precious moments were now wasted as he laid bare to Lochiel the suspicions he had long entertained about the fidelity of his General—a tirade to which the harassed Chief had no time to listen.

The Prince thereupon ordered Lord John Drummond, O'Sullivan, and the Duke of Perth, who had just come up from the rear, to go forward and interview Lord George. They overtook him by the farm of Knockbuie, or the Yellow Knoll, a little to the east of the ancient mansion of Kilravock, about six miles from their starting-point and a mile short of the place where Lord George proposed to cross the river. Lord John rode up to him and said in a low voice : " Why will you go on ? There is a gap in the line half a mile long. The men won't come up." The Duke of Perth, " who was as keen as any man in the army, crossed the narrow road with his horse, and said it was impossible the line could join."* Several of the officers that came up from the rear affirming that many of the men had left the ranks and had laid down—particularly in the Wood of Kilravock. Lord George wrote later : " This must have been occasioned by faintness for want of food, for it could not be weariness in a six-mile march."†

A halt was accordingly called ; and O'Sullivan told the General : " His Royal Highness would be very glad to have the attack made, but as Lord George Murray had the van and could judge of the time he left it to him whether to do it or not "‡—a message the gist of which the messenger chose later to forget.

Even without this latest message from the Prince Lord George

* Lord George's letter to Hamilton of Bangour.
† Ibid.
‡ Ibid.

would have been justified in ordering a retreat. As he said later, people " were resolved to lay the blame on someone, and I am pitched upon,"* but in the irregular Jacobite army the " practice had always been at critical junctures that the commanding officers did everything to their knowledge for the best. There was no officer of any distinction with the Prince (except Sir Thomas be reckoned one), they being all in the van. The Prince was a mile back and no way in the dark to ride through the wood but by the line where the men were, and in some places it was very narrow so it would be a work of considerable time to have sent back and forward."† Time was too precious to be wasted; and in any case Charles was too far in the rear to judge the situation.

The two Generals who had joined Lord George were well aware that the plan for a surprise assault upon the camp had woefully miscarried, for they knew by their repeating watches that it was already two o'clock. As Lord George said : " All the principal officers who were come to the van agreed that it was now impossible. A surprise was designed, but now it was palpable they could not even by a quick march advance two miles before daybreak. They must be two miles in the enemies' sight before they could come at them. Add to this that the officers were also convinced that they had not half the men that had been drawn up the day before."

Lord George was, however, resolved that everybody should be afforded an opportunity to state his views upon this vital matter. " It is a free Parliament," he said, " and I desire everybody to speak and give their opinion, for all are equally concerned." Brave old Hepburn of Keith, Hunter of Burnside, Anderson of Whitburgh, and other volunteers were all for carrying out the original design. " This opinion," Lord George afterwards observed, " showed abundance of courage for these gentlemen would have been in the first rank had there been any attack. But the officers were of different sentiments, as several of them expressed. Lochiel and his brother said they had been as much for the night attack as anybody could be, and it was not their fault that it had not been done ; but blamed those in the rear that had marched so slow and retarded the rest of the army."‡

* Lord George's letter to Hamilton of Bangour.
† Ibid.
‡ Particular Account.

Just then a drum beat. " ' Do you hear that ? ' said Lord George. ' The enemy are alarmed. We can't surprise them.' ' I never expected,' said Mr Hepburn, ' to find them asleep. But it is much better to march on and attack them than to retreat, for they will certainly follow and oblige us to fight when we shall be in a much worse state to fight them than we are now.' Lord George replied : ' It is too late. The day will begin to appear before we could arrive at the camp, and the enemy aware of our approach might take advantage of our situation and attack us while disordered and dispersed.' Mr Hepburn retorted : ' There will be no great harm done if we have a little daylight to assist the Highlanders in using their swords to advantage ' "* He and some other volunteers thought " the redcoats would be so drunk with solemnising the Duke's birthday "† that it would make little difference if it were light or not. But none of the officers were of that opinion. Someone declared that it was better to fight now with few men than with double the number after dawn. But the principal officers were convinced that dawn would break before they had marched two miles and the enemy would have time to point their cannon, draw up their men, and place their Cavalry so as to act in the most advantageous manner.‡ Lord George, who knew that the only hope of success had lain in a combined attack under cover of darkness, bluntly expressed his opinion that to fall upon Cumberland's men in the daylight " when they were prepared to receive them would be perfect madness."‡

O'Sullivan now thought it high time to intervene. He desired permission to speak to Lord George, and was told straightly " If you have anything to say above-board you can say it. But remember there is not a man here but has more to lose than you." " It may be very like, my Lord, I have only my life and honour to expose with pleasure for the King's service," averred the Irish soldier of fortune, " but I will answer you, my Lord, that I'll never lose my honour for all the wealth that you and these gentlemen can have." Lord George demanded impatiently if he had no more than this to say. O'Sullivan replied : " I ask pardon, my Lord, since you'll have me speak high. The Prince orders me to tell you that all his

* O'Sullivan.
† Lord George's letter to Hamilton of Bangour.
‡ Particular Account.

confidence is in you. The loss or gain of the Cause is in your hands, and depends entirely upon you. If you march upon the enemy it is morally sure you'll destroy them—having all manner of advantages, surprising them, and the spirits your men are in. You know the situation the Prince is in : neither money nor provisions. If you retire you discourage your men, who suffer enough already. You lose all your advantages and give them over to the enemy. If they come upon you in battle, superior as they are in Horse and Foot and Artillery, can you resist them ? "*

Menzies of Shian interrupted this stream of eloquence. He declared with an oath : " If we are to be killed let it be in plain day, when we can see how our neighbours behave." Another officer of the Atholl Brigade chimed in : " Those that are so much for fighting why don't they come with us ? " " I don't know to whom this discourse is addressed," retorted the Quartermaster-General. " If it be to me, you'll know that it was not the first time you saw me in action. You owned yourself, and said it openly, that you saw no other General but the Prince and me at the Battle of Falkirk. If Lord George will permit me, I'll offer to march in the first rank of the vanguard and will give my head off my shoulders, which is all I have to lose, if he does not succeed. And if he follows, I am sure you will, gentlemen."†

Such discourse was hardly likely to recommend the speaker to the General who had fought at Falkirk, nor to the other officers, for it had been the talk of the army that the Quartermaster-General had never been seen during the engagement. Fiery old Hepburn, ever noted for his impracticable ideas and strange prejudices, however, drew him aside and prayed him make a further attempt to prevail upon Lord George to change his mind. " It was an unhappy day that he joined the Prince," he added bitterly. " All knew he would ruin the Cause—this is the finishing stroke."‡

Just then Hay of Restalrig rode up with the false intelligence " that the line had joined."§ But retreat had now been decided upon. Fifteen minutes had been taken up by the discussion. " As it would be broad daylight before the Prince's army could arrive, the enemy would have abundance of time to make their dispositions, and discover the weakness of those who were coming against them."

* Conversation taken from O'Sullivan's ' Narrative.'
† Ibid.
‡ O'Sullivan's ' Narrative.'
§ Hay's Account.

Perth and his brother rode off as fast as the darkness permitted to order the men in the rear to turn about. " Come, gentlemen, go on. Follow the road I told you. The day is coming ; and I have taken my decision,"* said Lord George, turning to the Mackintosh officers, who were to lead him down to the road, since there was no longer any need for secrecy.

Hay " was generally esteemed a man of neither parts nor capacity by the army officers, and as men of that kind are apt to change their behaviour with their fortunes, he was reckoned to carry it too high to his superiors, which created him many enemies."† He turned upon them now, and " began to argue the point, but nobody minded him."‡ They justly regarded his criminal neglect to supply the army with rations as the chief reason why the march had to be abandoned. They were, in fact, so utterly weary of both him and O'Sullivan that they had already made up their minds to press for the removal of these two men from the positions in which they had done so much damage.

Enraged by Lord George's haughty indifference to his outpourings, Hay posted back to warn the Prince that " unless he came to the front and ordered his Lordship to go on, nothing would be done."§ The Prince was between the second column and the reserve, which now lagged so far behind as to form a third column. He started forward on horseback and met the men from his column about a hundred yards after they had wheeled about. " Where the devil are the men a-going ? " he called out. " We are ordered by the Duke of Perth to return to Culloden House," he was informed. " Where is the Duke ? Call him here,"‖ the Prince demanded. " I am betrayed ! What need have I to give orders when my orders are disobeyed ? "¶

The Duke of Perth and O'Sullivan, who rode with him, had evidently gone astray in the darkness. It transpired that Clanranald's men, who headed the second column, had marched on to within dangerous proximity of the enemy before discovering that their comrades had turned down to the road—a circumstance which proves the falsity of Hay's assertion that the columns had joined

* O'Sullivan's ' Narrative.'
† Lord Elcho's Journal.
‡ Lord George's letter to Hamilton of Bangour.
§ Hay's Account. Home's Appendix.
‖ Genuine Account of the Battle of Culloden, ' Lyon in Mourning.'
¶ Rev. George Innes's Account, ' Lyon in Mourning.'

before the decision was made to retreat. Wild confusion now reigned among the Prince's followers. Aides-de-camp rode from one column to another demanding: " For God's sake, what has become of his Lordship ? The Prince is in the utmost perplexity for want of him."*

At last the Duke of Perth presented himself before Charles and was asked: " What do you mean by ordering the men to turn about ? " " Lord George has turned back with the first column three-quarters of an hour ago," replied his Grace. " Good, God ! What can be the matter ? What does this mean ? " expostulated the Prince. " We were equal in numbers and could have blown them to the devil. Pray, Perth, can't you call them back yet ? Perhaps he has not gone too far."† The unhappy Duke, who was devoted to his young master, expressed his readiness to obey orders, but begged private speech with him. They went aside for a short time. They were joined by Lochiel, who said in forthright fashion : " It is now daylight. The project of surprising the Duke [Cumberland] has failed. It is better to be back than go on and attack the Duke, who would be prepared." Charles, " when he saw that nothing could be done, was in despair." On learning that " the decision had been taken in concert with Lochiel and others whom he never mistrusted, he did not know what to think, or what to do, except to blame Lord George's villainy for having " put panick in Lochiel." He went back to his men : " There's no help for it, my lads," he said. " March back. We shall meet them later and behave like brave fellows."‡

But Lord George's enemies were not slow to tell their master what they thought about the events of the night. O'Sullivan, as ready as Charles to forget the message he had been ordered to give the General, declared that Lord George had flagrantly disobeyed orders, and that there would have been ample time for an attack before dawn. And though day was already breaking, the statement was implicitly accepted as the truth by Charles. Other Irish officers " endeavoured by all manner of clandestine reports to cause it to be believed that in acting as he did on this occasion Lord George had betrayed the Prince." His fear of treachery became so great

---

* Captain Daniel's Progress.

† Genuine account. The Prince had set out with 4,000 men, whose numbers were probably reduced to 3,000. Cumberland commanded close on 9,000 men.

‡ Genuine account.

that he made " some of them promise to watch Lord George's motions, particularly in case of a battle : and they promised the Prince to shoot him if they could find he intended to betray him."*

The van had meanwhile reached the Inverness road, " the rest of the army following without knowing exactly whither, but daylight soon discovered the country and abundance of people were surprised to find themselves going back." It was quite light by the time the first column reached the Kirk of Croy two miles back from Kilravock. Most of the officers were convinced of the wisdom of not attacking the camp ; for, as Robert Strange wrote years later, it was " almost a moral certainty that we should have been cut off to a man ; the enemy, early astir, must have received us upon the point of their bayonets." But, as MacNab of Inishewen records : " The common soldiers reflected upon Lord George for the fatigue and the retreat—as if he had corresponded with the enemy." Hungry, footsore men, who knew nothing of the country or the distance to Balblair, suspected him of having led them by a route twice as long as needful. One of the " Articles of Impeachment " afterwards drawn up against Lord George anonymously, ran thus : " The Prince's army was by his means kept under arms, marching and counter-marching without rest, and half-starved for want of meat and drink, for forty-eight hours before the battle ; and therefore could not exert their wonted strength, on which, with their usual way of fighting, much depended."†

In spite of their ever-increasing hunger and weariness, the Highlanders trudged along the road with greater speed than they had marched over the moor. " As they did not shun passing houses as they had done in advancing, they marched very quick. They got to Culloden pretty early, so that the men had three or four hours' rest."‡ The vanguard reached Culloden House soon after five o'clock ; but the Prince was two hours later in arriving there. He had continued along the road to Inverness, a twelve-miles ride there and back, in a last-minute attempt to procure provisions for his men. Perth, though exhausted as the result of the exertions he was so unfit to undergo, was more alive to the danger of imminent attack than was Charles. The Prince's place, he felt, was with his army ;

* Elcho.
† Kirkconnel.
‡ Particular Account.

so he " followed him and engaged him to come back," very sensibly suggesting that Colonel O'Shea with his 100 troopers of FitzJames's Horse should be sent to the town with orders to bring back what provisions they could carry.

Charles consented to return to Culloden House. " The first person he met was Lord George. He taxed him with his behaviour of the night before—without the least anger," or so says O'Sullivan, whose statement does not tally with James Johnstone's assertion that " on entering the house His Royal Highness, enraged against Lord George Murray, publicly declared that no one in future should command the army but himself." However, he admitted years later that his General in the end convinced him " of the unavoidable necessity of retreating." But much valuable time was then wasted over an unedifying discussion as to whether Lord George or Lochiel had first spoken of turning back.

It was Lord George's maxim to give thought to doing better in the future rather than to brood and fret over past mistakes and failures. There was certainly much need to discuss what was to be done now if the day turned out better than it promised to be, and Cumberland decided to march from Nairn and give them battle. But in spite of his recent disappointment, " the Prince was so far from thinking of retreating that he would have taken it much amiss if anybody had doubted so far of a victory as to have asked him where the army should rendezvous. . . ."*

But everybody seemed to think of nothing but sleep. " Instead of deliberating about what was proper to be done at this critical juncture, they stared at one another in amazement. Everybody looked sullen and dejected ; those that had taken upon themselves to begin the retreat, as well as those that had not any share in it. The principal officers . . . were so tired that they never thought of calling a Council what was to be done. Every one laid himself down where he could, some on beds, others on tables, chairs, and on the floors, for the fatigue and hunger had been as much amongst the officers as soldiers."

After issuing orders that Inverness and the surrounding country must be ruthlessly ransacked for provisions, the weary Prince, who had been up for two nights and had marched much of the way on foot with his men, threw himself fully clad upon his bed to snatch a few hours' rest.

* Elcho.

CHAPTER XIII

CULLODEN

THE Prince and his exhausted followers had scarcely two hours' rest. " Their repose was interrupted in a very disagreeable manner."*

The day had not promised to be fair, and Lord George and many of the officers had hoped that the enemy would not advance. No organised patrol had been established to observe their activities at the camp—since the only troops whose horses were in a fit state for patrolling had been despatched to Inverness. But a few horsemen had been left behind to keep a look-out over the moor, and they and a lieutenant of the Camerons, who had fallen asleep near the spot where the vanguard halted, arrived at Culloden House before ten o'clock with the unwelcome news that the Government forces were upon the march. A party of Kingston's volunteer Cavalrymen were within two miles of Culloden, and the rest of the forces about two miles farther back.

Vivid descriptions have been given of how officers rode about the countryside rounding up men who had gone out to kill sheep and cattle, which they now had no time to eat. But greater still was the wild confusion that reigned in Culloden House. Officers, who had drunk up sixty hogsheads of claret and other choice wines in the Lord President's well-stocked cellars, hurried off to battle sustained only by cups of chocolate, which a thoughtful servant handed round on a tray. As they were rushing out the steward announced that " a roast side of lamb and two fowls were about to be placed on the table." " How can I sit down at such a time when my men are starving ? " the Prince asked him indignantly.

Charles had been in such a state of nervous irritability the previous morning that he had stigmatised as traitors any officers who suggested the advisability of forming plans in the event of a defeat. Thus no rendezvous was fixed where the army could reassemble— an omission that the absent Broughton could hardly credit when he came to hear of it. All was too much hurry and confusion for it to be thought of now. Lord George had no time to write out orders

* Henderson's ' History of the Rebellion of 1745.'

for battle, and those issued for the 14th and 15th April had perforce
to stand. It was fortunate indeed that these were afterwards printed
word for word in the Edinburgh ' Courant ' and other periodicals ;
for they proved that the lie about the Jacobites giving no quarter to
the enemy was a clumsy forgery added by the Whigs when the
butchery of Cumberland began to stink in the nostrils of the public.*

" The Prince and the Duke of Perth, Lord George Murray and
Lord John Drummond, mounted their horses, ordered the drums to
beat, and the pipes to play, which alarm caused great confusion
amongst people half-dead with fatigue." The Prince ordered
cannon to be fired to assemble the clansmen, who came streaming
through the parks of Culloden more or less in the order in which
they had been lying when roused. But many men had " slipt off to
take some refreshment in Inverness, Culloden and the neighbourhood . . . and the said refreshment so lulled them asleep that,
designing only to take one hour's rest, or two, they were afterwards
surprised and killed in their beds." So wrote Kirkconnel ; young
Johnstone endorses all he says :

> The Prince, who was always eager to give battle without
> reflecting on the consequences, was told that as the Highlanders
> were exhausted with fatigue, dispersed, and buried in deep sleep
> in the neighbouring hamlets and enclosures many could not

* " The lying order appeared in Marchant and Ray's contemporary
histories of the Rising, and it is amazing to find it repeated to-day in the
Dictionary of National Biography. Although Cumberland on the day after
the battle issued an order in which officers and men were desired to ' take
notice of the public orders of ye Rebells yesterday was to give no quarters,'
it is significant that no mention of this order was ever made in a Government
Gazette, or in any official account of the battle ; it is practically certain that
Cumberland must have known that no such order existed and suppressed
the knowledge for his justification. Four copies of Lord George's order are
known to be extant, all in his own handwriting. With the exception of
trifling variations in spelling and diction, they are practically identical. Two
are preserved at Blair Castle, one is among Cumberland's own papers, and
the fourth, now in the British Museum, belonged to Lord Hardwicke, who,
as Lord Chancellor, presided at the trial of the Jacobite peers in 1746.
Lord Kilmarnock, on the eve of execution, sent a petition to the Duke of
Cumberland in which he protested that he never heard of the ' no quarter '
order, and Balmerino on the scaffold emphatically corroborated this.
Although both the Duke of Cumberland and the Lord Chancellor must
have known that the order was a forgery, yet neither spoke out in response
to the appeals of the men whom they had brought to the scaffold, but allowed
the calumny to remain uncontradicted." ' Military History of Perthshire,'
edited by the Marchioness of Tullibardine.

possibly be present in the battle, from the difficulty of finding them. Besides, what could be expected from men in their situation, worn out with want of sleep and food, and quite exhausted with this night-march ; a thousand times worse than any march which had been made in England. They were not possessed of superhuman strength.

The Prince, over-sanguine in all his calculations, was dead to the suggestions of wisdom. It was useless to point out to him that " it was nothing short of downright madness to venture an issue that day," since the 3,000 famished and exhausted Highlanders, who had as yet appeared upon the scene, would have no chance against three times their number of well-fed, well-trained regular troops. " There was no manner of Council held upon the field, and indeed there was but one party [course] to take, which was to have crossed the Water of Nairn," observes Elcho. " What put a stop to all Councils was that the Prince always believed firmly that the Duke's army would be struck with panic ; so with those notions it was equal to him to have nine or only five thousand men." In vain the Marquis D'Eguilles flung himself on his knees and besought him not to risk an engagement. Charles would listen neither to him nor to the very reasonable plan laid before him by Lord George, and warmly seconded by Lochiel. As Lord George wrote :

> We still had time to cross the water and take up the ground which Brigadier Stapleton and Colonel Ker had viewed the day before, for our right was within three hundred paces of the water, and the banks were very steep which was nothing to hinder the Highlanders, and our Horse and cannon could have crossed at a small ford a mile further back. . . . That night or next morning we would have been near two thousand stronger. Had we passed that water in all probability we would not have fought that day. So that if the Duke of Cumberland had encamped that night upon the muir, which very possibly he might, we would have had a fair chance.
>
> Most of the clans, at least those I spoke with, were for this operation. His Royal Highness could have supported the fatigues as well as any person in the army. It's true Sir Thomas Sheridan, &c., could not have undergone it. So we were obliged to be undone for their ease. As to provisions, had I been allowed to have direction, we should not have wanted.*

Lord George's views were shared by Patullo, the Muster-master of the Jacobite army, who averred : " Sir Thomas Sheridan and

* Compounded from Lord George's accounts.

the officers from France, weary of the campaign and hoping no doubt for a miracle, urged the Prince to give battle, and prevailed."* The writer of an unsigned letter preserved among Lord George's papers had a great deal to say upon the subject :

> Lord George Murray . . . was for postponing fighting till the men were all come up, and to choose an advantageous field of battle, and to have provisions sent up to several of the inaccessible parts of the Highlands. All this was opposed by Sir Thomas, &c., as they feared nothing so much as a hill campaign. . . .
>
> Mr O'Sullivan chose that field of battle which proved so fatal, and I am certain that neither Scots officers or one single man of all the Highlanders would have agreed to it had their advice been asked—for there never could be more improper ground for Highlanders. What is remarkable though Mr O'Sullivan had all along acted as Quartermaster and Adjutant-General, yet he had no hand in choosing the former fields of battle. One reason for his not choosing the former fields of battle was that it must be done in face of the enemy—so it was left to the Highlanders and their officers to do it as they might ; which they did as much for their own advantage and the enemy's detriment as they could. But in this last Mr O'Sullivan had forty-eight hours to display his skill—and did it accordingly.†

Although the Prince had indisputably " given himself up altogether to the pernicious counsels of Sheridan and the Irish who governed him as they pleased," it would perhaps be more accurate to say that the Highland army was sacrificed at Culloden in a bid to save his self-esteem. Even Kirkconnel has to admit :

> He dreaded nothing so much as the appearance of fear at the approach of the Duke of Cumberland. He had too high an opinion of the bravery of his men ; he thought all irresistible. Hitherto they had never been worsted in any encounter ; every skirmish had ended to their advantage, and the enemy on every occasion had shewn the strongest symptoms of fear and diffidence. . . .
>
> Nothing was easier than to avoid an action for several days. The Prince had only to retire beyond Inverness, or beyond the river of Nairn ; but he thought either of these would be an argument of fear, an acknowledgment of the Duke of Cumberland's superiority, and discourage the army. . . . The enemy would not have attempted to force the town, or a strong camp,

* ' The Lyon in Mourning.'
† Unpublished letter at Blair Castle.

the same day they marched from Nairn.   But nothing of this
kind was concerted.   That unfortunate misunderstanding occasioned by the retreat, and improved by the suggestions of those
that had the Prince's ear, left no room for deliberation. . . . He
would not think of a retreat which he had never yielded to but
with the greatest reluctancy, and which on this occasion he
imagined would disperse the few men he had, and put an
inglorious end to his enterprise.

Since all the provisions had been stored there, Inverness would
have been a serious loss ; and, as ever, the Prince appeared to think
more of salvaging his baggage and clinging to an untenable town
than of the preserving the lives of the men who so trustingly followed
him.   The tragedy of Carlisle had left little impression upon him.
It had in no way weakened his confidence in his own judgment—
or rather in that of his flatterers.   His mistakes began as soon as the
regiments reached the moor.   It was not his fault that he knew little
of Highland traditions, for his father's courtiers were for the most
part Lowland gentlemen.   But it was owing to his persistence in
surrounding himself with those who spoke only to please that he
heard nothing of the Macdonalds' resentment at the prospect of
being deprived of their cherished place on the right—a fact
inadvertently revealed by O'Sullivan in his clumsy attempts to show
how at one time his perverse Lordship would " have it one way,
another time another."

> The Prince got a-horseback and went up on the moor with
> Lochiel's Regiment. . . . Lord George comes up and tells
> Sullivan, who had the honour to be near the Prince, that he must
> change the order of battle, that his regiment had the right yester-
> day.   " But, my Lord," says Sullivan, " there was no battle
> yesterday.   Besides it is no time to change the order of battle in
> the enemy's presence."   Lord George [replied], " Lead up the
> men then.   It's your business to set them in battle."*

It was, but the Adjutant-General had no desire to give himself
the exertion of altering the dispositions of the previous day although,
since the enemy was only three miles away, the army was now drawn
up on ground nearly a mile to the west of where it had been drawn
up the previous day.   Yet there was ample time to inspect this new
and wholly unreconnoitred ground in order to decide where the
regiments could be placed to the best advantage now that the morass

* O'Sullivan.

no longer protected the left wing. But Lord George was refused permission to do so. O'Sullivan continues :

> The Prince caressed Lord George, prayed him lead the men, and that he and Sullivan would make them follow in their ranks. " Gad, Sir," says Lord George, swearing : " It's very hard that my Regiment must have the right two days running." (When it was he himself would have it absolutely.)
>
> " Sir," says he again, " the ground is not reconnoitred. " I ask pardon," says Sullivan. " Here is as good a position as you could desire. You see that park before you which continues to the river with a wall six foot high. . . . The park here [Culloden] is to our left. If there is not ground enough we'll make use of the parks. I'll warrant you, my Lord," says O'Sullivan, " their Horse won't come to you there." He [Lord George] went off grumbling.

The Macdonalds were grumbling, too, as they marched out of the parks. Sir John Macdonald, much agitated after overhearing their conversation, sent Felix O'Neil to Sir Thomas to warn the Prince, if he thought fit, that " it was most important not to offend the clans."[*] He did not reflect that even if the Athollmen could be removed from the right, their place would automatically be taken by the Camerons, who had been next to them in the march, and who would be as averse as the Macdonalds from relinquishing this coveted post of honour. Meanwhile the Macdonald Chiefs sought out the Prince. " Clanranald, Keppoch, and I," says Lochgarry, " begged he would allow us our former right. But he entreated us for his sake we would not dispute it, as he had already agreed to give it to Lord George Murray and his Athollmen. And I have heard that he resented it much, and should never do the like again."[†]

" The Prince would not decide in a matter he was ignorant of, but as the thing had to be settled in some shape or other, he found it easier to prevail with the commanders of the Macdonalds to waive their pretensions than with Lord George to drop his claims," wrote Kirkconnel, equally unaware that it was O'Sullivan's warning about the danger of moving troops, and not Lord George's obstinacy, that kept the Athollmen on the right. Yet at the time many of Lord George's enemies knew of his offer to withdraw them ; for in the fantastic mock " Articles of Impeachment " drawn up by persons is recorded his great crime in wishing " the Camerons to have the

* Memoirs of Sir John Macdonald.
† Lochgarry's Account, Lockhart Papers.

right, well knowing that the Macdonalds, who from time immemorial held the right, would not fight under such an indignity."* They even went so far as to aver that Lord George had informed Cumberland that the Prince's left wing would be " quite inactive and useless " —thus causing that commander to strengthen his own left wing in anticipation of the main Jacobite attack.

Lord George, who, as he says himself, was unable to conceive how people could dispute over such matters at a time like the present, took up his position with the right wing—the only sector of the army where he was in full command that day. At eleven o'clock the Government army was still two miles away, marching along the wide plain that stretched away towards Nairn. The regiments were already in three lines, or two lines and a large *corps de reserve*, with the Cavalry on the wings.

" The Prince himself, in spite of his endeavours to the contrary, was not able to conceal that damp which his late night's disappointment had cast upon his spirits."† " This was the first time the Prince ever thought his affairs desperate. He saw his little army half-dead with hunger and fatigue."‡ He turned to an officer from a French regiment and asked him his opinion as to the outcome of the battle. The officer replied that he " feared it was already lost, for he had never seen men advance to the attack in so cool and regular a manner as did their enemies." Lord Elcho made a similar inquiry of Lord George, and received an equally pessimistic reply : " We are now putting an end to a bad affair." Lord Kilmarnock was also seized with a premonition of coming disaster as he watched the advancing troops. The Prince, however, contrived to hide his fears as he rode about the field on the fine horse that had been presented to him by Mr Dunbar of Thunderton :

> He . . . forgot nothing that was necessary to encourage everybody, shewing himself everywhere, talking to the particular officers, as well as to the private men, telling them in a gay way : " Here they are coming, my lads. We'll soon be with them. They don't forget Gladsmuir, nor Falkirk. You'll have the same arms and swords. Let me see yours," taking one of the men's swords. " I'll answer this will cut off some heads and arms

* So-called " Articles of Impeachment."
† Rev. George Innes's Account.
‡ Kirkconnel.

P

to-day. Go on, my lads. The day will be ours, and we'll want for nothing after." This and the like discourse heartened very much our men, tho' the Prince in the bottom had no great hopes.*

Neither had his eulogist, O'Sullivan, though he "kept the best countenance he could" when sent to interview Lord George. He told him how fortunate he was in being protected by a stone wall running the full length of the four farms whose fields stretched down to the river rather more than quarter of a mile away. John Cameron, then serving in Lochiel's Regiment, has left on record that Lord George had thought the same when he first rode out on to the moor. But on reaching the dyke and taking a " narrow view " of the land behind it, he realised at once that it would prevent the Jacobites from stopping a very possible attempt by the enemy to outflank them or take them in the rear. He blamed the Adjutant-General bitterly for never having even troubled to make a personal inspection of the ground he had chosen as a battlefield, and also for not sending men to throw down these obstructive walls while there was time to do so in safety. He himself was anxious even now to set about the task with his own men. " But as such a movement would have broken the line, the officers about him considered that the attempt would be dangerous, and he therefore did not make it."†

O'Sullivan made a jocose attempt to be consoling and conciliatory. " Never fear, my Lord," he said, " they can't come between you and the river unless they break down the walls of these two parks that are between you and them. You can't prevent them ; but I am sure they will not. My advice is that we should make a breach in this wall and set in the park Stonywood and the regiment that are behind you to take their Horse in the flank. With such a wall as this between them and those that fire on 'em, I'll answer they'll break. If they are broke the Foot will not stand. Besides, my Lord, if you march to the enemy, in case you're repulsed those same troops that you set in the Park will protect your retreat. I'd do more, my Lord. I'd set fifty men in each of these houses. I'd get the walls pierced—what we call crenelle. That will assure your retreat altogether in case of misfortune."‡

It was typical of O'Sullivan to ignore the fact that walls have

* O'Sullivan.
† Particular Account.
‡ O'Sullivan.

gates to afford admittance to the ground they enclose, and also that the farm of Culwhiniac and the two hovels beside it stood isolated in the middle of the spacious park. They could thus be by-passed with the greatest ease by any troops wishing to creep round to take the Jacobite army in the rear. Lord George had no intention of wasting troops in garrisoning them. He asked the Adjutant-General rather " huffingly " if he commanded the army ? O'Sullivan answered : " No : I only take the liberty to represent."*

Lord George, however, would listen to no more, but went off to confer with the Duke of Perth, who commanded the left wing. He soon hurried back when Lochiel sent an aide-de-camp to him with word that a large body of Argyll Militiamen had drawn away from the main body of the oncoming army with the evident intention of taking possession of the enclosed lands between the river and the Jacobite lines.

On returning to his own wing Lord George sent Ker of Graden, John Roy Stewart and O'Sullivan to examine the fields. Strangely enough, although they saw some Dragoons at the far end of the East Park of Culwhiniac, the two experienced colonels concurred in the Adjutant-General's opinion that " the river banks were so high that no Horse could come that way," and that it was impossible for them to approach the Jacobite army without first throwing down the walls.

Lord George knew that such a feat could be accomplished with ease, since the dykes were built of loose stones. His foreboding that the Dragoons were " coming to take him in the flank " was greatly increased by the report the officers brought that a party of them were already in the far corner of the East Park beside the river. O'Sullivan, though still persisting there was no danger, went off in search of the regiment of Aberdeen men commanded by Moir of Stonywood. Since it was on the extreme left of the second line Lord George was for some little time relieved of the presence of the Irishman.

On the way O'Sullivan evidently reported matters to the Prince, who sent word that the wall must be guarded. Somebody else had meanwhile suggested that it should be lined with troops—a plan warmly approved by Perth, who had ridden over from the left wing to join in the consultation. Lord George could not spare the hundred men required for such a duty ; but he ordered Lord

* O'Sullivan.

Ogilvy, whose two depleted battalions were immediately in his rear, to keep a close watch upon this danger spot, for he " doubted not that he would acquit himself as usual."* Then O'Sullivan, who had brought Stonywood and Avuchie's Regiments from the left wing to the rear of the right, was allowed to conduct a hundred of Stonywood's men into the Park " by a hollow way, so that the motion should not be seen, and post them, recommending them not to show themselves."† He also advised them to have one sentry to watch the Dragoons, and another to see that no one passed the river. Avuchie's men remained on the north side of the dyke ready to be sent into the Park if further reinforcements were required there.

It was only when the enemy were almost within cannon-shot that O'Sullivan (if his chronology of events is correct) seems to have realised that an Adjutant-General's duty was to set the army in battle array rather than to offer advice to the commander of one wing.

From right to left on the first line were the Athollmen, the Camerons, who had been behind them in the night march, the Appin Stewarts, and the Frasers, who had just marched in from the North and taken up their station by them as at Falkirk. Beyond this, to the left, everything was in a state of confusion. The rough-and-ready outflanking tactics which had procured a place on the right for the Macdonalds at Prestonpans and for the Macgregors at Falkirk, could not be put into practice at Culloden. The limited space between the Athollmen and the long stone dyke was already taken up with one of the three diminutive three-gun batteries placed in the centre and at each end of the Highland front line. But the offended Macdonalds showed the greatest reluctance to proceed farther than the centre of the line. There they were scarcely welcomed by Lord John, the commander of the centre, since the regiments allocated to that position had arrived upon the scene in good order to take up the posts assigned to them the previous day. The Duke of Perth, on the other hand, had no troops in his wing except small clan units such as the MacLeods, Grants, and others loosely attached to one or other of the Macdonald regiments.

The Macdonalds had only just moved (or had been moved) before

---

* John Cameron's Account, ' Lyon in Mourning.'
† O'Sullivan.

the Adjutant-General began his belated inspection of the disordered line. Unfortunately they had moved a great deal too far to the left —presumably they were anxious to secure the protection of a wall on the north side of the battlefield enclosing the Culloden parks. They were not protected by a bog as on the previous day. And though O'Sullivan had said a great deal to Lord George about the advantage of having walls on either flank of the army to guard against encircle-ment, he had not set the front line between these parallel dykes. Consequently the Jacobite lines were now thrown hopelessly askew. Writers who variously state that the contending armies lay three, four, or even five hundred yards apart are probably all correct in their assertions.

Trouble on the Jacobite left wing already threatened. The Duke of Perth, standing at the head of the Glengarry Regiment, heard the ominous muttering of the men behind him. Fully alive to the extreme gravity of the situation, he told the clansmen that " if they behaved with their usual valour they would make a right of the left, and that he would change his name to Macdonald."* O'Sullivan, however, did not wait long enough to foresee the impending disaster caused by his insistence that the Macdonalds should be on the left that day. Loud cries of " Close, close ! " were heard on his right. He had evidently come round to the left after a consultation with the Prince in the rear, and now that he turned to ride along the front line he was very much surprised to find gaps between the centre and the left wing.

The confusion that reigned in this quarter had nothing to do with Lord George, who was only responsible for the right wing that day —a fact overlooked by some historians of the campaign. Yet O'Sullivan reprimanded him for having placed his men too deep— six instead of the usual three or four—and complained that the gaps along the line were all his fault. Lord George would not reply to him—much to the indignation of the Irishman who strongly resented being ignored as if he had " spoke to a stone."† But having relieved his feelings in this fashion O'Sullivan hastened away to " rightify " the line by bringing up the Duke of Perth's and another regiment from the already dangerously weakened second line.

The enemy were now about six hundred paces away from the

* Chambers's ' History of the Rebellion of 1745.'
† O'Sullivan.

Prince's army. Their right wing was temporarily uncovered owing to a " piece of hollow swampy ground, which was so soft that the artillery horses sank and had to be unyoked." Soldiers could be seen unslinging their carbines and hurrying to assist in hauling the cannon to firm ground. Such a sight must have caused Charles to believe that O'Sullivan was indeed right in his assertion that Cumberland's Horse and Artillery could not operate successfully on the terrain he had chosen. He conceived that this was a heaven-sent opportunity to launch his attack. Afterwards he told John Roy Stewart that, had Lord George agreed to it, he " would have driven the enemy's front into the rear." But Inishewen stoutly maintains " 'twas no matter of surprise that Lord George was unwilling to engage with the few men that came up the hill at first—only seventeen hundred in our first line." On O'Sullivan's own showing these regiments were not all in place. Almost a third of the 6,000 men on the Prince's muster-roll were still missing, and the Prince, who stood fuming beside Lochiel, complained loudly that they were late in coming.

Rain now threatened, and a fierce gale was blowing from the north-east almost in the faces of the Jacobites. The men, who had stood for an hour or more exposed to this icy blast, were chilled as well as utterly weary before the fight began. Nor was it an exhilarating sensation to gaze upon Cumberland's imposing army. There were at least 8,000 regular soldiers and several hundred Argyll Militiamen. Six Infantry regiments made up the first line, six formed the second line, and there were three in reserve. There were " narrow intervals between them ; the two flags of each regiment rising from the centre, the officers standing at the extremities with their spontoons in their hands, and the drummers a little in advance beating their instruments."* It was a sight that must have filled with apprehension such of the Prince's officers as had had experience of regular warfare.

Whether the young Duke or his experienced generals were responsible for the disposition of the Government forces they were set in a manner best calculated to repel attack. Behind each space between the front-line regiments were two great guns ready to discharge their fire full in the faces of those who attempted to charge through these gaps. Men who had the hardihood to do so and to

* Chambers's ' History of the Rebellion of 1745.'

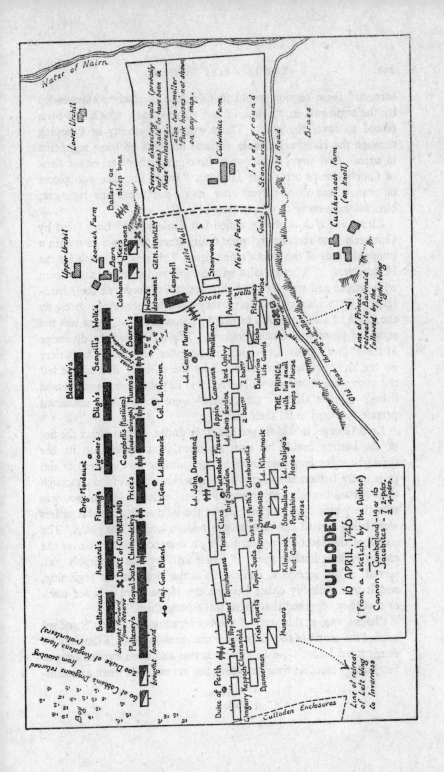

CULLODEN
16 APRIL 1746
(From a sketch by the Author)

Cannon — Cumberland — 14 or 16
Jacobites — 7 2-pdrs.
2 4-pdrs.

surround these cannon would in turn find themselves surrounded by the regiments in the second and reserve lines, which had been placed to cover the gaps. There was no possibility of sweeping through the Hanoverian ranks without breaking all these regiments in turn. And since there was a three-gun battery on either flank of Cumberland's army, the Jacobites " could not take two pieces of cannon, but three played upon them, nor break one regiment, but two were ready to supply their place."

About one o'clock the dandified but fearless Lord Bury (sent by Cumberland to reconnoitre) rode coolly across the moor to within a hundred yards of the Prince's first line. This was too much for the Highlanders. " Though faint with hunger and ready to drop down with fatigue and want of sleep they seemed to forget all their hardships. With alacrity and spirit they returned the shout given by the Duke of Cumberland's army."* Bonnets waved, there was the sound of pipes, and much shouting. There followed the discharge of the Prince's puny four- and two-pounder cannon. The battery on the right opened fire, followed by the others. But on the left the guns were " extremely ill served and ill pointed and soon ceased firing. Almost all the ' cannoneers ' were absent, and untrained private men had to fill their place."

Lord George, in addition to his other duties, had to direct the fire of the battery beside his own regiment, and it kept up its fire throughout the long cannonade. The gunners were ordered to aim principally behind the enemy's lines, where some officers through their glasses thought they perceived Cumberland. He, in fact, was so actively employed in riding about the field seeing that his orders were being carried out, that he was seldom long in one place. The sound of the Jacobite cannon was soon drowned by the roar of the enemy sixteen heavier guns. " Their artillery was admirably well served. They seemed to aim chiefly at the Horse in the beginning, and it was probably either because the Horse were a better mark or that they supposed the Prince was among them."†

Charles was, at this stage of the battle, stationed by his Standard behind the centre of the second line and surrounded by Kilmarnock's dismounted Horse Guards. Their horses had been handed over to FitzJames's men, for theirs had been lost at sea. But when a cannon-

* Kirkconnel.
† Ibid.

ball killed a led horse and a groom two hundred yards in the Prince's rear, it was deemed expedient for him to move. He took up his new position behind the right wing on a little hillock close to the north-east corner of the enclosures around Culchuinach Farm, and there he remained, guarded by sixteen of FitzJames's troopers and Balmerino's Life Guards. These Guards and the larger troop commanded by Elcho had been placed, as at Falkirk, on the right of the Reserve, the left being protected by the few remaining Hussars and Strathallan's newly raised Perthshire Horse in which Pitsligo's dwindling troop had been amalgamated. The new vantage-point was a suitable enough post from which to direct operations had the Prince been an experienced commander of well-drilled regular troops about to engage in a set battle in the usual manner of the time. But Falkirk had shown that it was a hopeless task to keep track of the whirlwind movements of Highland troops from so far back. More-over, intermittent showers of snow and sleet began to impede his view of the field.

Earlier that morning he had told his brave but simple followers that " victory depended upon a bold stroke."* But in this hour of crisis, when for the first time he was sole commander of his army, free to act exactly as he wished, his own boldness forsook him. He allowed the Highlanders " too much leisure to contemplate an enemy more than double their number,"† instead of unleashing them when their blood was high and before their instinctive horror of cannon-fire (so innocuous at Prestonpans) was renewed by the sight of the carnage taking place around them.

Never before had the young Prince been obliged to think for himself. Now his trusted advisers failed him in his hour of need. O'Sullivan knew well that when two armies were drawn up, both in a position of defence, the one with the weaker artillery must in the end be forced to charge—and he had said as much to Lord George. But he dared not risk falling out of favour by advocating a course which, in view of the odds against the Jacobites, would, in all probability, lead to disaster. Neither could old Sir Thomas, who had insisted upon a battle, give his erstwhile pupil instructions how to fight it. Hitherto their royal puppet had danced in spirited fashion to their piping. Now that they had ceased to pull the strings

* O'Sullivan.
† Kirkconnel.

he appeared incapable of movement. Uncertain of himself, and of how to act, the Prince remained for more than half an hour in a state of bewildered indecision—still clinging to the vain hope that Cumberland, with the wind at his back, would begin the attack.

Cumberland, finding his cannon rapidly thinning the Jacobite ranks without experiencing any loss in return, had no desire to charge. Under the expert supervision of Colonel Belford and his experienced gunners his cannon tore great gaps in the serried Highland lines. At the same time he made good use of the time so obligingly offered to him to strengthen his own position. The manœuvring on the Jacobite left wing was at first taken by the enemy as a feint, and later as an indication that the main attack would be launched upon their right wing. Cumberland accordingly took his stand at this supposed danger-point. From the Reserve he called up Pulteney and Battereau's Regiments to extend the right of his first and second lines, which had become outflanked when O'Sullivan stretched the Prince's first line to such unwieldy length. The Duke also summoned the Duke of Kingston's Light Horse, a volunteer force left in the rear, to guard the right flank of his first line which, unlike the second, was unprotected by the wide morass that stretched away towards Culloden House. On the left his second line extended beyond the first. He therefore ordered the furthermost regiment—Wolfe's—to move past Barrel's in the front line and draw up at the side at right angles to it. Each one of these fresh dispositions was to prove most disadvantageous to the Jacobites.

A company of Loudoun's men from across the Firth, and the two companies of Argyll Militiamen whom the Duke had spared from guarding his baggage, had stolen westward by the river—screened from view by the rising ground on which stood the farms of Upper and Lower Urchil. Between these holdings and the East Park of Culwhiniac Farm a sunken lane ran from the river to the moor where Cumberland's first line was drawn up. His regular Cavalry were posted on this side of the army in readiness to make for the outflanking movement which Lord George had expected. They consisted of 200 of Cobham's Dragoons (10th Hussars) under Lord Ancrum, and 300 of Lord Mark Kerr's Dragoons (11th Hussars) under Major-General Bland. Led by a Campbell scout, these five squadrons, commanded by General Hawley, filed down the hollow

land and entered the Culwhiniac enclosures through a breach made
by the Militiamen at the corner of the walls beside the river. They
were now making their way westwards along the farthest dyke by
the Water of Nairn. One company of Campbells was marching
northward along the inner side of the wall running parallel with
the lane. Another Campbell company, Loudoun's men, were
advancing in a slanting direction up the East Park of Culwhiniac,
supported by a squadron of Dragoons which Hawley had foolishly
allowed to be sighted by Ker and his companions, confirming Lord
George's surmise that Cumberland had indeed sent Cavalry to the
right in order to outflank the Jacobites. The Campbells entered
the West Park after beating down part of a low wall that ran up to a
point in the outer dyke between Lord George's and Lord Ogilvy's
regiments. Kirkconnel, the major of the Life Guards stationed
behind the Ogilvies, is a reliable witness of what happened in that
quarter :

> Lord George Murray seeing a squadron of the enemy's
> Dragoons and the Campbells . . . judged that they intended to
> outflank the Highlanders, or come upon the rear of the army
> when it was engaged in front. To prevent these inconveniences,
> he made Avuchie's battalion advance towards the Campbells . . .
> and . . . ordered the Guards and FitzJames's Horse quite to
> the right flank, and made them form opposite the Dragoons. . . .
> The Campbells advanced no further, and Avuchie's battalion was
> ordered to watch their motions.

It would have been a trial to seasoned troops to remain steady
under such destructive cannonading as the Prince's followers were
still enduring. The Highlanders, only partially inured to cannon-
fire, " were greatly surprised and disordered by it."* By reason of
their nearness to the enemy the Athollmen and Camerons were the
greatest sufferers ; and their commanders were obliged to stand
helplessly by, bearing as best they could the sight of this needless
slaughter. At last Lochiel sent word to Lord George that he could
not hold his clansmen in check much longer. The men were
" galled by the enemy's cannon, and were turned so impatient that
they were like to break their ranks."† Lord George sent Ker
hurrying with this intelligence to the Prince. Charles ordered an
attack. Colonel Ker conveyed the order first to the Duke of Perth,

---

* ' Scots Magazine.'
† Particular Account.

whose wing was set so much farther back. Unluckily the young MacLachlan officer despatched with a similar order to Lord George was killed by grape-shot on his way to the front line. O'Sullivan, however, came up to him with what seems an incomprehensible message " to pray him march directly upon the enemy, and . . . to have troops in the Park [to] take the Horse in flank when . . . marching upon them."*

Brigadier Stapleton, the commander of the second line, hastened up in his wake, but did not reach the right wing until after the charge began. In the centre of the first line the mackintoshes had become exasperated beyond endurance, and were quite out of Lord John's control. With a wild cry they started forward, followed by the Macleans and MacLachlans on their immediate left. Midway in their career a burst of fire from the enemy's centre and right wing caused them to swerve sharply to the right, and the Mackintoshes were, in fact, the first regiment to charge upon Cumberland's left wing. As Elcho put it : " The centre joined with the right, and in a sort of mob, without order or distinction of corps, mixed together and attacked."

Lord George went straight to his objective. But the Frasers, Stewarts, Camerons, and Athollmen whom he commanded could hardly wield their swords, so closely pressed were they between the regiments from the centre and the fatal long stone dyke. From behind its shelter 200 Campbells poured a death-dealing fire on them. So also did the men of Wolfe's Regiment and the gunners from the three-gun battery on the rising ground in the Urchil enclosures.† The Highlanders could not return this devastating fire, for, as usual, they had flung away their muskets before charging —some on this occasion without having fired a shot. Many, too, had left their targes behind them on the night march and were, in consequence, wholly unprotected from this flank attack and from the direct fire of the men of Barrel's and Munro's Regiments against which they hurled themselves.

Undeterred by the losses they were suffering on their exposed right flank, the men of Atholl, Appin and Lochaber swept in upon

---

    * O'Sullivan's ' Narrative.'

    † A crowd of beggars had collected there ready to swoop down upon the battlefield when the fight was ended and rifle the bodies of the slain. These beggars were among the forty persons burned to death in the Leanach barn, where many wounded officers and men had sought shelter. It was burned by Cumberland's orders.

Barrel's Grenadiers*—by a most unlucky chance the very men who had withstood the Highlanders at Falkirk. Posted on the extreme left of Cumberland's first line, they were numerically one of the weakest of his regiments (owing to the losses sustained in that engagement). But they were undoubtedly his steadiest. Though " a little staggered " by the shock of attack by four regiments at once, the " Old Tangiereers " (as these veterans who had seen so much foreign service were nicknamed) behaved with great bravery, and received their adversaries on the point of the bayonet. They had, moreover, been trained in a new method of using this weapon. Instead of having his blade deflected by the targe of the Highlander who attacked him, each soldier was instructed to thrust at the sword-arm of the man on his assailant's left—unprotected from so unexpected a blow.

The Atholl Brigade charged through the gap between Barrel's and Munro's Regiments in the face of the two great guns—of which they made themselves masters, but they found themselves confronting the centre of Sempill's Regiment which, with Bligh's, had been brought forward by General Huske, the commander of the second line. These were soon reinforced by many of Barrel's men, who, pushed aside by the violence of the Highland onslaught, had dashed to the rear to assist their comrades there. The steady fire from Sempill's men, and Bligh's, who were posted on their right, played havoc among the vanguard of the Highlanders and caused them to recoil. But only for an instant. " Maddened by despair, and utterly regardless of their lives, they rushed on the enemy whom they felt, but could not see, amid the cloud of smoke in which their assailants were buried. . . . All that courage, all that despair could do, was done. . . . Almost every man in their front ranks, Chief, and gentleman, fell before the deadly weapons which they braved."† Those who flung themselves upon these fresh unbroken regiments, in an heroic but desperate attempt to penetrate the enemy's second line, died as they fell. Their comrades were forced back among the front-line Infantrymen. But the men of Barrel's Regiment, and that half of Munro's which had been attacked, recovered from their disorder and closed their ranks upon the

---

* The Appin Banner (one of the few saved from Culloden) was carried to Edinburgh Castle by Lord George's descendant Lord James Stewart Murray, later ninth Duke of Atholl. It was placed in the Museum beside that of Barrel's Regiment.

† Chambers's ' History of the Rebellion of 1745.'

retreating clansmen. The Highlanders fought desperately to hack their way back to their own second line, but in doing so they sustained cruel losses, for Munro's soldiers gave no quarter. Half the Government's three hundred casualties occurred among Barrel's and Munro's regiments. But it was claimed afterwards by the survivors that most of them had dispatched two Highlanders a-piece with their spontoons and bayonets.

Lord George had " attacked at the head of his Athollmen with all the bravery imaginable."* But when he had passed the cannon his horse reared and plunged so violently that, thinking it was wounded, he quitted his stirrups and was thrown. Once again he lost his bonnet and wig. Covered with blood and dirt, and with several bayonet cuts in his coat, he fought his way back through the seething Infantrymen, and hurried to bring up reinforcements to his sorely pressed men.

The Prince had not sent forward his second line to assist the first. The reason was all too apparent, and Lord George found to his dismay that the whole Jacobite army stood in danger of encirclement. The Campbells had come into the adjacent park " without receiving one shot from the two battalions that were placed there to observe their motions." They were now firing upon the Ogilvies, who, fortunately for themselves, were at too great a distance to suffer serious casualties. Far more alarming was the sight of the Dragoons at the west end of the park preparing to file through a gate into another sunken lane; for this led towards the hillock where the Prince had taken up his stand.

From this eminence Charles had a better opportunity than anybody else of gauging what was taking place in the enclosures, but after all the messages he had sent to Lord George to spare men to guard the dyke, he despatched no reinforcements to those already there, and they were slaughtered almost to a man by the Campbells. As at Falkirk, he displayed no aptitude for leadership and, as Elcho scornfully records, he seems to have lost his head. Instead of " carrying out these manœuvres which he wished to see executed,"† he remained inert, irresolute and immobile, wholly incapable of

---

* ' The Battle of Culloden,' by Colonel Ker of Graden.
  † Chevalier Johnstone.

judging where the regiments in the reserve could best be sent.
Fortunately Stapleton, as ever, acted with sound good sense, and
ordered a battalion of Lord Lewis Gordon's Regiment to support
the Ogilvies. But it was owing to Lord George's foresight in
having sent FitzJames's Horse and Elcho's Life Guards to guard
the right flank that the entire Jacobite army was saved from
encirclement.

Bards have sung (and rightly so) of the valour of the clansmen who
so heroically, and so vainly, flung themselves upon the ranks of the
Government forces. But not one historian of the battle has ever
thought to bestow a word of praise upon the gallant Irishman,
Robert O'Shea, and Lord Elcho, who prevented Cumberland's
Cavalry from cutting off the Jacobites' retreat. The commander of
FitzJames's Horse had but 60 men with him, and Lord Elcho fewer,
for his much diminished troop had never consisted of more than
100 gentlemen troopers—and many of them had asked that day to
serve as volunteers with the Atholl Brigade.* With horses as worn-
out and half-starved as were the men, it required courage to go
forward and attack between four and five hundred well mounted,
well trained regular troopers. But they unhesitatingly advanced
upon them as they streamed into the lane. The steep banks prevented them from charging upon one another and, providentially,
Cumberland's Dragoons seemed averse to spilling their own blood
that day—and, in fact, lost only eight men. Nevertheless they
inflicted many losses upon the small but gallant force which now
withstood them, aided only by Avuchie's men—for the Prince
neither spared his own Guards nor sent Bagot's Hussars or Strathallan's Horse to their relief.

Lord George could not make his usual attempt to rectify the
mistakes made by his royal commander. His immediate task was
to bring up reinforcements to his own sorely pressed men. With
Glenbucket's Regiment and the remaining battalion of Lord Lewis's
Regiment he hurried forward to their support. But nothing
could be done. By this time all was lost. In the desperate
contest between broadsword and bayonet the bayonet had for the
first time won the day. Unable to sustain their unequal conflict
with adversaries so superior in numbers and in arms—in everything

* The Jacobite Cavalry now numbered less than 200.

but courage—the Highlanders were now in full retreat to their own lines.

Modern writers have drawn imaginary pictures of offended Macdonalds in the left wing standing immovable, jabbing at the heather with their swords. In fact they only formed a part of that wing, and their regiments were so weakened by recent desertion that had they remained immobile it would have made no difference to the outcome of the battle. But Lord George, O'Sullivan, Home, and Cumberland in his official account of the engagement, have all left on record that the clansmen of the left wing marched (though they did not charge) upon the foe. " While the Highland regiments on the right and centre . . . made their attack, those on the left, consisting of Roy Stewart's Regiment, the Farquharsons, and the three Macdonald Regiments, did not advance at the same time or in the same manner. They came so near enough to the English troops to draw some fire upon themselves, which they returned with a general discharge."* Three times during their advance they paused and seemed about to retire, halted by the " regular and nourished fire " levelled upon them by the men of the three first ranks of Cumberland's front-line regiments, the first kneeling, the second crouching, and the third standing upright. These Infantrymen's muskets seemed to be forever at their shoulders ; for, like the Artillerymen, they were supplied with packed ammunition which facilitated rapid firing. When about a hundred paces from the enemy, a rift in the cloud of smoke revealed to the advancing Highlanders that their comrades on the right were in full retreat, and that a wide undefended strip of moor lay between the two wings. They, too, began to retreat. As they did so sixty of Cobham's Dragoons, who had returned from scouting and stationed themselves beside Pulteney's Regiment, darted off in pursuit of them, followed by two hundred of the Duke of Kingston's volunteer Cavalrymen from Nottinghamshire. The Macdonald officers made a gallant charge upon the oncoming foe, and in doing so most of them met their death.

Meanwhile, on the right wing, for ten vital minutes Lord Elcho and Colonel O'Shea, aided by the gallant Gordon of Avuchie and his men, prevented the Dragoons from breaking out from the lane and galloping out upon the moor to cut off the main body of the

* Home's ' History of the Rebellion of 1745.'

LORD GEORGE'S FUNERAL HATCHMENT

(Description overleaf)

[*Facing p.* 240

LORD GEORGE MURRAY'S HATCHMENT

The Funeral Hatchment of Lord George Murray, hanging over his memorial in the church at Medemblik, Holland, where he was buried.

The Hatchment is of special local interest; for it includes the Royal Arms of the Netherlands, indicating Lord George's descent from William the Silent, Prince of Orange, founder of the Dutch Republic.

Between four skulls with crossed bones (*memento mori*) on a black background spattered with tear-drops and inscribed with his initials LGM, are Lord George's Arms (the Atholl quarterings personally differenced by a crowned Douglas heart taken from the shield of his mother's family) and the ducal supporters to which he was next heir, but with the old Tullibardine motto TOUT PREST and peacock's-head crest. These are surrounded by what are intended to be his *seize-quartiers* : the Arms of the sixteen families to which his great-great-grandparents belonged. But in error, instead of the eight shields of his mother's side, the eight shields of his maternal grandmother's side have been given, and Villiers has been repeated in place of the Arms of Sir George Villier's wife, Mary Beaumont, Countess of Buckingham.

Correctly, the families of Lord George's great-great-grandparents were : 1. Murray, Duke of Atholl. 2. Stewart, Earl of Atholl. 3. Campbell of Glenorchy (later Earl of Breadalbane). 4. Lord Sinclair. 5. Stanley, Earl of Derby. 6. De Vere, Earl of Oxford. 7. La Tremoille, Duc de Thouars. 8. Nassau, Prince of Orange. 9. The Red Douglas, Earl of Angus (later Duke of Douglas). 10. Lord Oliphant. 11. The Cock o' the North, Marquis of Huntly (later Duke of Gordon). 12. Stuart d'Aubigny, Duke of Lennox. 13. Hamilton, Duke of Hamilton. 14. Cunningham, Earl of Glencairn. 15. Feilding, Earl of Denbigh. 16. Villiers (later Duke of Buckingham).

One generation further back, Lord George's ancestry included the great French houses of Bourbon and Montmorency, and the talented English stock of Cecil, Lord Burghley ; while through the Stanleys, Lord George descended from King Henry VII, and thus from the vigorous Tudor and Plantagenet Blood Royal.

[*Facing p.* 241

Jacobite army.* When at last they were forced to give way before the onslaught of the two Regiments of Dragoons, FitzJames's Horse reformed in a solid square to protect the retreating Highlanders. But they had hardly done so when O'Sullivan, who had remained to the rear of the left wing, rushed up to O'Shea, crying out : " All is going to pot ! You can be of no great succour. Before the general rout, which will be soon, seize upon the Prince and take him off ! "

Back they galloped to the Prince who had been forced to move off in the direction of Balvraid. Old Sir Thomas was agitatedly begging him to quit the field—a course repellent to the Prince who would have liked to make some attempt to rally his men. O'Sullivan used more forceful methods ; he seized the royal bridal rein and turned the horse's head, and dragged him away. It was perhaps fitting that Charles was led from the battlefield by these two evil geniuses whose pernicious advice had brought about this fearful carnage among his faithful Scottish followers.

Because the Government Infantry regiments, records Elcho, " continued to pursue in order of battle, always firing their cannon and platoons in advancing, there was not so many people killed or taken as there would have been had they detached corps to pursue." Lord George's and Lochiel's men, owing to their exposure to flank fire, suffered more severely than other regiments, for the whole

---

* Cumberland, the soldier, seems to have had a clearer perception than the historians of how Elcho's stand against his Dragoons prevented a general massacre of the Highland and Lowland troops. In the unpublished part of Elcho's ' Journal,' when referring to his efforts to obtain a pardon, Elcho attributes his failure to the animosity of the Duke :

" I learned since then that the Duke of Cumberland had a great hatred of me : and that as he wished to discredit with the nation all those who were joined to Prince Stuart, treating them as of no account in point of birth, others as ruined gentlemen, and being unable to say such things of me, he had given out that I had counselled the Prince to cut off the thumbs of all the soldiers that fell into their hands to prevent them serving against him any more. This atrocious lie, which I had never given any occasion for by my words, was generally believed in Great Britain.

" An anecdote that one of my relatives recounted to me will show to what a pitch the Duke of Cumberland carried his animosity against me. An English officer named Crou, whose life I had had the happiness to save at the Battle of Falkirk, having heard his brother officers say that I was a very cruel man, took my part and declared that but for me he would have been slaughtered at the Battle of Falkirk. Some time afterwards, this officer Crou received a letter from the Duke of Cumberland wherein the Duke threatened to cashier him if ever he thought proper to take my side again."

Q

length of the interminable dykes seemed to be lined with their hereditary foes, a party of whom emerged from the park and came to grips with the Camerons. But though he lost more men on the retreat than when advancing, Lord George was able to weld the shattered right wing with the reserve regiments he had with him and to march them off the field in good order. The men of Lord Lewis Gordon's other battalion had done useful work in holding up the soldiers who had attempted to come out of the enclosures. Lord Ogilvy's almost unbroken regiment, during the early stages of the retreat, turned about several times and held up Hawley's Dragoons who, Kirkconnel records with scorn, " made no attack where there was any body of the Prince's men together, but contented themselves with sabering such unfortunate people as came in their way single and disarmed."

The soldiers in the French service, who had no need to fear being taken prisoners, remained for long on the battlefield, and the Irish Piquets sustained grievous casualties and lost their commander, Brigadier Stapleton, while bringing off some of the Macdonalds who were almost surrounded by Kingston's Horse. The Royal Scots also faced about and held the oncoming Horse at bay while the Macdonalds, at last clear of the Culloden enclosures which had impeded their progress, took the road to Inverness. Not many reached their goal, for they were pursued to within a mile of the town by Cumberland's Cavalry and slaughtered upon the road. Three of the Duke of Kingston's Nottingham volunteers, all butchers by profession, received special praise from Cumberland for the services they performed that day.

Thus ended the fatal Battle of Culloden, the first and last occasion on which the Prince had supreme command of his army. He, who so longed for martial glory, had presented that notoriously bad general, Cumberland, with the only victory of his career. His brave and trusty Highlanders " had done all that their system of warfare had taught them, and all their natural strength had enabled them to perform ; but they had found this vain." All was lost. The Stuarts' Cause lay in ruins, and Charles's hopes were forever shattered.

CHAPTER XIV

THE AFTERMATH

THE apparently well-informed Whig historian previously quoted states clearly that Lord George " was the first and last on the field " —contradicting Sir John Macdonald and O'Sullivan's assertions that he and his were the first to flee. " He resolutely faced the greatest danger ; he commanded that wing that made the only (and indeed desperate) effort, and had he been seconded the victory should have been dearly purchased,"* adds the Whig writer. His testimony is confirmed by Colonel Ker, who wrote that, had the public " been witnesses of his zeal and activity from the time he joined in that affair to the last of it—his exposing his person wherever occasion offered, and in particular at the Battle of Culloden, where he went on with the first and came not off till the last, they would have done him more justice."†

After breaking off the engagement Lord George led the remnants of the right and centre lines to Balvraid, and on for another four miles to the Ford of Faillie, where they could strike across into the wild hilly country to the south. At this spot, where Wade's military bridge spanned the Water of Nairn, the Prince had already made his crossing, continuing on a westerly course. He paused a little distance beyond the bridge to hold a consultation with his favoured advisers. Lord Elcho describes the scene :

> As he had taken it into his head that he had been betrayed and particularly by Lord George Murray, he seemed very diffident of everybody except the Irish officers. . . . He neither spoke to any of the Scots officers present, or enquired after any of the absent (nor at any of the preceding battles he never enquired after any of the wounded officers). He appeared very uneasy as long as the Scots were about him, and in a short time ordered them all to go to Ruthven of Badenoch, where he would send them orders. . . . He was so prepossessed against the Scots, that he was afraid they would give him up to make their peace with the Government ; for some of the Irish were at pains

* ' History of the Rebellion in the Years 1745 and 1746.'
† ' The Battle of Culloden,' by Colonel Ker of Graden.

to relate to him in very strong terms, how the Scots had already sold his great-grandfather to the English. As he was naturally of a suspicious temper it was no difficult matter to persuade him of it. He always believed it until the fidelity the Highlanders showed him during the long time he was hid in their country convinced him and everybody else to the contrary.

The Prince had, however, ordered Æneas Macdonald, the Paris banker who had sailed with him to Scotland, to distribute among his needy followers 500 Spanish pistoles, which had been left with his equipage at Ruthven. Mr Macdonald and the mounted officers and gentlemen volunteers, who had accompanied their master thus far on his flight, waited by the river to tell Lord George of the rendezvous. Together, with heavy hearts, they then set out upon the road to Ruthven—the place where thirty years before Mar's army had gathered before its final dispersal.

Most of the officers and men slept that night upon the heather. Next morning, at Dalmagarry by the shores of Loch Moy, they fell in with Cluny and between three and four hundred of his clansmen. On their way to Culloden they had been told of the disaster by some of FitzJames's troopers. Lord George " ordered the Macphersons to remain till the rear of the defeated army came up, which might take about two hours, and then to cover their retreat to Badenoch with the utmost attention, as it was doubtful what steps the Grants might take. The main body of the army marched to Ruthven that night, but the ' nobility ' and some horsemen lodged all night at Aviemore guarded by Cluny's Regiment."*

By the loch Lord George also met his brother William, who had been lying ill in Inverness, unfit to fight in the battle. On hearing of its outcome he had hurried in the direction taken by the Prince, anxious to share his hazards. But on being told that his master desired no followers to impede his movements or to draw attention to his whereabouts, the Duke had sadly turned aside and with Lord Nairne had spent the night at Corrybrough House. Lord Nairne had with him his son and twelve survivors of his regiment. It had suffered more than any other. " Robert Stewart of Killiechassie, who commanded the right flank company of the battalion on the right, consisting of thirty-four men, stated that only himself and three men came off."† Nairne's brother, Robert Mercer, had been shot

* General Stewart of Garth's Papers.
† Ibid.

through the head during the charge, and his son, a mere child in years, was also thought to be among the slain, as was their cousin, Lord Strathallan.

When they all reached Ruthven Lord George sent out patrols to guard the approaches to Badenoch. He also despatched an aide-de-camp to tell the Prince that a great part of his army was assembled there. According to James Johnstone, some of the younger officers were eager to carry on the campaign. So, too, was Lord Elcho, who believed that " if only things were properly directed " the Highlanders could still be rallied, though if the Prince " should go into hiding or, worse still, leave the island, every man would think of himself and provide for his own safety."*

Elcho had remained at his master's side after FitzJames's troopers had turned back to surrender to the Government forces, as the Royal Scots had done, and the Irish Piquets too, after their gallant commander Walter Stapleton had received his death-wound. The Prince's other companions were his Secretary, Hay, his aide-de-camp, MacLeod, his confessor, Macdonald (an officer in one of the Macdonald regiments), the inevitable O'Sullivan, and Sir Thomas Sheridan, who was accompanied by his nephew Michael. Sir John Macdonald was not among them. He chose to give himself up rather than face the discomforts and dangers of a flight to the Highlands which he so detested.

The fugitive's first halt was at Gortuleg, where the aged Lord Lovat was then residing. The Jesuit Father, Guilio Cesare Cordara, gives a vivid account of the scene that took place when the young commander of the Life Guards made his impassioned appeal to the Prince not to fly to France in the elusive hope of obtaining French troops with which to renew hostilities :

> " If only Your Royal Highness will listen to me, no one today shall persuade you either to fly or conceal yourself. Do not act in such a way that so many valiant men ready to lay down their lives for you should look in vain for their beloved Prince and Captain. Betake yourself at once to the mountains of Lochaber and Badenoch. There I hope we shall soon be able to collect a sufficient force, which we shall be ready to lead wherever you may order."

He was speaking in this fine way when Sheridan, either from

* ' The Expedition of Charles Edward Stuart,' by the Jesuit Guilio Cordara.

some secret grudge or from his natural sourness, or—and I think
this is nearer the truth—from weariness at all they had endured,
burst forth and reproached Elcho with his poor defence of the
Spey :—

" Captain Elcho, it is useless now to play the undaunted hero ;
you ought to have done so elsewhere. Now we have been ruined
by you, we must bear patiently that which cannot be remedied
and adapt ourselves to what needs must be. You must think the
enemy a fool to be willing to leave us time to get the army together
again. On the contrary, from every side he is pursuing us with
his victorious troops. He is closing the passes. Victory flows
unrestrainedly, and possibly while we are deliberating about the
remedy, the enemy will surprise us and finish it. And suppose—
though I have no hope of it—that he is slack and gives us time,
shall we, who, with eight thousand brave and well-trained soldiers,
suffered defeat like ours, with much less people and more timid
recruits, without money, or arms, or food, face the conqueror ?
Unless I am entirely mistaken, I can see no help for it except that
the Prince should get off to the Continent and reserve himself for
better times, if only they will come."

This bitter speech exasperated Elcho beyond all measure, as
he saw that the unhappy issue of the war was imputed to him.
Flushed with anger and indignation, he declared that he had been
insulted by this impudent villain and would have his revenge.

The Prince intervened, and by praying them not to ruin the
common cause by a private quarrel, put a stop to the nascent
discord and gave orders for others to speak freely their opinion.

During Sheridan's speech Sullivan appeared : he added his
reasons for hastening the departure for the Continent. Lovat at
first seemed to hold with Elcho ; then after a better consideration
of the circumstances, was undecided and said nothing. The
others, because in evil fortune no advice is safe, thought it better
to listen than give counsel which might turn out ill. But not one
of them declined to do whatever he could for the safety of the
Prince. In this alone all agreed.*

Although he planned to make for the coast that very night, the
Prince allowed his aide-de-camp, Sawnie MacLeod, to write to
Cluny :

DEAR SIR,—You have [heard] no doubt ere now of the ruffle
we met with this forenoon. We have suffered a good deal ; but

* Sir Walter Scott's story of Elcho's open quarrel with the Prince is
without foundation. He knew a nephew of Elcho who late in life probably
gave muddled and unreliable versions of stories such as the above which he
had heard second-hand in his youth.

hope we shall soon pay Cumberland in his own coin. We are to review tomorrow at Fort Augustus, the Frasers, Camerons, Stewarts, Clanranald's and Keppoch's people. His R.H. expects your people will be with us at furthest Friday morning. Dispatch is the more necessary that His Highness has something in view which will make ample amends for this day's ruffle. I am, Dear Sir, Yours, etc.

GORTULEG, 16th April, 9 at night.

We have sent an express to Lord Cromartie, Glengyle, and Barisdale, to join us by Beauly. For God's sake make haste to join us ; and bring with you all the people can possibly be got together. Take care in particular of Lumisden and Sheridan, as they carry with them the sinews of war.*

Michael Sheridan, who brought the letter, seems to have let out the fact that the Prince was by now on his way to Glengarry. For on the back of it Lord George wrote : " Mr McLeod's letter seems to be a state of politicks I do not comprehend."

It was undoubtedly the opinion of a great number of officers that their master had ordered rendezvous at both Ruthven and Fort Augustus for the purpose of deceiving Cumberland as to his whereabouts, and thus saving himself from pursuit. Elcho bears witness that those whom he met on the western seaboard were aghast at Charles's desertion of his troops, and were " surprised that he had not acquainted any of them of it, or so much as ever wrote to thank them for any of the services they had rendered him. The commonalty were enraged because he used always to tell them he would never abandon them while two of them would stand by him."

But the gentlemen at Ruthven had yet more cause for indignation when they learned that their royal leader, finding himself pinched for money (" he had only one shirt on his back "),† had apparently sent the young Irishman to bring him all the money he had left with his equipage at Ruthven. His own wants had evidently made him regret the instructions he had given to Æneas Macdonald to distribute money to his followers. " It is a very hard case," protested Lord George, " that the Prince carries away the money while so many gentlemen who have sacrificed their fortunes for him are

* Jacobite Correspondence of the Atholl Family.
† O'Sullivan.

starving. Damn it! If I had ten guineas in the world I'd with all my heart and soul share it with them."*

It was then that, filled with burning indignation, he wrote the well-known letter to the Prince:

RUTHVEN IN BADENOCH, 1st *April* 1746.

May it please your Royal Highness,

As no person in the Kingdom ventured more frankly in the Cause than myself, and that nobody had more at stake, and in some respect not so much, I cannot but be deeply affected at our late loss and present situation. But I declare that next to the safety of your R.H. person, the loss of the Cause, with the present unhappy situation of my countrymen, is the only thing grieves me. For I thank God I have resolution to bear with my own and family's ruin without a grudge.

I hope, Sir, you will upon this occasion pardon me if I mention some truths which most of the gentlemen of our army seemed sensible of.

It was surely wrong to set up the Royal Standard without having positive assurance from his most Christian Majesty that he would assist you with all his might, and as your Royal Family lost the Crown of these Realms by their adherence to France, the world did (and had reason to) expect that H.M.C.M. would lay hold of the first favourable opportunity to do his utmost to restore your august family. As for what regards the management of your army, we were all fully convinced that Mr O'Sullivan, whom your R.H. trusted with the most essential things in regard to your operations, was exceedingly unfit for it, and committed gross blunders on many occasions. He, whose business it was, did not so much as visit the ground where we were to draw up in line of battle. And it was a fatal error yesterday to allow the enemy so fair a field for their horse and cannon, and those walls to the left, which made it impossible for our right to break them, and we were exposed both their front and flank fire. Colonel Ker can testify that I urged Mr O'Sullivan to take the ground on the south side of the Water of Nairn, which was strong ground, and very favourable for Highlanders, and which Brigadier Stapleton and Colonel Ker had visited the day before at my desire. In short never was more improper ground for High-landers than that where we fought. Our Athollmen and others on the right lost half their officers and men. Happy had it been for us that Mr O'Sullivan had never got any other charge or

* O'Sullivan.

office in our army than the care of the baggage and equipages, which I am told he had been brought up to and understood. For my own part, I never see'd him in time of action, neither at Gladsmuir, Falkirk, nor this last. The want of provisions was another misfortune which had the most fatal consequences. Mr Hay, who your R.H. trusted with the principal direction and superintendency of them things of late (and without whose orders not a boll of meal or one farthing of money was to be delivered), has served your R.H. most egregious ill ; when I told him of the consequence of provisions, he said it was ordered, the thing was done, it would be got, &c. But your R.H. knows the strait we were in. Had this gentleman done his duty, which by the trust reposed in him your R.H. had reason to expect, our ruin might have been probably prevented. The last three days (which were so critical) our army was starved, and this was a great cause of our night march proving abortive, when we possibly might have surprised the enemy and defeat them at Nairn, but for want of provisions a third of our army was scattered, and went to Inverness and other places, and those who did march went so slow that precious time was lost. The next day, the fatal day, if we had got plenty of provisions, we might have not only crossed the Water of Nairn, but by the strength of our position made it so dangerous for the enemy to have attacked us, that probably they would not have ventured to have done it, and by that means the rest of our army would have had time to have joined us, and we could have had it in our power to have attacked them night or day when we pleased.

Mr Hay and Mr O'Sullivan had rendered themselves so odious to all the army that they were resolved to have applied to your R.H. for redress if they had had time before the battle. As for my part, I never had any particular discussion with either of them ; but this much I will venture to say, had our field of battle been right choice, and if we had got plenty of provisions, in all human probability we would have done by the enemy as they have unhappily done by us.

Your R.H. knows I had no design to have continued in the army, even if things had succeeded, gladly would I have laid down my commission, particularly lately when I returned from Atholl, but my friends told me, and persuaded me, that it would be a prejudice to the Cause at that juncture. I hope your R.H. will now accept of my demission, and whatever commands you have for me in any other station you will please honour me with them, being with great zeal, Sir,

Your R.H.s most Dutiful and Faithful Humble Servant,

GEORGE MURRAY.

> I have desired Mr Sheridan to leave £500 of the money he has
> with him with Cluny, for the use of many who are in want. We
> will wait for your R.H.'s directions for that and other things.*

Hunter of Burnside and a number of officers, equally indignant on
hearing that the Prince had taken for his own use money owing to
his unpaid and starving men, wished to set out in immediate pursuit
of his emissary. But Lord George told them " that he was well
mounted, and that they would not overtake him."† Had they done
so, Charles might never have received Lord George's letter, which
increased his dislike of him a thousandfold.

To have heaped reproaches upon a fallen Prince is described as
an unworthy action by many commentators, who never pause to
reflect upon the feelings of a commander who had lost half the men
of his three regiments—victims of the obstinate folly of a Prince
who lacked the rudiments of military knowledge. Lord George
had had nineteen officers killed and four wounded—men who were
his friends, as were also the humbler followers, who at his call had
left their homes to die so needlessly and uselessly upon the fatal
field of Culloden. Nor did Charles evince the slightest remorse
for the havoc wrought by his insistence upon fighting a battle—
and upon such ground. He did not even hasten to send instructions
to his three Generals at Ruthven who, in great perplexity, were
awaiting his commands. They had with them 1,500 men—not
2,000 or 3,000 as has been often stated. The Macpherson and
Ogilvy Regiments were intact, but the rest of the Highlanders at
Ruthven were leaderless men from broken regiments. Except for
Cluny and Ardshiel (who had lost seventeen officers and an unbelievable number of his 250 Appin men) " the Chiefs were a-missing."
Lochiel was wounded in both ankles ; and Keppoch, that other
flawless model of a Highland Chief, had fallen with his brother
Donald in a last brave charge against the oncoming Hanoverian
Cavalry. Perth, whose valiant spirit alone had enabled him to carry
out his duties during the last few weeks, was within three weeks of
his death. Even he, brave and self-sacrificing as he was, could do
no more.

Before the Battle of Culloden Lord George had maintained that,
if an engagement was avoided, the Highlanders " could have made

---

* Atholl Chronicles.
† O'Sullivan.

a summer campaign without risk of any misfortune; they could have marched through the hills . . . by ways that regular troops could not have followed . . . and might have fallen upon the enemy when least expected."* But the chance of carrying on guerilla warfare had been lost by the Prince's stubborn refusal to send to the High-lands the provisions and ammunition which his enemies had now seized in Inverness. " Besides our defeat, there was neither money nor provisions to give, so no hopes were left," the General wrote sadly in his ' Marches of the Highland Army.'

The writer of a pamphlet printed soon after the battle accused Lord George of anxiety to get meal and to hold out in order to obtain terms. His anonymous defender, who had evidently been at Ruthven, waxed indignant over such an accusation. He wrote :

> He indeed sent Cluny to Lochiel who was lying wounded at two miles distance to know what he proposed to do. Everybody agreed that things were desperate. As it was known the Prince had past Fort Augustus without stopping and had sent away all the Scots who had attended him, and was gone a very different road from that which would have led him amongst his own troops, it was evident he had no thought of heading his men any more.
>
> Lord George Murray was perhaps the only man that could never expect terms. It was the third time he had taken up arms against the House of Hanover. And it's well known they were more exasperate at him than all the others put together.

Even such faithful admirers of the Prince as John Roy Stewart, who had expected every hour to hear from him, began to say that " it was high time for every one of them to do the best he could for himself." Two days after they had assembled at Ruthven a message did arrive from their master. " Let every man seek his safety in the best way he can," was the curt command brought to them by his aide-de-camp MacLeod. The order was read out to the officers and men by Lord George Murray and Lord John Drummond.

The Duke of Atholl, Lord George and Lord Nairne accompanied the vast body of men who made their way to Perthshire. There they parted and went their separate ways. Lord Nairne procured a chaise in which to convey his invalid brother-in-law, Robertson

* Particular Account.
† Unpublished letter at Blair Castle.

of Drumachine, and the now frail Lord Pitsligo to a hiding-place
in Glenshee. Duke William, accompanied by the Prince's lost and
forlorn Italian valet, decided to make for the coast in the hope of
procuring a passage to the Isle of Man—a possession of the Atholl
family where fugitives from English laws were afforded sanctuary.

One of Lord Glenorchy's spies reported having seen the Duke
in Glendochart " skulking miserably in a little house." Another
met " Lord George with only two with him, retiring to the hills."*
He was said to have been seen at Rannoch and near Castle Menzies
(an unlikely place as it was held by Government troops). Others
thought they had seen him in Edinburgh. There was probably
more truth in the report of secret visits to his home. A contemporary
commentator of events expressed the general surprise that for many
months after the dispersal of the Jacobite army nothing was heard
about the General who had commanded it. Lord George never
revealed where he had lain hidden—for fear of implicating those
who had befriended him. But thirty years after his death an aged
Highlander wrote to Lord George's son, General James Murray,
telling how he had carried his father's sword, belt, and plaid to
Tullibardine when he retreated to Glenartney.

Unlike most people of his day, Lord George had a true appreciation
of scenery—a waterfall, a raging torrent, or a snow-clad mountain
awakened in him the poetic feeling inherent in his family. Both he
and his eldest brother had always felt the need of occasional spells
of " retiredness " in the country; and on many of his sporting
trips to the Highlands Lord George's love of sport had given way
to love of meditation. At such times he was apt to indulge in
introspection. Conscious now of a tendency to imagine slights
where none were intended, he seems to have suspected that he had
magnified his recent rebuffs, and to have believed that the Prince's
actions, as William had always said of those of their brother James,
were occasioned by his having fallen into bad hands. Now that the
din of battle was over, and for the first time for many months he
had time to think of anything beyond the pressing needs of the
moment, he was, apparently, seized with a morbid conviction that
during that time of stress his own manner towards his sovereign's
son had been brusque, impatient, and lacking in respect. Ever
ready to acknowledge his faults, he now frequently expressed

* Marnore MS.

" concern and regret that he had been too often guilty of contradicting and thwarting the Prince in the measures he proposed."*

Lord George remained in hiding for eight months—exactly the same period as after the defeat at Glenshiel. Then he and his servant had only one book between them—a Bible : now he was close enough to his home to be supplied with books from the well-stocked library at Tullibardine. The study of heraldry, architecture, astronomy, Egyptology, and the history of his own and other countries must have helped to beguile his hours of solitude, and also to fill in the gaps of his early education. Best of all he loved the works of Marcus Aurelius and Montaigne. Even in the days of his early exile he had been something of a philosopher, firmly believing that all was ordered for the best ; although, as he grimly commented, it was sometimes extremely difficult to see it. As he told his wife : " To expect evil often softens the weight when it happens."† He was therefore less crushed than many other Jacobites by the disaster that had overtaken the Cause.

Lord George had need of all his philosophy when he heard of the fate of friends who had shared his perils. The Duke of Perth died on board the ship that bore Lord Elcho, Lord John Drummond, Kirkconnel, and other fugitives to safety. Cluny and Ardshiel skulked in their own country ; Lord Ogilvy and James Johnstone hid in Angus, the one in Glen Clova and the other in Glenprosen, until they eventually made their way to France and obtained commissions in the French army. Lord George's cousins, Lord Nairne, Oliphant of Gask and their sons also escaped abroad, as did their nephew the new Lord Strathallan. But Duke William was less fortunate, for he fell into the Government's clutches before reaching the coast. The hardships he endured on the voyage to London sapped what little strength remained in him. He died three weeks after entering the Tower, where his gentleness and sweetness of character won him the regard of grim old General Williamson, who proved so harsh a jailer to the other Jacobites. Lord Kilmarnock and Lord Balermino, captured at Culloden, both laid down their lives on Tower Hill.

The hearts of all loyal Jacobites were riven with anxiety for the safety of the Prince who roamed, homeless and hunted, through the Highlands and Islands. Charles's hairbreadth escapes and adven-

* ' The Lyon in Mourning.'
† Unpublished letter at Blair Castle.

tures shed a glamour of romance about his name which, fortunately for him, two men who well knew the weakness of his character did nothing to dispel when they set down the events of the campaign. His Secretary, Broughton, remained silent out of affection for him. And his Lieutenant-General, Lord George, out of love for his royal father and loyalty to the Cause, did not inform the world of what he had suffered from the moods, ill-humour, and secretiveness of his capricious young commander. What Lord George said about the Prince he had said straightforwardly and to his face, and His Royal Highness had not liked it. But in his writings he set down nothing about him but what he would have said (and probably did say) to the King himself—namely, that the Prince was bold to the verge of rashness. In his notes for a projected history of the Rising, presumably jotted down soon after Culloden, he wrote with less restraint. But when three years later he compiled from them his ' Marches of the Highland Army,' his bitterness had lessened. He described events without dipping too deeply into the causes of the failures and disasters ; and he purposely omitted harsh things that he had said of Sheridan, who had died broken-hearted after being reproached by King James for having encouraged the Prince to embark upon an adventure that cost the lives of so many valiant men.

After long months of anxiety there came the news that on 20th September a ship had borne the royal fugitive back to France. On 16th December Lord George also took his last farewell of his beloved native land. On Christmas Day he landed in Holland.

When he had left that country twenty-six years before his one grief had been that he had not the happiness of seeing his King before he left for home. But he was no longer " wandering about the world as the most miserable strolling vagabond,"* as during his earlier exile. His wife had been able to supply him with money, and he had sufficient to undertake the journey to Rome, which he reached by way of Venice—a city he had visited in his youth when in search of military employment.

On 21st March 1747 King James wrote to the Prince in Paris :

> I must tell you that I was much surprised t'other day at the arrival of Lord George Murray in this place. After having absconded many months in Scotland, he found means to come

* Lord Tullibardine to Lord George.

to Holland, and thence by Venice here. By what Bramston [code name for O'Sullivan] says, I am sorry to find that you have not been pleased with him, but tho' I questioned Bramston much about him, yet I own I don't see any motive to suspect his fidelity and loyalty. People may have an odd, and even a wrong way of thinking, and may even fail in something towards ourselves, but may be men of honour and honesty with all that ; so that consider-ing his birth, and the figure he made in your service, and that you had never writ to me about him yourself, I thought it would be very wrong in me not to receive him with all kindness, and even distinction. I don't know how long he will stay here, or how he proposes to dispose of himself, but I understand he has a mind to bring over his lady, and to live privately with her in some retired place. He is publicly here, for he has no measures to keep ; and I must do him the justice to say that he never speaks of you but with great respect, and even *éloge*. He told me he had left Lord Marischal at Venice as well as Lord Elcho : he says the last was endeavouring to make his peace with the English Government, but that he does not believe he will succeed, and that he thinks of staying in Italy till he sees the success of his endeavours. I remarked he brought me no messages from him.*

On 3rd April the Prince wrote from Paris, adding this postscript to his letter :

I have just received for certain account that L. George Murray past ye Carnivall at Venice with Lord Elcho and Earl Marischal, from thence he proceed to Room. If it be so it is of Laste Import-ance he should be well secured there until He can justifie himself to me for his past Conduct, of which putting it in ye best light, one will finde severall demonstrative acts of disobedience, insolency, and creating dissention ; *En fin* besides for what he deserves I humbly represent your Majesty, it would be of ye most Dangerous Consequences iff such a Divill was not secured immediatly in sum Castle where he might be at his ease, but without being able to escape, or have ye Liberty of Pen or paper.†

King James replied with his usual restraint :

I am truly sorry to find you in the way of thinking you are to Lord George Murray. I spoke very fully about him to O'Sullivan, who should be with you before you get this, and by all he said to me I really cannot see any just reason to suspect his loyalty and fidelity. And I remark you do not now tax him with anything on those points. One who had been guilty in that respect would have rather exceeded in point of flattery than in want of respect,

* Browne's ' History of the Highland Clans.' Appendix.
† Stuart Papers. Printed in Blaikie's Itinerary.

and the fact that he has lost what he had, and the expectation of much more ; that he does not pretend to be in our secrets, or a charge on us, and that he has no other view at present but to get over his Lady from Scotland, and to live privately and quietly with her at Cleves, and all this does not, I am sure, denote any ill disposition or design.

If he has been on several occasions of a different opinion from you or other people, I don't see what crime there is in that, and this would be a very unfit time to enter into such sort of discussions ; and as to what he may have failled against you personally, he has owned his fault to me, for tho' but too many people have failled towards me, yet I scarce ever remember that anyone made such an act of submission as he has done. All he seeks is your forgiveness, and to be restored to your favour, which you are, I am sure, incapable of refusing him, and which he proposes to do himself in person in a short time, and after having made his court to you and your brother for a few days, to go on to Cleves. But as I find you are much exasperated against him, I shall endeavour to have it so contrived that he may stay here till I get your answer to this, for, whatever you may think, it would certainly be of disservice to you should he meet with an unkind reception from you ; for, as having him secured, I think in my conscience it would be an injustice, and tho' it were not such an act of despotism, would do us more hurt in our own country than any he could do us, were he the worst of men. The appearance he made in your service is publick as well as what he suffers by it, whereas his faults and mistakes are not ; and I know he has amongst his own people his friends as well as his enemies, and he may, on another occasion, be of great service to you. So that all put together, any hard or unkind usage he might receive from you would be really unchristian, unprincely, and impolitick. You may think I have enlarged too much on this subject, but I have done so more on your account than Lord George's, because I take your behaviour towards him on this occasion to be of some importance to you, by the inferences the public may draw from it of your personal qualities and character.*

King James, as he told his son in another letter, was beginning to think that the Prince would never succeed in anything on account of the way he managed matters and handled people. His recent letters had become yet more wild, for he now asserted that his late General was " in click "† with Broughton, who had turned King's Evidence. He also believed that some sinister purpose lay behind

* Browne's ' History.'
† The Prince's letter to King James.

LORD GEORGE'S TOMBSTONE

Set in the floor of the Church at Medemblik

his meeting with Elcho on his way to Rome—actually a wholly
unexpected encounter in a Venetian theatre. The King dismissed
such accusations as ridiculous ; and as if to atone in some measure
for his son's conduct, it was noted by all that he treated Lord George
" with particular marks of favour."* Scottish newspapers published
sensational accounts of the late commander of the Jacobite army
being fêted by Roman society and even being granted an audience
by the Pope.

O'Sullivan was in Rome from 15th March to 18th April. True
to his habit of saying only what would please his hearer he spoke
well enough of Lord George to King James. But the favour shown
to his former rival was evidently more than he could bear. He
wrote of him with great venom in his subsequent 'Narrative' of the
campaign—in spite of King James's stipulation that " such a paper
should be composed with nice regard to truth and prudence, so as
. . . not to disgust, much less wrong, any particular persons."† On
rejoining the Prince in Paris he undoubtedly did all he could to increase
Charles's bitterness against the object of their mutual aversion.

Meanwhile Lord George lingered on in Rome—a city full of
interest to anyone so widely read as he, his visit being rendered
the more pleasant because he had kept up his Italian as well as
his French by reading such foreign periodicals as his brother
John had been able to procure for him in London. He renewed
friendships with comrades of the earlier Jacobite campaign, particularly with the King's Secretary, James Edgar, a godson of his
uncle the Earl of Panmure, at whose lodgings the two young men
had spent much time during their exile at Avignon. But Lord
George's greatest joy was the renewal of his friendship with his old
master, marred only by the consciousness of his inability to express
his heart-felt gratitude for "so many transcendent marks of so much
undeserved grace, royal goodness and bountiful favours " and by
the sad certainty that it would never be in his power to render any
further service in return.

The King's next letter to his son was sent from Rome on 2nd May:

> I should have been glad to keep Lord George here untill I
> had your answer to what I writ to you last post about him, but
> he is impatient to go nearer home, to be better able to look after

* Jacobite Gleanings.
† ' The Forty-Five and After ': Alasdair and Henrietta Tayler.

R

his private affairs and bring over his Lady. I did not think it
was fit to constrain him, and so he parts in a few days, but I
don't believe he will be at Paris before the middle of June, for
he goes by Venice and Switzerland. He has again spoke to me
with much concern for lying under your displeasure, and if you
could have seen how sincerely he owned his faults, and how
penitent he was for them, I am sure you would have been touched
with it. It is certainly a very great mistake to think he has anything to do with John Murray. Nothing can be more different
than their present situations and behaviour, and I hope you won't
do yourself the wrong, nor give me the new mortification as not
to give him a good reception, and make himself sensible that you
have forgiven him, which I should think should cost you very
little, since there is no question of his staying with you, or your
trusting and employing him.*

This letter was followed by another a week later :

Lord George Murray parted from hence last Sunday. I beg
of you when you see him to receive his submissions with goodness,
and since he owns so frankly that he has been in the wrong towards
you, don't put yourself in the wrong by an unkind, and by
consequence even impolitick behaviour towards him for the few
days he proposes to stay in Paris . . . Lord George is persuaded
he will get no favour from the Government, and I understand
he thinks of passing some time at Bologna. Persons like him
may do both good and hurt, and it is prudent to manage them,
and would manifestly be of prejudice could they be able to say
that their former services had been disregarded.†

Neither of these missives mollified the Prince, who was not in a
mood to see reason. His renewed threats of imprisoning his former
Lieutenant-General greatly perturbed his royal father. But King
James learned from a letter received by his Secretary, James Edgar,
from Balhaldy, that Lord George had not yet reached Paris :

Lord George Murray is not yet arrived here. I am hopeful
we will find in him when he does arrive something equal to the
character men of best sense and greatest spirit were in the Prince's
army, give of him.‡

Early in May Lord George, who never wearied of travel either
by land or sea, left Rome for Bologna. In this ancient city King

* Browne's ' History.'
† Ibid.
‡ Ibid.

James had once held his Court; and there his marriage to Queen
Clementina had been solemnised, with Lord George's kinsman
Lord Dunbar standing as proxy for the royal bridegroom. Lord
George then rejoined the Earl Marischal and Lord Elcho, who were
still in Venice. Elcho has been stigmatised as a traitor for his vain
attempts to obtain a pardon, as many a Jacobite had done after the
failure of the previous Risings. The Scottish Jacobites of his own
day did not so regard him. He was one of the first guests to stay
in the house in which Lord George settled down at Cleves for the
winter.

After witnessing the famous Venetian Fête of the Ascension, the
three friends proceeded to Padua to attend that of St Anthony.
Three days later Lord George set out for Paris. On his arrival there
he interviewed the heads of the Scots College, and requested them
to collect in writing any charges levelled against him in order that
he might refute them. But, as Inishewen has left on record, not a
single allegation was handed in to the Fathers. Neither could Sir
James Stuart of Goodtrees induce any of Lord George's detractors
to set down on paper the things of which they accused him. Such
accusations as appear in print in Scotland were all the work of
anonymous writers.

But Lord George's main purpose in visiting the French capital
was to pay his homage and to offer his apologies to the Prince for
any former lapses of respect towards him. The moment was,
however, unpropitious for such a purpose, for Charles was just then
seething with rage over his brother's acceptance of a Cardinal's hat
—an act which would most surely deal a death-blow to the Jacobite
Cause. The Duke of York had fled to Rome; but Lord George
was in Paris, and he at least could be punished in some degree for
the offence he had given to his royal commander. On hearing that
his late General wished to wait upon him, Charles sent him a curt
command not to seek an audience. Cut to the quick, Lord George
wrote a Memorandum which he sent two days later with a letter
to the King in Rome :

PARIS, 13th July 1747.

SIR,—However unwilling I am to give your Majesty the trouble
of a letter, yet I think it my duty to acquaint your Majesty that,
having arrived here on the 10th at night, I next day informed
myself where H.R.H. the Prince of Wales stayed. I designed to

R 2

have gone out early the 12th to St Ouen to have paid my dutiful respects to him, but having received the inclosed message, I prepared myself to set out for Germany, and I hope to be able to leave this place in a few days. In any part of the world I may happen to be in, and in whatever situation, I shall pray for your Majesty's prosperity, and that of your sons, and my distressed country. Whatsoever misfortunes may attend me, I shall look upon as small in comparison with what you all suffer, being with the most devoted attachment,

May it please your Majesty,

Yr. Majesty's most dutyfull and faithful

Subject & Servant,

GEORGE MURRAY.*

PARIS, 11th July 1747, 9 at night.

I was at this moment called to the door by a gentleman who delivered me the following message, That he was just then sent by H.R.H. the Prince of Wales at St Ouen, who had heard that I was come to town, that his R.H. desired I should not come near him, for that he would not see me, and that I would do well to leave Paris as soon as I could.

I asked the Gentleman his name, who, after assuring me he would not have delivered such a message without orders, he at last told me his name was Mr Stafford. I desired he would acquaint H.R.H. that I had come to France with no other design but to pay my respects to him, and that I should punctually obey his orders, which I hoped Mr Stafford would assure H.R.H. of.

GEORGE MURRAY.

The moment Mr Stafford was gone I sat down and wrote what had passed, not to trust too much to my memory.†

" This Irishman, who called himself Stafford, said he had orders from the Prince to tell him to leave Paris—otherwise he would have him put in the Bastille," recorded the indignant Elcho in his Journal. " Lord George insisted upon seeing this order in writing, and Mr

* Browne's 'History.'
† Ibid. A copy of this note was found by Lady George among her husband's papers after his death, and was forwarded by her to her two eldest children for their inspection. " It shows the return our father met with for the much he had done and all he had sacrificed," John grimly observed when posting it to his sister. " From the manner of the writing [it] must have made a most deep impression on our father's heart," was Amie's comment.

Stafford gave it to him signed by the Prince's hand. No one has rendered such great services to the Prince in Scotland as my Lord George. He raised 1,000 men on the lands of his brother the Duke of Atholl, who served the Prince well throughout the campaign ; and he was cherished and respected by the whole of the Prince's army. One may judge of the Prince's character from the way in which he treated Lord George. My Lord Marischal from his knowledge of the Prince's character predicted to Lord George all that came to pass. But my Lord George, knowing that he had nothing to reproach himself with, did not believe such treatment possible from a Prince for whom he had sacrificed everything."*

Gravely concerned about the discourteous behaviour of his son, King James wrote to his faithful friend and servant :

I received last week your letter of the 6th August from Boulogne. Could I have foreseen what happen'd to you at Paris, I would certainly have advised you before you left this to have gone into Flanders by another road ; but neither before nor since I have never heard any particular thing that appears to me to affect your character, which I think too well established, especially by your late public behaviour in the good Cause, not to make you superior to all that may come from ignorant or malitious tongues. I am persuaded this storm against you will blow over at last, and in the meantime if my good opinion of, & kindness for you, can be of any comfort or advantage to you, you may be well assured of both.

I am heartily sorry to find that even your Lady personally should share with you in your sufferings on our account, and I heartily wish I were in a condition to supply you in a manner suitable to your merit, & my own inclination. But what little I have in my power I do it at least with good will, & shall send by next French post my orders to George Waters, l'aine at Paris, to pay to your order 400 louis p. month, beginning with the month of July last inclusive. I hope this will find your Lady in good health with you. I desire she may find here many kind compliments from me, & heartily wish you both all the comfort and satisfaction which your present melancholly situation can allow of.

JAMES *R.*†

Lord George, who, straitened though he was, had not solicited a pension, must have been touched by his royal master's realisation

---

* Unpublished part of **Lord Elcho's Journal.**
† Atholl Chronicles.

of the extra expense which he had incurred (and could so ill afford), in journeying to Cleves by way of Paris for no other purpose than to pay homage to the Prince. " As much as in me lies, you will always find me a true friend to you on all occasions and in all circumstances," the King assured him ; and as in all other instances, King James kept his word.

The Prince and his General never met again. Both were destined to pass the remainder of their lives far from the land where their memory was to be forever enshrined, and their deeds of daring remembered. Henceforward their paths were to be as widely divergent as the manner in which each faced up to the problem of adjusting himself to the dreary and hopeless future that lay ahead. Lord George, who had lost everything he possessed through his adherence to the Stuart Cause, faced his trials with the same steady courage with which he had faced his enemies upon the field of battle. But Charles who, in point of fact, had lost nothing that he had ever in reality possessed—except the bright hopes and dreams of glory and of conquest that had braced his spirits in his youth—had not the strength of character to comport himself with courage and with dignity in the time of misfortune. He refused to return to his home, where a loving welcome would have been extended to him by his father, and the King was left to pass the remaining nineteen years of his life in solitude—racked by anxiety about the well-being and whereabouts of his son who would not even visit him upon his death-bed. Lost soon were the good-looks and charm that had made this romantic young Prince the idol of so many Scottish hearts ; and more and more accentuated became the faults and weaknesses that had been his through life. In these years of bitter disillusionment and disappointment he gave way entirely to the excessive fondness for wine that had caused King James acute concern even before the days of his Great Adventure, and which had been noted with dismay by Lord Elcho on the road to Derby—the road which Charles had so fondly supposed would lead him to St James's.

EPILOGUE

LORD GEORGE now had to endure, not only exile, but separation from his family, who were already suffering as the result of the course he had taken. That spring his wife was turned out of Tullibardine by Duke James, who had previously removed all the family furniture left in the Castle during his brother's tenancy. When writing to tell her of the new house he had secured in Cleves, Lord George ended his letter sadly :

> I beg your pardon in the first place, and entreat my children to excuse me for having imprudently engaged myself in the 'Forty-Five, by which means I have brought ruin on you all. I shall only say my intentions were upright, and I thought to have saved my country. Sure, I have acted an honest and disinterested part, but I am afraid I have much to answer for. . . . My heart is melted when I reflect and think on you, my Guardian Angel, and it is a pleasant reflection for me to think, whatever may become of me, my children lose nothing so long as God spares you to them.*

" All my children are equally dear to me," he told her in this letter. But the greatest weight that lay upon his heavily burdened mind was the thought of the injury he had done his eldest son. Family affairs prevented Lady George from joining him at Cleves that winter ; and during those first dreary months there her husband braced himself to make a sacrifice of greater magnitude than he had already made. Lord Elcho recorded in his Journal :

> Lord George Murray left in the commencement of February 1748 for Königsberg, and wrote me from there and from Cracow in Poland. His intention, as far as I could divine it, was to buy an estate and to go and take up his residence there under an assumed name, and circulate a report of his death so that his eldest son might enjoy the title and the lands of his uncle the Duke of Atholl, that would otherwise have fallen to Lord George, and would, in consequence, have been confiscated.†

* Record of Invercauld.
† Unpublished part of Lord Elcho's Journal.

For the sake of his King and country Lord George had cut himself off for ever from his own much-loved land. Now for the sake of his own son, and in the hope of preserving the power and prestige of the family of Atholl, he was prepared to cut himself off from the being he loved so deeply, and who alone could make life dear to him. But his wife would not permit him to make this sacrifice. In October she had lost the little daughter born shortly after the Battle of Falkirk, and she could not contemplate the thought of losing her husband too. Moreover, in November their niece, the seventeen-year-old Lady Jean, died of a fever at Utrecht six months after her elopement with Lord Crawford. Her sister Charlotte, whom Lady George had always preferred to lovely, lively Jean, was heiress now to the Atholl lands. She might eventually become the bride of Johny, to whom Duke James still extended his favour— though only on the strict understanding that the young man never- more saw or corresponded with his rebel father. If the Duke had sufficient influence at Court, an Act of Parliament could be passed enabling his nephew and son-in-law to succeed to the ducal honours.

So Lord George returned to his house in the pleasant old-world town beside the Rhine, where his wife and blooming sixteen-year-old daughter joined him in the autumn. Their stay was cut short by the death of Lady Strowan. Financial burdens were lightened by Lady George's accession to her mother's estates; but their adminis- tration, and the need to supervise the education of the younger children, kept her much in Scotland. Lord George had no mind to jeopardise his children's future by allowing them to share his exile; nor would he deprive them of their mother's care. The early days of his exile were thus extremely lonely. He deeply felt the " change from a society he had loved to a loneliness far easier felt than described." However, he did not repine, for as he had always maintained " It is not those that have the greatest plenty, but those who can make the most of everything that falls in their way that are happy." In his fourteen years of exile Lord George found a peace that had not been his during his last years in Scotland when he had been torn in two between his duty to his King and to the House of Atholl. His allegiance was no longer divided; and to the end of his life he remained in happy correspondence with his well-loved master, for whose sake he was able to bear his own and his family's ruin without a grudge. The kindly letters which King James sent him from time to time did much to brighten the dark days of Lord George's exile.

Thinking perhaps of the great walled garden (the first of its kind in that part of Scotland) which he had made for his mother-in-law at sunny Arnhall, he wrote to his wife that, as a sun-drenched wall throws back heat to the fruit along its trellises, so the happy knowledge of the welfare of his dear ones warmed and comforted his lonely heart. He was never to see his eldest and his youngest sons again ; but Jamie came out to live with him for some time before entering the service of the Elector of Saxony ; and after twenty-three years of married life Lady George gave birth to another child—Charlotte—who was the light of her father's declining years.

Johny, now the Laird of Strowan and in charge of the other estates, became the husband of his gentle cousin Charlotte, and the father of a numerous family of sons and daughters whose descendants would carry on the fine traditions of the House of Atholl. Amie somewhat horrified her father by wedding the aged Lord Sinclair—with whom he had essayed to fight a duel in the year '15 ; but, widowed within a few months of her marriage, she made a more suitable match with her second cousin Farquharson of Invercauld, whom Lord George had once captured along with Cope's baggage after the Battle of Prestonpans. Georgie, after leaving Edinburgh High School, became a midshipman in the British Navy.*

From then onward Lady George was seldom separated from her husband, who never knew true happiness unless she was at his side. Until 1759 they chiefly lived at Emmerick near Cleves, and received visits from several old friends who were also in exile. They then moved to Medemblik in North Holland, where Lord George was much respected by all the townsfolk. His health, which had remained good throughout the earlier part of his exile, now began to fail. On the eve of his sixty-sixth birthday he was taken ill, and he died eight days later, on 11th October 1760.

Lord George had come to believe that it mattered little where a man's mortal remains reposed after death. He was laid to rest in the large church at Medemblik—far from his own land and the little

---

* Lord George's eldest son, John, became the third Duke of Atholl. James eventually became a General in the British Army. George rose to the rank of Admiral.

Chapel of Tullibardine where he had once hoped that his dust would mingle with that of his forebears, the old Lairds and Earls of Tullibardine.

The memory of the great Scots "mylord" who spent his last years at Medemblik lingers in the minds of the inhabitants of this once thriving port upon the shores of the Zuyder Zee. They point out the house where he is said to have lived; they respect his tombstone, and the funeral hatchment on which are emblazoned the arms of the House of Orange.

Like his illustrious ancestor William the Silent, Lord George had fought to free his country from foreign domination. But he had failed to do so. Unlike the great Stadtholder, he was not the head of a ruling house. He had not even been permitted to act as the head of the army which he had been appointed to command. His enemies had frustrated his efforts; and their calumnies had blackened his character. A cloud has hung over his name which historians, who endeavoured to explain his actions, have long failed to pierce. But the long unpublished writings of men who fought beside him, and who burned with indignation at the aspersions cast upon him, have revealed with startling clarity his every action throughout the ill-fated campaign. The mists of obscurity have rolled away, and Lord George Murray stands revealed as the devoted servant of the House of Stuart and among the finest of the military leaders his country has produced.

ACKNOWLEDGEMENTS

I AM indebted to many people for giving their time and thought towards helping me with the book, and I am particularly grateful to the following :—

The Duke of Atholl, for permission to reproduce the five portraits and two miniatures from the collection in Blair Castle, and the sketch of the Castle from ' The History of the Siege of Blair Castle in 1746 ' ;

Captain and Lady Victoria Wemyss, for the photograph of the portrait of Lord Elcho, and for lending me the copy of Lord Elcho's unpublished ' Journal ' ;

Captain Iain Moncreiffe of Easter Moncreiffe, for his encouragement, and for his expert description of Lord George's Funeral Hatchment ;

Sir David Ogilvy of Winton House, for permission to reproduce the Allan Ramsay portrait of Lord Ogilvy ;

The Trustees of the Duke of Newcastle, for permitting me to include extracts from the unpublished MSS. at Nottingham University ;

Dr C. A. Malcolm, O.B.E., Ph.D., of the Signet Library, Edinburgh, for his invaluable help and advice concerning Jacobite books ;

Miss Margaret Stephen, of the Library, King's College, Aberdeen University, for her valuable help in sending me Jacobite letters from among the Blair Papers at present at Aberdeen ;

Miss Amice Lee, for information from family letters about the Highlanders on the march to and from Derby ;

The Curators of the West Highland Museum, Fort William, for permission to reproduce the portrait of Lochiel and the miniature of James, Duke of Perth ;

Major A. L. Murray, 3rd Carabineers, Prince of Wales's Dragoon Guards, for obtaining the photographs of Lord George's Tombstone and Funeral Hatchment at Mademblik, Holland ;

Captain David Wilson, R.N., of Messrs William Blackwood & Sons Ltd., for his help throughout.

Among the many books and publications consulted I select the following for special mention :—

Lord George Murray's Unpublished Notes for a projected History of the Rising.
Lord George Murray's Unpublished Letters at Blair Castle.
Lord George Murray's ' Battle of Falkirk.'
Lord George Murray's ' Retreat from Falkirk.'

Lord George Murray's "Marches of the Highland Army." Printed in
'Jacobite Memoirs.'

'Chronicles of the Atholl and Tullibardine Families.'

The Jacobite Correspondence of the Atholl Family.

'The Siege of Blair Castle.' The Seventh Duke of Atholl.

'A Military History of Perthshire.' Edited by the Marchioness of
Tullibardine.

'Lord George Murray and the Forty-Five.' Winifred Duke.

'Memoirs of the Jacobites.' Thomson (including 'Life' of Lord George
Murray).

'Memoirs of the Pretenders and their Adherents.' Jesse (with article on
Lord George Murray).

'Maxwell's Narrative of Charles Prince of Wales's Expedition, 1745.'
Maxwell of Kirkconnel.

'The Affairs of Scotland.' Lord Elcho.

'Memoir of David, Lord Elcho.' Hon. Evan Charteris.

"Lord Elcho's Journal." Printed in 'Jacobite Miscellany.' Edited by
H. Tayler.

"Memoirs of Sir John Macdonald." 'Jacobite Miscellany.' Edited by
H. Tayler.

"O'Sullivan's Narrative." Printed in 'The Forty-Five and After.' Edited
by H. Tayler.

'Memoirs of the Rebellion, 1745-46.' Chevalier de Johnstone.

'The Memorials of Murray of Broughton.'

'Genuine Memoirs of John Murray, Esqr.'

Lochgarry's Narrative. Printed in the Lockhart Papers.

Strathmashie's Narrative. Printed in the 'Lyon in Mourning.'

'Memoirs of Sir Robert Strange and Andrew Lumisden.'

"Captain Daniel's Progress with Prince Charles." Printed in 'Origins of
the Forty-Five.'

'Ascanius, or The Young Adventurer.'

'The Wanderer, or Surprizing Escape.'

'The Young Juba.' Michele Vezossi.

'Memoirs of Prince Charles Stuart.' C. L. Klosse.

'The Life and Times of Prince Charles Stuart.' A. C. Ewald.

'The Life and Adventures of Prince Charles Edward Stuart.' W. Drummond
Norrie.

'Bonnie Prince Charlie.' Clennel Wilkinson.

'Prince Charles Edward Stuart, the Young Chevalier.' Andrew Lang.

'Prince Charles Edward.' D. B. Chidsey.

'Prince Charles Edward.' Carola Oman.

'Prince Charles Edward and the Forty-Five.' Cuthbert Hadden.

'Prince Charles Edward and the Forty-Five.' Winifred Duke.

'The Rash Adventurer.' Winifred Duke.

'In the Footsteps of Bonnie Prince Charlie.' Winifred Duke.

'In the Footsteps of Prince Charlie.' Augustus Muir.

'Charles, Prince Regent.' A. G. Goyder.

'Prince Charlie.' Compton Mackenzie.

'The Young Pretender.' C. Sandford Terry.

'Prince Charlie on the Borderland.' D. G. Beattie.

'Prince Charlie's Country.' Donald B. MacCulloch.

'Edinburgh in the Time of Prince Charles.' W. B. Blaikie.
'The Errant Prince.' Dumont-Wilden.
'The Young Adventurer.' Donald Nicholas.
'The Quest Forlorn.' Cyril Hughes Hartmann.
'Death of a Legend.' Peter de Polnay.
'The White Cockade.' Baron Porcelli.
'Argyll and the Forty-Five.' Sir James Fergusson.
'History of the Rebellion in the Years 1745 and 1746.' (Anon.) Edited by H. Tayler.
'History of the Rebellions of 1689 and 1715.' Robert Chambers.
'History of the Rebellion of 1745.' Robert Chambers.
'History of the Rebellion, 1745.' Henderson.
'A Compleat History of the Rebellion.' James Rae.
'An Impartial History of the late Rebellion.' Boyse.
"History of the Rebellion of 1745 and 1746." Extracted from the 'Scots Magazine.'
'History of the Rebellion of 1745.' Home.
'The Forty-Five.' Lord Mahon.
'The Medical Heroes of the Forty-Five.' W. A. Macnaughton.
'Memorials of the 'Forty-Five.' Rev. A. Macdonald.
'Memoir of Macdonald of Keppoch.' Dr Angus Macdonald.
'Jacobite Sidelights.'
'Jacobite Gleanings from State Manuscripts.' J. Macbeath Forbes.
'The Jacobites and the Union.' C. Sandford Terry.
'The Forty-Five from Contemporary Accounts.' C. Sandford Terry.
'The Last Jacobite Rising.' C. Sandford Terry.
'The Jacobite Risings of 1715 and 1745.' Rupert C. Jarvis.
'The Forty-Five and After.' Alasdair and Henrietta Tayler.
'Jacobite Epilogue.' Henrietta Tayler.
'Jacobite Miscellany.' Henrietta Tayler.
'The Stuart Papers at Windsor.' Alasdair and Henrietta Tayler.
'The Stuart Court in Rome.' Alasdair and Henrietta Tayler.
'The Old Chevalier.' Alasdair and Henrietta Tayler.
'The Chevalier de St George.' C. Sandford Terry.
'The King over the Water.' Andrew Lang and Alice Shiel.
'Jacobites of Aberdeenshire and Banffshire in the Forty-Five.' H. Tayler.
'The Jacobite Letters to Lord Pitsligo.' Alasdair and Henrietta Tayler.
'Irishmen in the Forty-Five.' Sir Charles Petrie.
'The Jacobite Movement.' Sir Charles Petrie.
'The Scottish Jacobite Movement.' George Pratt Insh.
'Papers relating to the Jacobite Period, 1690 to 1750.' Col. Jas. Allardice.
'The Lyon in Mourning.' Bishop Forbes.
'Jacobite Memoirs.' Robert Chambers.
The Lockhart Papers.
The Culloden Papers.
The Woodhouselee MS.
'Origins of the Forty-Five.' Walter Blaikie.
'Itinerary of Prince Charles Edward Stuart.' Walter Blaikie.
'History of the Highland Clans.' J. F. Browne.
'Derby and the Forty-Five.' Major Eardley Simpson.
'Intercepted Post.' Donald Nicholas.

' The House of Airlie.' Rev. W. Wilson.
' Wolfe in Scotland.' J. T. Findley.
' Sketches of the Characters of the Highlanders.' General Stewart of Garth.
The Unpublished Newcastle MSS.
' The Battle of Culloden.' Colonel Ker of Graden.
' British Battles on Land and Sea.'
' Guide to Culloden Moor.' Peter Anderson.
' Culloden : the Forty-Five.' Major-General Sir A. B. Tulloch.
' The Mystery of Culloden Battlefield.' D. Murray Rose.
Local Histories of Perth, Stirling, Cumberland, Westmorland and Lancashire.

INDEX

(References to Footnotes in italics)

Agnew, Sir Andrew, 183-187, 192, 194-195.
Anne, Queen, 2.
Ardshiel, Stewart of, 57, 128, 129, 155, 250, 253.
Argyll, Archibald, 3rd Duke of, 159.
Argyll, John, 2nd Duke of, 172.
Atholl, Amelia, Marchioness of, 1.
Atholl, James, 2nd Duke of, 1-3, 6, 10, 12-14, 16-18, 20, 23-25, 38, 78, 165, 183-184, 186-187, 189, 193, 252, 263-*265*.
Atholl, Jean, Duchess of, 12.
Atholl, John, 1st Duke of, 1, 2, 3, 14, 189.
Atholl, John, Marquis of, 1, 9.
Atholl, Katherine, Duchess of, 1.
Atholl, William, *de jure* Duke of (*see* Tullibardine).
Avuchie, Gordon of, 179, 228, 235, 239-240.

Balhaldy, Drummond of, 58, 258.
Balmerino, Arthur, Lord, *61*, 93, 152, 178-179, *220*, 233, 253.
Balnacree, Stewart of, 185.
Barrymore, Lord, 102-103.
Berwick, James, 2nd Duke of, 54.
Blair Castle, Prince at, 18, 23 ; Siege of, 184-196.
Blairfettie, Robertson of, 34, 35, 114, 176, 183.
Blairfettie, Lady, 183.
Blakeney, General, 159, 169-170.
Bland, General, 235.
Blind Jack of Knaresborough, 187.
Bohally, Charles Stewart of, 183.
Breadalbane, John, 2nd Earl of, 49.
Broughton, John Murray of, 8, *18*, 23, 32, 36-37, 48, 52, 54, 59-61, 66, 76, 80-82, 85, 90-95, 112-113, 116, 120, 161-164, 166, 168, 173, 175-176, 189, 219, 254, 256, 258.

Broughton, Mrs Murray of, 118, 168.
Brown, Captain, 93-94, 102, 134, 158-159.
Burnside, Hunter of, 212, 250.
Bury, Lord, 232.
Buttivant, Lord, 103.

Cameron, Dr Archibald, 212.
Cameron, Daniel, 148.
Cameron, Rev. John, 169, 226.
Campbell, General, 181.
Campbell, Sheriff, 49.
Carlisle, Siege of, 74-76 ; Jacobites at, 77-90 ; Return to, 133-134.
Charles I., 44, 55, 59, 60, 99, 100.
Charles, II., 55, 60, 162.
Charles, Prince, 5, 12-13, 17-20, 26-30, 32-34, 36-38, 40, 43, 51-52, 55-56, 58-64, 66-70, 74-77, 79-82, 85-86, 88, 91-96, 98-99, 102-103, 105-113, 115-121, 123-124, 126, 128, 130-134, 137-140, 143, 145, 147, 149, 152-154, 156, 158-164, 167-175, 180, 191, 196-227, 229-230, 232-235, 238-239, *241*, 242-263.
Cholmondeley, Brigadier, 147.
Clanranald, The Young, 28, 45, 57, 145, 150, 215, 224, 247.
Clementina, Queen, 53, 58, 259.
Clifton, Battle of, 127-133.
Cluny Macpherson, 57, 112, 124, 129-132, 164, 175, 182, 184, 188-189, 196, 201, 244, *246*, 250-252.
Cobham, Lord, 135.
Cope, General Sir John, 16, 18, 51, 73, 90.
Craigie, Lord Advocate, 8, 13, 16.
Crawford, John, 17th Earl of, 192-195, 264.
Cromartie, George, 3rd Earl of, 142, 180.